# Revivals, Awakenings, and Reform

*Chicago History of*
*American Religion*

*A Series Edited by*
*Martin E. Marty*

# Revivals, Awakenings, and Reform

*An Essay on Religion
and Social Change
in America, 1607–1977*

*William G. McLoughlin*

*The Univeristy of Chicago Press*
*Chicago and London*

*I dedicate this book to my
friend and mentor, Oscar Handlin*

The University of Chicago Press, Chicago 60637
The University of Chicago Press, Ltd., London

© 1978 by The University of Chicago
All rights reserved. Published 1978
Printed in the United States of America
82 81 80 79 78      9 8 7 6 5 4 3 2 1

WILLIAM G. MCLOUGHLIN is professor of history at
Brown University. His previous books include
*Modern Revivalism: Charles Grandison Finney to
Billy Graham* (1959); *American Evangelicals,
1800-1900* (1968); and *New England Dissent,
1630-1833: The Baptists and the Separation of
Church and State*, 3 vols. (1971).

**Library of Congress Cataloging in Publication Data**

McLoughlin, William Gerald.
 Revivals, awakenings, and reform.

 (Chicago history of American religion)
 Bibliography: p.
 Includes index.
  1. Revivals—United States.   2. United States—
Church history.   3. United States—Civilization.
I. Title.
BV3773.M32      269'.2'0973      77-27830
ISBN 0-226-56091-0

# Contents

# Foreword

Individuals do not ordinarily live their lives at a single pitch of intensity. Periods of high drama are interspersed among longer periods of mild boredom. After times of vitality come stretches of exhaustion. As with individuals, so with cultures. The people who make them up could not sustain "peak experiences" every day or every year, yet after barren or serene periods they almost welcome disturbances and challenges. Historians measure cultures both by the way they endure ebbs or enervations and enjoy flows or revitalizations.

William G. McLoughlin has written an essay on revitalizations in the culture of America, or at least in many of the subcultures that make up the nation. The fact that these times of agitation and fresh impetus appear to him to have a religious dimension or that they sometimes are even fundamentally religious does not result merely from his assignment to write a book in a series on American religious history. His is a full-length illustration of a theme in the writings of Paul Tillich: that religion is the soul of culture and culture the form of religion. Whether in the discovery and settlement of the New World, the revolutionary struggles to shape the nation, the Civil War agonies to preserve it, or the recurrent times of troubles or new dedication, deeply religious themes come to light. The writings of Christopher Columbus, Thomas Jefferson, and Abraham Lincoln or the inaugural addresses of numerous presidents illustrate this bonding of national and spiritual themes.

At times the revitalizations begin and even run their course as religious movements. As such they often can go unnoticed by historians who have their eyes trained chiefly on economic or political indicators, on tariff debates or diplomatic treaties. Even the most significant religious events often appear to be so diffuse and subtle that "hard news" reporters and historians tend to neglect them. To take an example: in the year of the American Bicentennial numerous polls of historians and news reporters ranked the most important events in American history. Never did the First Great Awakening of the 1730s and 1740s show up in the one hundred top selections. Yet scrutiny of colonial life on the part of specialists turns up evidence that this Great Awakening was perhaps the most extensive intercolonial event; that it reached into virtually every kind of community and crossroads; that its effects were at first profoundly unsettling to the established order and then became creative elements in establishing a new order; and that indirect lines connect many of its impulses to those of the War of Independence and nation-building endeavors. Perry Miller and Alan Heimert argue with considerable effect that the awakening began "a new era, not merely of American Protestantism, but in the evolution of the American mind," that it was a watershed, a break with the Middle Ages, a turning point, a "crisis."

If this First Great Awakening, its Second counterpart, sixty years later, and two or three later eruptions were so revitalizing, why, it may fairly be asked, are they so obscure and neglected in national consciousness? Certainly their diffuse character or their elusiveness cannot be the only reason; historians welcome the challenge to style past cultural trends and to give a shape to intellectual phenomena that are hard to chart. We must look elsewhere for answers to the question. One possible answer comes from the character of the American academy in what many call a secular period and a pluralist society. With the birth of the modern university and its accompanying division of labor, the study of religious history was edged into segregated seminaries and divinity schools. Especially with the rise of public tax-supported institutions the study of religion became problematic. Add to this the fact that many intellectuals were themselves in rebellion against what they experienced as repressive and limiting childhood religion, and it is easy to see why the study of awakenings did not draw notice the way charting of military conflicts or presidential elections did.

While the academy was isolating and pushing aside the religious subject, the study of revitalizations, then, tended to become "church property." Historians of the movements tended to denominationalize the experience and argue over it along the lines of their sectarian preserves. As a result, some of them chose to define revivals and awakenings as precisely and as narrowly as possible. In church life you can hear intense debates over whether the terms "revival" or "awakening" are more appropriate than others; whether Baptists or Methodists were most responsible for them; whether non-Protestants were caught up in the ethos of renewal; whether the hand of Providence must be seen in such movements or whether ordinary social and psychological explanations are in order. As a result, it is easy to see the majority of people who are not members of the contending parties yawning and serenely ignoring the whole discussion.

Professor McLoughlin is as gifted and persistent as any of the specialists in these churches in his efforts to track the trails of revivalists. He has written the most extensive general history to date in his *Modern Revivalism*, and his biographies, *Billy Sunday Was His Real Name* and *Billy Graham: Revivalist in a Secular Age*, have been lively contributions to the literature. McLoughlin does not choose, however, to fence in the revivalists or put narrow borders around awakenings. In the present essay he moves more boldly than anyone I have yet read to extend the study of American awakening into culture-wide phenomena called "revitalization movements." The reader must be forewarned not to expect fully conventional uses of sectarian terms in this book; the same reader must be forewarned against the idea that he or she can, after reading this, settle back comfortably with unchanged views of American culture.

The task of conceiving, chartering, eliciting, and seeing to fruition a book of this sort from preoccupied and busy scholars takes a number of years. My first correspondence with McLoughlin, the author, dates back more than ten years before the time of publication. Around 1967 not many Americans were speaking about revivals or awakenings. They were aware, of course, of the durable efforts of evangelist Billy Graham, but for the rest revivalism smelled of the old sawdust trail and the southern rivers of baptism. Agitation over the Vietnamese War or the movements of

Black Power swept campuses, and most collegians would have been embarrassed to be caught knowing what "born again" meant, to say nothing of being seen at a prayer meeting.

In the same late sixties, however, many Americans were beginning to send out subtle signals that a change was in the air. Some of the protest against the war turned pacific; "flower children" replaced the militants, and some of them retreated to communes where interest centered in Zen Buddhism, macrobiotic diets, or the Children of God. In the cultural avant-garde, people sang of an impending Age of Aquarius and began to consult their friendly neighborhood astrologer. Eastern religions found Western embodiments on campuses and in cities. Suddenly the long-latent fundamentalist, evangelical, and pentecostal movements erupted closer to the mainstream and Middle American cultures. By 1976 the two presidential candidates were part of prayer-revival movements, and the more flamboyantly "born again" of the two became president. The best-selling books in the nation touted the experience of revival and awakening, and celebrities never tired of revealing their horoscopes or laying bare their experience of the Holy Spirit. Professor McLoughlin, who dates "The Fourth Great Awakening" from 1960, found himself writing in the midst of cultural changes that few had anticipated.

The reader will note that the final chapter heading looks beyond the present to 1990—with a question mark. No one can know how long the ferment will last. Some of the noisier hucksters on the revivalist trail claim that a new epoch of the Spirit, a time of permanent Awakening, is at hand. The more sober have learned from history that there are what Emile Durkheim called "moments of effervescence," "periods of creation and renewal," times when people "are brought into more intimate relations with one another, when meetings and assemblies are more frequent, relationships more solid and the exchange of ideas more active." They also know that, after crises pass, "all that has been said, done, thought and felt during the period of fertile upheaval survives only as a memory . . . an idea, a set of ideas." More than a memory, these "flows" leave a sediment, a changed cultural landscape.

Cultural fads, crazes, and manias come and go; as the date of publication nears, there are signs that many of the more effervescent phenomena have already lost some of their bubble and fizz. It is possible that before long the "meetings and assemblies" will lose their hold, that their partisans will turn schismatic and see their vitality diminish. The basic secular aspects of the culture may not have been decisively altered. If people regain confidence in their political and technical processes, some of the passion for personal experience of a religious character may be diverted into other channels. Should that day come soon, this essay by William McLoughlin is likely to be recognized as one of the more helpful efforts to put a name on this complex set of events and to place it in the much longer context of Americal history.

Martin E. Marty
The University of Chicago

# Preface

In part this essay is designed to distinguish between America's "great awakenings" and the religious revivalism that accompanies them. Revivalism is the Protestant ritual (at first spontaneous, but, since 1830, routinized) in which charismatic evangelists convey "the Word" of God to large masses of people who, under this influence, experience what Protestants call conversion, salvation, regeneration, or spiritual rebirth. Awakenings—the most vital and yet most mysterious of all folk arts—are periods of cultural revitalization that begin in a general crisis of beliefs and values and extend over a period of a generation or so, during which time a profound reorientation in beliefs and values takes place. Revivals alter the lives of individuals; awakenings alter the world view of a whole people or culture.

Psychologists and theologians study transformations in individual outlook and behavior; historians, sociologists, and anthropologists study transformations of cultural outlook and behavior. Insofar as a theological position (say, Calvinism, deism, Evangelicalism, Liberal Protestantism, Humanism) is an ideology, that is, gives meaning and order to the lives of a people, it is subject to reinterpretation (or dissolution) in the light of significant changes in the economic, demographic, political, or social affairs of the people who hold it. The intellectual historian who attempts to explain the complex relationship between ideologies and social change faces the task of comprehending the whole social order of a community over time. This essay, in seeking to explain America's five great awakenings, or periods of ideological transformation, is thus an interpretation of

American cultural history from 1607 to the present. As such, it can hope to provide in a relatively short book only a suggestive model of social change.

In addition, I hope to stimulate a more coherent approach to the history of religion in America than we have had. We cannot study one aspect of one awakening (say, the New England phase of the First Great Awakening) and hope to comprehend the total phenomenon; nor, in summarizing one awakening, can we comprehend why the phenomenon seems constantly to repeat itself. This essay suggests that beneath the recurring pattern of ideological (or theological) change lies a common core of beliefs that has provided continuity and shape to American culture (insofar as our culture, which is really a subculture of Western civilization, has a distinctive ideology or national character). Consequently, the reader is asked to trace the evolutionary changes in a group of interlocking myths, hopes, and ideals that have shaped, and been reshaped by, the events of our history. At the heart of our culture are the beliefs that Americans are a chosen people; that they have a manifest (or latent) destiny to lead the world to the millennium; that their democratic-republican institutions, their bountiful natural resources, and their concept of the free and morally responsible individual operate under a body of higher moral laws (to transgress which is to threaten our destiny); and that the Judeo-Christian personal and social ethic (especially in the formulation described by Max Weber as "the Protestant ethic" and called by recent generations "the success myth," "the work ethic," and "the American dream") causes the general welfare to thrive by allowing the greatest possible free play and equal opportunity to each individual to fulfill his or her potential.

This individualistic, pietistic, perfectionist, millenarian ideology has from time to time been variously defined and explained to meet changing experience and contingencies in our history, but the fundamental belief that freedom and responsibility will perfect not only the individual and the nation but the world (because they are in harmony with the supreme laws of nature—and of nature's God) has been constant. American history is thus best understood as a millenarian movement. The five periods of social and ideological crisis that have produced our great awakenings have served essentially to sustain this common core of cultural myths (which even the most recent immigrants rapidly assimilate, if they do not arrive possessing them).

In this essay I endeavor to explain the sources of our recurrent ideological crises and the process of reorientation and redefinition of the core of beliefs and values that has enabled us to emerge from each crisis with renewed self-confidence as a people. This renewed confidence in turn produces those recurrent eras of social and institutional reform that (taken as a whole) constitute the American liberal tradtion. As God sheds "new" or "further light" on our mission, we refashion our pattern of life and enculturation to enable rising generations to cope with the unfolding complexities of human redemption. In a concluding chapter I suggest that, since 1960, we have been in the process of what may well be the most traumatic and drastic transformation of our ideology that has yet occurred.

Because this is an essay and not a scholarly monograph, I have avoided the use of footnotes by identifying in the text the principal sources upon which I have drawn. I must also acknowledge, of course, that I have drawn upon the writings and thoughts of a host of colleagues, friends, and students. To any who find their ideas intermixed in this book with mine, without acknowledgment, I offer my apologies and my thanks. I also wish to extend special appreciation to David Buchdahl for much help with chapter 6 and to my daughter, Jeremy, for her assistance with that chapter. Above all, as ever, I am thankful to Virginia.

# 1 *Awakenings as Revitalizations of Culture*

## *Revivalism and Protestant Hegemony*

Awakenings have been the shaping power of American culture from its inception. The first settlers came to British North America in the midst of the great Puritan Awakening in England bringing with them the basic beliefs and values that provided the original core of our culture.

Our Revolution came after the First Great Awakening on American soil had made the thirteen colonies into a cohesive unit (*e pluribus unum*), had given them a sense of unique nationality, and had inspired them with the belief that they were, "and of right ought to be," a free and independent people.

Shortly after the Constitution had launched the American republic, a second era of religious revivals created the definitions of what it meant to be "an American" and what the manifest destiny of the new nation was. After the Civil War had cemented our sense of the Union ("One nation, indivisible under God, with liberty and justice for all"), the Third Great Awakening helped us to understand the meaning of evolutionary science and industrial progress and led us into the crusades "to make the world safe for democracy" in 1917 and 1941.

Since 1960, Americans have been in the midst of their Fourth Great Awakening (or their fifth, if we include the Puritan Awakening). Once again we are in a difficult period of reorientation, seeking an understanding of who we are, how we relate to the rest of the universe, and what the meaning is of the manifold crises that threaten our sense of order at home and our commitments as a world power abroad.

Great awakenings (and the revivals that are part of them) are the results, not of depressions, wars, or epidemics, but of critical disjunctions in our self-understanding. They are not brief outbursts of mass emotionalism by one group or another but profound cultural transformations affecting all Americans and extending over a generation or more. Awakenings begin in periods of cultural distortion and grave personal stress, when we lose faith in the legitimacy of our norms, the viability of our institutions, and the authority of our leaders in church and state. They eventuate in basic restructurings of our institutions and redefinitions of our social goals.

Great awakenings are not periods of social neurosis (though they begin in times of cultural confusion). They are times of revitalization. They are therapeutic and cathartic, not pathological. They restore our cultural verve and our self-confidence, helping us to maintain faith in ourselves, our ideals, and our "covenant with God" even while they compel us to reinterpret that covenant in the light of new experience. Through awakenings a nation grows in wisdom, in respect for itself, and into more harmonious relations with other peoples and the physical universe. Without them our social order would cease to be dynamic; our culture would wither, fragment, and dissolve in confusion, as many civilizations have done before.

Revivals and awakenings occur in all cultures. They are essentially folk movements, the means by which a people or a nation reshapes its identity, transforms its patterns of thought and action, and sustains a healthy relationship with environmental and social change. To understand the functions of American revivalism and revitalization is to understand the power and meaning of America as a civilization. Until the present generation these periods of cultural readjustment have been associated almost wholly with the Protestant churches. The association of awakenings with revivalism derives from the fact that Protestant ideology has, until recently, been so dominant in our culture that other faiths have not really counted, or have not been counted, in measuring the growth of the nation in it efforts to redeem the world.

Until recently, most Americans assumed that the progress of their nation toward the millennium could be measured in the growing adherence of people here and around the world to some form of Protestantism. Protestants assumed that the preaching of God's Word (especially by gifted evangelists or missionaries) would eventually bring the whole world into a right relationship with God. Periods of mass conversion were seen as evidence of God's favor and of man's obedience to his will. R. H. Tawney said, in *Religion and the Rise of Capitalism*, that "Calvin did for the bourgeoisie of the sixteenth century what Marx did for the proletariat of the nineteenth . . . ; the doctrine of predestination satisfied the same hunger for an assurance that the forces of the universe are on the side of the elect as was to be assuaged in a different age by the theory of materialism." Americans, whose nation began with the upthrust of Calvinism in England and whose prosperity rose with the success of capitalist enterprise, have always felt that they were the elect of God, and the growth in church membership (which in seventeenth-century New England included about 20 percent of the population) to close to two-thirds of the population in the 1970s confirmed the view that God had blessed America spiritually as he had blessed it materially.

The success of the British colonists against the pagan Indians and their Catholic Spanish and French allies prior to 1776 seemed proof of this. Our successful revolution against British tyranny, our rapid expansion to the Pacific, our rise to industrial power, our triumphal role in the great European wars, and our assumption of global power after World War II added further conviction that we were indeed God's chosen people. But that conviction rested on the ideological assumption that Protestants had replaced Catholics as the true church after 1517 just as Christians had replaced Jews after the death of Christ. Protestant church growth was the measure of Christianity's success, and revivalistic evangelism was the means of that growth.

The first inkling of the possibility that evangelical Protestantism might not remain the dominant religious ideology of the new nation came with the massive immigration of Irish Catholics in the second quarter of the nineteeth century. Their resistance to evangelistic effort produced a great fear among pious Protestants that the safety and progress of the nation were endangered. Fear as well as hope has been a spur to revivalism ever since. Evangelistic efforts to reach the unchurched redoubled after 1830, and a host of "professional" revivalists arose to sustain Protestant church growth. After the Civil War, when the cities were described by home missionaries as seething caldrons of foreign, godless, and radical immorality among "the masses," new evangelistic techniques were directed toward "winning the cities for Christ." Revivalists like D. L. Moody, J. Wilbur Chapman, Sam P. Jones, and Billy Sunday led elaborate revival campaigns in cities across the country. Because they were thought to have a special gift for "reaching the masses," they were given broad Protestant support and publicity. Their success, however, proved limited.

After World War I, when it became statistically evident that non-Protestant church membership was rising more rapidly than Protestant membership and when the split between Fundamentalists and Modernists led many of the rising generation to abandon formal church affiliation for agnosticism, humanism, or atheism, xenophobic fears became so great that the nation's first immigration-restriction laws were passed. These were specifically written to exclude immigrants from non-Protestant countries (just as earlier laws and agreements had specifically excluded Oriental immigrants).

## The New Pluralism

Fundamentalist Protestants began to adopt a premillennial perspective on human history at the end of the nineteenth century because their conception of America's covenant with God ceased to be dominant among the largest denominations. Pervaded by gloom as the non-Protestant immigrants increased and as Protestant leaders abandoned belief in a literally infallible Bible, the Fundamentalists concluded that they were the saving remnant. Yet they doubted whether they alone could save America or the world from the imminent Apocalypse. The Modernists or Liberal Protestants, accommodating the Bible to the higher criticism of the Bible and to Darwinian evolution, assumed that God still intended to work

through America to redeem mankind. However, they yielded
considerable authority to the scientists (including sociologists,
psychologists, economists, and political scientists) in working out
man's progress toward the millennium. The nonchurchgoing
humanists and agnostics, relying on science rather than revelation
or the churches, had more in common with the Modernists than
with the Fundamentalists. And, for the first time, Liberals (whether
Modernist Protestants or lapsed-Protestant humanists) made
gestures of including Catholic and Jewish liberals in their efforts to
overcome the roadblocks to the millennium. After all, many of the
poor, and many members of the working class, were recent
immigrants; to uplift them, to allow them to participate fully in the
working-out of America's millennial mission, could be construed to
be as much the task of the Catholic and the Jew as of the Liberal
Protestant and the progressive humanist.

Unfortunately, this tentative ecumenism was still tainted with
superciliousness on the part of the native-born; their general
support of restrictions on immigration and their feeling that
Catholic and Jewish immigrants needed to be "uplifted" from
their "backward" and "superstitious" ignorance scarcely contributed to religious equality. However, when the Bolshevik
Revolution in 1917 created a revolutionary force in the world that
rivaled the potential power of the Americal Revolution as a source
of hope for the oppressed of the world, a new kind of ecumenism
began to develop among conservative Fundamentalists, Catholics,
and Jews.

Fearing that Communism represented the Anti-Christ, aware
that it threatened not only private property and American
capitalism but the Judeo-Christian faith, many Fundamentalists
and Catholics found common ground in defending "the Cross and
the Flag" against this satanic foreign conspiracy. The creation of
the State of Israel in 1948 (following Hitler's efforts to eliminate
the Jews from human history) provided a link between conservative
Evangelical Christians and Jews. According to Fundamentalist
exegesis of the Bible, the redemption of the human race included a
role for the Jews; particularly noted was the prediction that in "the
latter days" a sign of the millennium would be the return of the
Jews to their homeland. Defense of religious liberty, of capitalist

hegemony in the world, of "inalienable natural rights" against tyrannical fascists and communists alike, also united Liberal Protestants and humanists behind a common front with Catholics and Jews after 1950.

At this point Americans at last accepted the concept of a pluralistic nation, at least to the extent, as Will Herberg put it in 1955, of agreeing that "to be a Protestant, a Catholic, or a Jew are today the alternative ways of being an American." The election of a Roman Catholic to the presidency in 1960 and the admiration for Henry Kissinger (a foreign-born Jew) as secretary of state after 1968 were outward symbols of this pluralism. Although Orientals were still only a tiny group in the nation, their religious outlook gained respectability in the 1950s when the rising generation found the ecumenism of the new pluralistic "establishment" too fear-ridden, conservative, and culture-bound. The interest in Zen Buddhism suggested that ecumenism should be worldwide rather than American or Western.

When a tremendous upsurge of interest in religion began in the 1960s, many journalists and social critics found signs that a new awakening was at hand, but they found them at first in the older symbols of revivalism. Protestant evangelists like Billy Graham, Oral Roberts, and Katheryn Kuhlman resurrected the tradition of mass revivalism in the cities, while Catholics like Monsignor Fulton J. Sheen and Jews like Rabbi Joshua Liebman aroused tremendous popular response within their faiths. Revivalism seemed more ecumenical but not essentially different. What did not fit the old pattern was the new interest in Zen Buddhism, magic, astrology, satanism, and the occult. It seemed that, while the older generation of Americans was ready to reaffirm its Judeo-Christian heritage, a large proportion of the younger generation was ready to abandon it. There was also a renewed interest in atheistic Marxism in the 1960s, not to mention the continued appeal of scientism, evident in Scientology, Esalen, and est. Faith in the Holy Spirit was matched by faith in ESP. Revivalism was present, but it did not seem to be at the center of the new awakening. The emergence of the Jesus People and the new popularity of neo-Evangelicalism (personified in President Jimmy Carter and his faith-healing sister) were matched by the death-of-God movement and the new rural communes, which seemed to reject the nation's Judeo-Christian heritage. To explain all this, a new definition of an "awakening" was necessary.

## Toward a New Definition of an Awakening

The purpose of this essay is to indicate why the key to a great awakening is no longer to be found simply in Protestant (or even ecumenical) mass revivalism. Most historians, although they note a serious ideological shift in American culture between 1890 and 1920, do not describe that period (as I shall here) as America's Third Great Awakening. They do not because they rightly see that Dwight. L. Moody, Billy Sunday, and Aimee Semple MacPherson were not really at the heart of that ideological reorientation in the same sense that Jonathan Edwards was at the center of our First Great Awakening and Lyman Beecher at the center of our Second. Nevertheless, these four great eras of ideological reorientation (along with the Puritan movement) are similar. What we need, therefore, is a model that can abstract the causes, functions, and results of such reorientations from the Protestant revivalism that originally characterized them.

If we can rid ourselves of the old Protestant definition of revivalism and awakenings and think more sociologically and anthropologically about religion, we will better understand our past as well as our present times of concern with man's place in the universe. Ever since the first applications of psychological analysis to religious experiences in the 1890s there has been a tendency to denigrate their spiritual quality. But while such analysis freed us from doctrinal explanation of conversions, it also tended to deny their religious dimension. Despite the best efforts of William James, most psychologists, whether Freudian or behaviorist, have reduced religious experiences to secular terms by stressing latent versus manifest content. The scientific analyst of religion has also stressed the "primitive," "backward," "culturally impoverished," "economically deprived," "socially ostracized," or privately "neurotic" aspects of religious experience. But reductionism is not explanation. Nor does it help to say simply, as anthropologists have, that all cultures construct rituals to help the child transform himself into a man or herself into a woman. To call conversion a *rite de passage* still begs the question of periodic mass awakenings. It explains what a culturally normal event is, but it does not explain the culturally abnormal event. Hence the new interest among anthropologists since 1960 in ghost-dance religions and cargo cults.

Some religious experiences are undoubtedly the results of pathological problems. Still, I would say with William James and Erik Erikson that, even in what may seem extreme cases, the results may be heuristic or cathartic. By and large, most religious converts move from states of anxiety and inhibition to states of functionally constructive personal and social action. Similarly, the abnormal cultural events that we call religious awakenings or revivals— movements that grip whole communities or nations for many years —are not only fruitful but necessary if a culture is to survive the traumas of social change.

I propose, therefore, to view the five great awakenings that have shaped and reshaped our culture since 1607 as periods of fundamental ideological transformation necessary to the dynamic growth of the nation in adapting to basic social, ecological, psychological, and economic changes. The conversion of great numbers of people from an old to a new world view (a new ideological or religious understanding of their place in the cosmos) is a natural and necessary aspect of social change. It constitutes the awakening of a people caught in an outmoded, dysfunctional world view to the necessity of converting their mindset, their behavior, and their institutions to more relevant or more functionally useful ways of understanding and coping with the changes in the world they live in.

The Protestant theologian speaks of great awakenings or revival times as divine manifestations of concern for the "salvation of Adam's children from the bondage of Satan," as signs of "the coming Kingdom of God on earth," or as *kairos* (the invasion of the temporal by the eternal). What I have to say will not necessarily contradict the faith system of either the behavioral psychologist or the Judeo-Christian theologian. My concern is with the social function of religious systems and with achieving a historical perspective on their periodic transformations.

Since there is agreement that widespread expressions of religious

concern have recurred periodically in American history, the task of
the historian is to explain why they occurred in those particular
spans of time, in that particular place, among those particular
people, in that particular way. Such attempts have of course been
made before (especially concerning what our textbooks describe as
the First Great Awakening in the 1740s and the Second Great
Awakening in the early nineteenth century). These explanations
have included efforts to associate revivals of religion with great
natural catastrophes (floods, earthquakes, volcanoes, tidal waves),
or with epidemics, wars, and depressions, but without convincing
correlations. Some historians have argued that charismatic individuals have the power to sway multitudes at will, but history is not the
biographies of great men. Others have traced revivals to the rise and
decline of religious institutions, to the decadence of one ecclesiastical system and its challenge by a new one. Still others have
explained these awakenings in terms of the conflict of ideas—the
impact upon old theological dogmas of new modes of thought
about the nature of the universe or the nature of man—as though
religion were simply the rational process of convincing people that
one world view is more consistent than another.

The causes of great awakenings and the revivalism that is part of
them seem to me to lie in more complex social and intellectual
relationships. There can be no single cause for such wide-ranging
transformations in thought and behavior upon which millions are
ready to stake their lives.

Human institutions generally assume that there is a fixed or
normative relationship of one man or group to another, of one
generation to another. They prepare men for continuity, not
change; they are the means by which men try to insure stability,
order, regularity, and predictability in their lives. The child-rearing
practices of the family, the husband-wife relationship, the legal
system, the schools, the churches, the government, all assume
permanent relationships and therefore impose sanctions on deviations from these social norms. But times change; the world changes;
people change; and therefore institutions, world views, and cultural
systems must change.

In this study I have adapted a formulation of cultural change
described by the anthropologist Anthony F. C. Wallace in his essay

"Revitalization Movements" (*American Anthropology*, 1956).
Because Wallace derived his theory from studies of so-called
primitive peoples (preliterate and homogeneous), it is not totally
applicable to the complex, pluralistic, and highly literate people of
the United States. Wallace speaks of a single prophet's inaugurat-
ing a revitalization movement and transforming a whole society,
because he is concerned with the Seneca Indians and the Handsome
Lake religious movement. Nevertheless, the general configuration
of his model can be applied to American history, and he himself
explicitly says that it applies to movements as broad and complex as
the rise of Christianity, Islam, Buddhism, or Wesleyan Methodism.

I shall treat each of the five awakenings as a period of fundamental social and intellectual reorientation of the American belief-
value system, behavior patterns, and institutional structure. But I
shall also contend that these reorientations have revolved around a
constant culture core of rather broadly stated beliefs. These beliefs
(though radically altered in definition during each awakening) have
provided the continuity that sustains the culture. In short, great
awakenings are periods when the cultural system has had to be
revitalized in order to overcome jarring disjunctions between norms
and experience, old beliefs and new realities, dying patterns and
emerging patterns of behavior. Each of the awakenings has to be
studied as a process of social change taking place in various stages
over a thirty- to forty-year period. The specific revivals and revival
leaders within these broad periods generate or articulate not a single
theological system (as Handsome Lake did for the Seneca's revitalization movement) but a set of commonly shared beliefs and
practices that cut across the specific denominational lines that
divide American ecclesiastical life. Denominational organizations,
sects, and cults provide alternative strategies within the grand
overall design of revitalization suitable to the various regional,
class, color, ethnic, or educational groups within the nation as they
cope with the broad necessities of social change.

While I should not like to be held strictly to the dating, I would
roughly describe our periods of awakening as follows: the Puritan
Awakening, 1610–40; the First Great Awakening (in America),
1730–60; the Second Great Awakening, 1800–1830; the Third
Great Awakening, 1890–1920; and the Fourth Great Awakening,

1960–90(?). These generations of transition were confusing and
tumultuous, but it is important at the outset to stress the positive,
unifying results of each of them. The Puritan Awakening led to the
beginning of constitutional monarchy in England; America's First
Great Awakening led to the creation of the American republic; our
Second Awakening led to the solidification of the Union and the
rise of Jacksonian participatory democracy; our Third Awakening
led to the rejection of unregulated capitalistic exploitation and the
beginning of the welfare state; and our Fourth Awakening appears
headed toward a rejection of unregulated exploitation of human-
kind and of nature and toward a series of regional and international
consortiums for the conservation and optimal use of the world's
resources.

Robert Bellah in *The Broken Covenant* (1975) stated well the
reasons why the study of a nation's changing religious system is at
least as important as a study of its political or economic system and,
hence, why a book on America's great awakenings is relevant to
those who do not share the religious concerns of the current
awakening:

> It is one of the oldest of sociological generalizations that any coherent
> and viable society rests on a common set of moral understandings about
> good and bad, right and wrong, in the realm of individual and social
> action. It is almost as widely held that these common moral under-
> standings must also in turn rest upon a common set of religious
> understandings that provide a picture of the universe in terms of which
> the moral understandings make sense. Such moral and religious under-
> standings produce both a basic cultural legitimation for a society which
> is viewed as at least approximately in accord with them, and a standard
> of judgment for the criticism of a society that is seen as deviating too
> far from them.

Our five awakenings came about when, by the standards of our
culture core and the experiences of daily life, our society deviated
too far from the moral and religious understandings that legiti-
mized authority in church and state. Not surprisingly, each of our
awakenings in the past (and undoubtedly the same will hold for our
current one as well) has been followed by a period of drastic (once,
truly revolutionary) restructuring of our social, political, and
economic institutions.

## Awakenings as Revitalizations of Culture

A great awakening occurs, Wallace says, when a society finds that its day-to-day behavior has deviated so far from the accepted (traditional) norms that neither individuals nor large groups can honestly (consistently) sustain the common set of religious under-standings by which they believe (have been taught) they should act. When parents can no longer adequately guide their own lives or their children's, when schools and churches provide conflicting ethical guidelines for economic and political behavior, and when courts impose sanctions upon acts commonly recognized as neces-sary (or accepted) deviations from old rules, then a period of profound cultural disorientation results. Then leaders lose their authority and institutions the respect essential for their effective operation. Then men begin to doubt their sense and their sanity and to search about for new gods, new ways to perceive and comprehend the power that guides the universe. If they are lucky, they will find leaders able to articulate a new accommodation with "reality," a new sense of reality, of identity, and of self-confidence, and, above all, a revision of their institutional structure that will return daily life to regularity and order. If they are unlucky, their culture will disintegrate: their birthrate will decline, psychic dis-order will increase, and some wild ghost-dance religion will mark the final sputtering-out.

In the perception of this crisis of legitimacy and the effort to cope with it lies the beginning of what Wallace calls a revitalization movement. Such movements follow certain patterns of evolution. The first stage he calls "the period of individual stress," when, one by one, people lose their bearings, become psychically or physically ill, show what appear to be signs of neurosis, psychosis, or madness, and may either break out in acts of violence against family, friends, and authorities or become apathetic, catatonic, incapable of func-tioning. Emile Durkheim described this as "anomie," or loss of identity. Often anomic individuals destroy themselves by drugs, alcohol, or suicide. By their friends, and by society in general, these early victims of social disjunction are seen as deviants, misfits, persons too weak or too psychologically infirm to cope with life. They are sent to ministerial or psychological counselors (medicine

men) or to hospitals and asylums to be cured or to "readjust." But
as the number of these individuals increases, the institutional
bonds of society begin to snap. Families are the first to suffer as
husbands and wives quarrel, divorce, and neglect or mistreat their
children.

The second state of the revitalization movement Wallace calls the
"period of cultural distortion." Gradually people conclude that
the problems are not personal but are resulting from institutional
malfunction. The churches do not offer solace and acceptance of
the prevailing order; the schools cannot maintain discipline over
their pupils; the police and courts cannot maintain orderly processes
of action (they often infringe the very laws they are supposed to
enforce); the hospitals cannot cure; the jails burst at their seams;
and, finally, the government itself fails to function with the respect
and authority it requires. Political rebellion in the streets and
schismatic behavior in churches create civil and ecclesiastical disorder, to which the authorities in church and state can react only by
more sanctions, more censures, more punishments.

In a viable, healthy, effectively functioning society there are always,
of course, strains and stresses, but the system is prepared to handle
them. Every culture has stress-reduction mechanisms built into it.
For individuals these include appeals to God through churchly
offices, the medical assistance of doctors, and various legitimate
outlets for aggression in recreation or sports. But in a period of
cultural distortion the stresses are abnormal, the ordinary stress-
reduction techniques fail to help those who resort to them, and the
decreasing efficiency of these mechanisms leads to severe and
widespread personality disorders. Similarly, when a culture is
functioning harmoniously, it is able to cope with major natural
disorders (floods, earthquakes, epidemics) and to pull its people
together in a common cause against external dangers (military
invasion, subversion, economic dislocations). However, in periods
of cultural distortion the populace is at odds with itself. The
people cannot agree on proper measures for coping with dangers;
instead of joining together to meet it, they quarrel and divide,
often blaming those in authority. They refuse to unite on any
scheme. They may even flout the establishment by unpatriotic
acts, seeming thus to give aid and comfort to the enemy.

At this early stage of revitalization, Wallace notes, there almost always arises a nativist or traditionalist movement within the culture, that is, an attempt by those with rigid personalities or with much at stake in the older order to argue that the danger comes from the failure of the populace to adhere more strictly to the old beliefs, values, and behavior patterns. Generally these traditionalists are found among the older generations, those in authority or closely associated with the hierarchy in various institutions. In the ecclesiastical system they point out that God is displeased because the old rituals have not been adhered to; in the civil system they point to the rise of crime and insist that disrespect for law and order lies at the root of the problem. They mistake symptoms for causes. Their solution is double-edged. First they call for a return to the "old-time religion," "the ways of our fathers," and "respect for the flag" (or other symbols of the old order). Second, they tend to find scapegoats in their midst (aliens, witches, conspirators, foreigners, traitors) upon whom they can project their fear; then, by punishing these "outsiders," they can set an example of revived authority. The nativists, denying any cause for disorder, often blame the younger generation for unjustifiable deviation from the right ways. "Rigid persons," Wallace says, "apparently prefer to tolerate high levels of chronic stress rather than make systematic changes" in their ways of thought or behavior. They are reactionaries who look backward to a golden time, "the period of homeostasis," when the system worked; they insist that it will still work if only everyone will conform to the old standards.

Wallace used the term "mazeways" to describe the enculturated patterns of thought and behavior that guide individuals in their daily lives. At the basis of any culture is a generally understood and accepted world view by which each adult orients himself or herself to the family, the neighbors, the employers, the rulers, the social order in general. Through the child-rearing process the individual learns what his role is in his own town and what his place is in the universal scheme of things. He learns that he should act in conformity with man-made laws because they are the ways prescribed by the power that controls the universe. "Culture," as Wallace says, "depends relatively more on the ability of constituent units autonomously to perceive the system of which they are a part, to receive and transmit information, and to act in accordance with the necessities of the system" than it depends on the compulsory authority of any "central administration." Each individual maintains "a mental image of the society and its culture" and knows how to act automatically in any normal or normally-abnormal situation. But in periods of cultural distortion these routine mazeways become blocked, and the individual, unable to react automatically, becomes stymied and frustrated. His normal responses do not lead to the expected results. Fear and anxiety increase as he struggles to find a solution that lies outside his accepted patterns of thought.

Robert K. Merton defines a stressful or anxiety-ridden situation as one in which there is a "dissociation between culturally prescribed aspirations and socially structured avenues for realizing these aspirations." Seymour M. Lipset speaks of the need for "a dynamic equilibrium" in any social system between autonomous action and changing experiences: "a complex society is under constant pressure to adjust its institutions to its central value system in order to alleviate strains created by changes in social relations." A religious revival or a great awakening begins when accumulated pressures for change produce such acute personal and social stress that the whole culture must break the crust of custom, crash through the blocks in the mazeways, and find new socially structured avenues along which the members of the society may pursue their course in mutual harmony with one another.

So stressful a situation inevitably produces profound and widespread emotional confusion and excitement. People must be found who can help to formulate a new consensus, create new mazeways. These new mazeways must be understood to be in harmony not only with daily experience but also with the way in which that experience is understood to reflect the realities of the mysterious power that controls the universe. As Clifford Geertz puts it, "In religious belief and practice a group's ethos is rendered intellectually reasonable by being shown to represent a way of life ideally adapted to the actual state of affairs the world view describes, while the world view is rendered emotionally convincing by being presented as an image of an actual state of affairs peculiarly well-arranged to accommodate such a way of life.'' This is what occurs in the religious excitement of an awakening.

The final stages of a great awakening arrive with the building of the new world view or mazeway and the restructuring of old institutions. The most rigid and reactionary nativists are seldom able to make this transition; they continue, as much as they can, to follow the old ways, but they now represent the minority, the dissident view in the new consensus. But many who at first adopted the traditionalist stance gradually drift into the new consensus when they find it more satisfactory or when they conclude that they cannot sustain the old order. Wallace puts forth as the third stage of the revitalization movement the appearance of a prophet who (like Moses, Mohammed, Martin Luther, or Handsome Lake) personally undergoes a traumatic religious experience that epitomizes the crisis of the culture. Often such prophets have hallucinatory visions or dreams (for them as vividly real as any physical experience) in which they directly confront the deity. From that confrontation they receive (or have revealed to them) new formulations of divine law. Thereafter the prophet reveals (as God's chosen messenger) this new way to his fellow men. Gradually he develops a band of disciples or followers, whom he appoints (or anoints), and they fan out through the social system to proselytize for the new religious order. Among the precepts they inculcate are not only theological statements regarding the nature and will of God and how he is to be worshiped but also (more or less explicitly) a new set of social norms for individual and group behavior. Those who come in contact with the prophet or his charismatic disciples are ''touched'' by the same divine experience, and this validates both the prophet's vision and the new mazeway he inculcates as God's will for his people.

There has been no single prophet in America's five awakenings and no national displacement of the Judeo-Christian tradition. There have, of course, been individual religious leaders, of great force, who founded new denominations or cults: Joseph Smith and Brigham Young among the Mormons; Ann Lee among the Shakers; Aimee Semple McPherson and the International Church of the Foursquare Gospel; William J. Seymour among the black Pentecostalists; William Miller and Ellen White among the Adventists;

Mary Baker Eddy, founder of Christian Science; Charles Taze Russell founder of Jehovah's Witnesses. These leaders have sustained a core of believers, not by repudiating Christianity, but by supplementing or modifying it. They all fall within the Judeo-Christian tradition in major aspects of their theology, and, despite some eccentricities, they generally conform to the prevailing codes of behavior. They have not deflected the mainstream of American culture and, in fact, generally claim to represent a better version of it.

America's revivalistic movements consequently fall outside Wallace's model, and it is useful to cite Peter Worsley's work *The Trumpet Shall Sound* (1968) to supplement it. Worsley argues that "charisma—sociologically viewed—is a social relationship, not an attribute of individual personality or a mystical quality." Charisma provides "more than an abstract ideological rationale. . . . It is a legitimation grounded in a relationship of loyalty and identification in which the leader is followed simply because he embodies values in which the followers have an 'interest' . . . The followers . . . in a dialectical way, create, by selecting them out, the leaders who in turn *command* on the basis of this newly-accorded legitimacy. . . . He articulates and consolidates their aspirations." He specifies and converts aspirations into "beliefs which can be validated by reference to experience." Worsley maintains that the message is more important than the medium in revitalization. "It is indeed highly probable that a prophetic movement will generate not a centrally focussed, single authority-structure but a fissiparous dispersion of leadership in the persons of numerous leaders, particularly where inspiration is open to all."

Worsley's view seems particularly relevant to American religious leadership. Because we have had a voluntaristic religious and political structure, together with fundamental religious freedom, leadership in our awakenings has been widely dispersed, differing in emphasis or tone in different regions and groups. We shall have to seek for the common elements among a wide variety of prophets in each awakening and choose as key spokespersons those who articulate and consolidate the new world view for the mainstream majority—in short, those whose appeal is interdenominational rather than denominational. Such persons have never repudiated the older world views entirely; instead, they have claimed merely to shed new light on them, that is, to look upon old truths from a new perspective.

The concept of "new light" from God is intrinsic in the Judeo-Christian tradition, which thus has within itself the power of self-renewal. Each of the Old Testament prophets, though castigating God's chosen for departing from the old ways, shed new light on those traditions. Jesus of Nazareth, the last of these prophets, urged the Jews to live more truly by the old laws, not to abandon them. Martin Luther claimed to be returning the Christian churches to their original apostolic truths in his reformation of Catholicism. When John Robinson bade the Pilgrims godspeed from Holland to New England, he reminded them that their dissent from Anglican orthodoxy was justified: "The Lord has more truth and light yet to break forth out of his holy word." The belief that "God has yet further light to shed upon his revelations" has been a constant theme of English and American revivalism. Part of the strength of the new lights in every awakening comes from their placing the burden of corruption upon those who are illuminated by an older, dimmer light. Orthodoxy in America has been progressive or syncretic, offering new definitions for old truths. God is, of course, always and everywhere the same, but his spirit manifests itself in new ways to meet new needs. It is the old lights in each of our awakenings (variously called "Old Sides," "Old School," "Old divinity," or "Fundamentalists") who have clung to the letter and ignored the spirit of God's will. Their reliance on dead formalism and shibboleths that have lost their meaning has enabled the new lights to capture the imagination of a confused people and lead them out of the old churches and into new ones, constantly revitalizing the mazeways.

There is no conservative tradition in America because God is not a conservative. God is an innovator. American culture is thus always in the making but never complete. It will be completed, according to one of our most cherished cultural myths, at the end of human time, the beginning of God's Kingdom, the coming of the millennium. Exactly how and when that will occur is itself constantly subject to new light. America, the New World, has easily become a metaphor for the New Eden; it is "the new Garden in the West," where, unspoiled by old and corrupt institutions (monarchy,

an established church, a nobility), man might create a perfect
moral order with perfect moral freedom. From its first settlements,
not only in Pilgrim Plymouth but in almost every colony, America
has been a utopian experiment in achieving the Kingdom of God
on earth. Our Revolution was justified on these terms in 1776. Our
history has been essentially the history of one long millenarian
movement. Americans, in their cultural mythology, are God's
chosen, leading the world to perfection. Every awakening has
revived, revitalized, and redefined that culture core.

To return to our model of cultural reorientation, Wallace says
that the fourth state of revitalization begins when the prophet (or
prophets) of the new-light vision begin to attract the more flexible
(usually the younger) members of the society, who are willing to
experiment with new mazeways or life-styles. These persons "try
out various limited mazeway changes in their personal lives,"
Wallace says, in order to relieve the stresses they feel. They leave
home or school and travel to other parts of the country. They join
informal groups trying out new communal (or utopian) forms of
social relationship. Often they experiment with new economic,
political, and familial arrangements or new sexual mores. Every
awakening has brought new kinds of "communes" or communities
of this sort. But some of these experiments become psychologically
regressive, violent and destructive. There is a negative side to every
new-light movement, and often the most pietistic and perfectionist
new lights become the most destructive. They make transvaluation
of all values the measure of their separatism from a corrupt order.
They practice as truth what formerly was called demonic; they deify
their leaders, invert Christian rituals, denigrate the individual.
Eventually the more moderate new lights repudiate such extremists
in order to establish their own stability and order.

But even among the moderate new lights there is at first
considerable emotionalism (or enthusiasm); many are carried away
in transports of hysteria by their vision of God in revivalistic
meetings. It is considered a measure of one's commitment to the
new ways that he or she experience a violent psychological break
with the past through a direct confrontation with God (under the
aegis of the new prophets). So profound are these confrontations
that the convert from the old to the new way of belief feels that

God's power has totally transformed him, regenerated him, made him a new man. From that cataclysmic conversion experience he dates his "new birth," and many see the world thereafter through such different eyes that they seem to friends and relatives to be truly reborn. Their behavioral patterns are transformed. Frequently these persons conclude that God's spirit has come to dwell in them, for how else can they explain the different aspect in which they view the world?

In all awakenings the concept of divine immanence as opposed to divine transcendence becomes a central issue. The Calvinist tradition, so central to American culture, emphasized the separateness of God from his creation and the separation of man from God (through Adam's fall). However, in times of cultural stress, when institutionalized religion is unable to sustain, even among the faithful, a sense of regular communion with God in formal church rites, the distance between Creator and created becomes intolerably great; men sink in fear and loneliness. Then the pendulum swings to the pole of divine immanence (dating back, perhaps, to more primitive, animistic, or pantheistic religious feelings). God's absence from the churches is compensated for by his spiritual presence in nature; regular churchly practices begin to appear as a barrier rather than as a bridge to God. People seek him elsewhere. The assumption grows that he is more really present in this world than his priests have let on and more readily available to all. He has left the temple and entered the world around it. God's spirit, sensing man's need, makes itself known to man in new ways, appearing unbidden in visions and speaking through even the most humble people. In an awakening, the gap between this world and the next disappears. The spiritual and physical worlds intermingle. God can be discerned as easily in a flower, a blade of grass, or a child as in a church. He can be spoken to directly, confronted personally, and his spirit takes up its dwelling in all of creation. God is all in all.

By the same token, the spiritual power of evil also becomes more immanent. The distraught see God and the devil locked in conflict for men's souls; both are at arm's length, seeking to possess men with their power. The most frightening, and heartening, of spiritual possiblities seem imminent. Then logic yields to intuition

as a source of knowledge or truth; self-discipline yields to impulse,
science to magic, formal worship to vision. Man having lost control
of himself and his world, other forces seek to control him and it.
Anything is possible.

In this crisis the new-light prophets and their apostles offer a
vision of God as a guardian spirit, capable of helping those who
seek it, ready to define new rules of conduct to bring back order and
tranquillity. But they also preach that, if God's new rules are not
adhered to, some terrible catastrophe—the end of the world
itself—will surely follow. Part of the American culture core has
been its myth that we are a "covenanted people" (successors to the
apostate Jewish nation as God's chosen people). As such, God has a
special interest in helping, and a special reason for punishing, us.
This covenant applies both to individuals and to the nation as a
whole. But if each does his or her part to adhere to the new rules,
then God promises, according to his prophets, a glorious new day
of peace, fraternity, and perfection—a time in which all human
needs will be met, both physical and spiritual. Thus the experience
of hearing, yielding to, and experiencing this call is one of ecstatic
release from the burden of guilt and fear.

The revivalism of an awakening is the ritual process by which this
transformation or regeneration takes places both individually and
en masse. All revitalization movements are replete with symbols of
death and rebirth—death to the old Adam, the old errors, the old
sins, the old ways, and rebirth into bodily rejuvenation and
spiritual renewal. A revival meeting is at once a funeral service and
a christening. In many cases this rebirth includes the healing of old
bodily ailments, and faith healing has been a constant feature of
revivalism. In extreme perfectionist cults the claim has been made
that the converted will never die.

Wallace points out, however, that successful prophets never
"lose their sense of personal identity." They bear God's message
but are not God incarnate. To revitalize their society, their message
must spread beyond them geographically and chronologically. This
means that they must skillfully argue down the old-light opposition
and skillfully keep their followers from total civil suppression. They
must learn to distinguish between what is God's and what is
Caesar's In addition, they must be able to organize their followers

and routinize their charisma. The spontaneous, ecstatic experience
of a revival meeting during an awakening must be canalized,
ritualized, linked to regular services. The followers who hang on the
revivalist's words and long to be in his presence must learn to
sublimate that feeling in regular church services under anointed
apostles, and these in turn must create means to raise up successors
from the gifted laity. In each of our awakenings the successful
new-light prophets have achieved this important organizational
transition. When the Puritan movement died, the evangelistic
spirit within it was reborn in Congregationalism and Presbyterianism and was later revitalized by the Baptists, Methodists, Campbellites, Disciples of Christ, and by Progressive, Liberal Protestants.

Finally, in the last phase of a revitalization movement, the
prophets succeed in winning over that large group of undecided
folk who, though they have not themselves experienced the ecstasy
of conversion, have been sufficiently impressed with the doctrines
and behavior of the new lights to see the relevance of their new
guidelines and to accept their practices. Even many of the former
old lights are won over to the new consensus in this final stage. Now
control of the old religious institutions passes to the new leadership.
From the thesis and antithesis of the revival generation a new
synthesis emerges. But the old light never quite dies, and the
process is never finished.

As the new lights become dominant and the mazeways are
cleared, there is considerable revision of the institutional structure,
often through political action. Familial patterns change, sex roles
alter, schools reform their curriculums and teaching methods,
courts revise their interpretations, governments enact new laws and
reorganize their recruitment of civil servants. It frequently happens
that the spiritual fervor released by this unblocking of the mazeways, this renewal of the convenant, produces an uncontrollable
effort to reform the most basic aspects of the older social order: the
relations of sons to fathers or husbands to wives, new concepts of
property rights, new economic practices. It was through following
the new guidelines of our revitalization movements that Americans
abandoned allegiance to the king, abolished human slavery,
regulated business enterprise, empowered labor unions, and is now

trying to equalize the rights of women, blacks, Indians, and other minorities.

More often than not this reunited sense of national millenarian purpose has led Americans into war in the effort to speed up the fulfillment of their manifest destiny. It might be more accurately said that our periods of great awakening have produced wars rather than resulted from them. All our wars, like Cromwell's against Charles I, have been understood as holy crusades against error within and evil without. Cromwell first destroyed the monarchy and its Cavaliers and then tried to eradicate the Celtic Catholics in Ireland. The colonists, after the First Awakening, first defeated the French and Indians and then threw off the corrupt king and Parliament. The Americans, after the Second Awakening, first eliminated the Indians and Mexicans and British from the West and then attacked those who would secede from the covenant in order to uphold black slavery. At the height of their Third Awakening, Americans stopped attacking big business and turned against "the Hun" to save the world for democracy; the war against Naziism was simply a continuation of that effort. From our Fourth Great Awakening we may expect a similar crusade, unless the new light of this revitalization drastically alters the millenarian concept of manifest destiny (as it fortunately shows signs of doing).

Wallace concludes his essay on "Revitalization Movements" by noting their drive toward "extensive cultural changes" and their implementation of "an enthusiastic embarkation on some organized program" of reform, which generally includes "projects of further social, political, and economic reform." This being so, our effort in the following pages cannot help being a rather cursory summary of the whole of American history, so closely intertwined are revivalism and awakenings with our culture.

# 2 The Puritan Awakening and the Culture Core

## The Puritan Revitalization Movement: 1610–40

America was born in an awakening. Its settlements arose from the tremendous energy unleashed in the Puritan revitalization movement in England in the decades preceding 1640. It took a profound commitment to God's will and faith in his oversight to encourage tens of thousands of men, women, and children to uproot themselves from their homes and embark in frail, cramped ships for the steaming forest or frigid rocks of the New World. In setting sail for "an howling wilderness" inhabited only by savage beasts and beastly savages, the first settlers had to be driven by conscience and faith as much as by the hope of bettering their condition.

Perry Miller defined Puritanism as "that point of view, that philosophy of life, that code of values which was carried to New England by the first settlers." But it was also carried by early settlers to Virginia and other colonies as well, though in different forms of Puritanism. "Puritanism," as Miller said, "was not only a religious creed, it was a philosophy and a metaphysic; it was an organization of man's whole life, emotional and intellectual." In his introduction to *The Puritans* (1938) Miller noted that "Puritan culture as a whole [shared] about ninety percent of the intellectual life, scientific knowledge, morality, manners, customs, notions and prejudices . . . of all Englishmen." Yet the other 10 percent "made all the difference"; it dyed the whole barrel; it changed the whole nature of a person's outlook. Puritanism was a different world view from Anglicanism, with which it was in conflict.

Starting as a quarrel over the purification of the Church of England, the Puritan movement spread to include a host of political and economic issues until, by 1630, "the gulf between the belief of those Puritans and the majority in the Church of England grew so wide that at last there was no bridging it at all." In effect, England had two antagonistic ideologies; Puritanism had become the counterculture, the "new light" to the Anglican "old light." And while the Puritan Revolution did not succeed, it brought to a head those basic dysfunctions within their society which Englishmen had to resolve if their culture was to remain dynamic. The king and his church, the aristocracy and its feudal rights, simply could not withstand forever the forces of social change for which the Puritan movement spoke. Though Cromwell's Bible Commonwealth failed, the gentry class did rise to power, the Commons did seize the initiative in Parliament, the king's prerogatives were limited by constitutional bounds, and commerce in a market economy did replace the feudal, agrarian way of life. England went through two political revolutions (one in 1642, the other in 1688) in the process of accommodating to these forces of social change.

The American colonies were a direct offshoot of this cultural revolution. They were settled at its height and retained so much of its thrust as to give the colonies an accelerating trajectory out of the orbit of the motherland. The Puritan Awakening in effect gave America its own culture core, its sense of being a differently constituted people, covenanted with God on a special errand into the wilderness. The millennial hopes of the colonists, their pietistic perfectionism, their belief in further light and a higher law, their commitment to freedom of conscience and separation of church and state, and, above all, their profound sense of individual piety made the Americans different. The colonies of North America attracted from their beginning a special kind of people who found this cultural outlook more appealing than that of old England. It was a land committed to the reformation of God's world and the freedom of the individual in his calling, though its settlers also possessed a large share of self-interest, aggression, and acquisitiveness.

The Puritan awakening in England was a reaction against the established order that had grown out of the English Reformation a century earlier. The religious excitement that climaxed in Henry VIII's break with the Church of Rome in 1523 continued to boil through the reigns of Edward VI and Mary but finally settled down under the compromise system of Elizabeth I. The more fanatical reformers, who had fled to Europe during Mary's efforts to return England to Catholicism in the 1550s, returned under Elizabeth but were unsatisfied with her halfway measures. Too small a minority to do much about it, they could only mutter among themselves as the Anglican Church developed its own world view and won the allegiance of the vast majority of Englishmen. But the reign of Elizabeth was filled with other aspects of social change, and these slowly built up to a new period of tension under her successors.

The discovery of the New World, leading to the first exploitative settlements in Central and South America, opened new interest in trade and discovery in Europe and greatly enhanced Spanish wealth and power. The Catholic Counter-Reformation stemmed the southward advance of Luther's and Calvin's Protestant revolt (though Calvinism gained in these years a strong hold over the people of Scotland). The gold and silver of the Aztecs and Incas stimulated new economic development in Europe, particularly in the textile industry. Trade routes expanded to the East, and cities arose at crossroads and seaports, housing a new class of middlemen (tradesmen, merchants, craftsmen, lawyers, businessmen) between the peasants and the nobility. England was at first isolated from these changes; and until it defeated the Spanish Armada in 1588, it was in danger of being conquered by Spain and returned to Catholicism. After that victory England entered into its own age of discovery, trade, and colonization. Then Britain began its phenomenal rise to world power through its navy and merchant marine. The early years of the seventeenth century were seething with social ferment, and Puritanism provided a congenial "new light" on what this meant for England's God-ordained future greatness. R. H. Tawney summarized the ideological conflict between Anglicanism and Puritanism in *Religion and the Rise of Capitalism* (1926):

> If a philosophy of society is to be effective, it must be as mobile and realistic as the forces which it would control. The weakness of an attitude which met the onset of insurgent economic interests with a generalized appeal to traditional morality and an idealization of the past

[as the English king and bishops did] was only too obvious. Shocked,
confused, thrown on to a helpless, if courageous and eloquent, defensive
by changes even in the slowly moving world of agriculture, medieval
social theory, to which the most representative minds of the English
church still clung, found itself swept off its feet after the middle of the
century by the swift rise of a commercial civilization in which all traditional landmarks seemed one by one to be submerged.

Tawney exaggerated somewhat, but in essence the philosophy of
Puritanism did challenge not only the theology and polity of the
Anglican Church but also its social theory. Englishmen, especially
in the middling class, who prior to 1600 had little use for
Puritanism, began to find that it had much to commend it.

The ascendancy of James VI of Scotland to the throne of England
in 1604 seemed to give the Puritan reformers the chance they had
been waiting for. James had been raised in Scotland and was an
ardent Calvinist theologian. But to their dismay he rejected the
petition asking him to do away with the rule by bishops in the
church and to abolish other corrupt rituals left over from Catholic
times. His famous statement, "No bishop, no king," reflected his
faith in an older tradition, one that was to end a generation later
when his son was beheaded, along with the archbishop of Canter-
bury, in the Puritan Revolution. In large part, however, James I's
opposition to Puritanism was based less on theology than on his
commitment to the theory of the divine right of kings and his
defense of the royal prerogative. In pursuing this royalist theory the
Stuart monarchs of the seventeenth century ran strongly against the
rising currents of what the middle class considered its own prerogatives. Good Anglicans, who did not mind if James I and Charles I
harried religious fanatics out of the realm, could not tolerate their
laying taxes without assent of Parliament upon those engaged in
trade and textiles. Nor could they stomach the bishops' use of
ecclesiastical courts to restrain and punish economic practices
essential to capitalist expansion (on the grounds that such practices
ran counter to medieval religious morality).

The Puritans' new light on God's will argued that men must be
diligent in business and that, if they were among the predestined
saints, their business ventures would thrive. The "Protestant
ethic," as Max Weber pointed out, offered a new set of social

virtues more in harmony with capitalist practice than the medieval condemnation of usury, "filthy lucre," and rugged individualism. Thrift, industry, frugality, scrupulous financial honesty, a horror of debt, and the integrity of credit were all prime virtues to the Calvinist. True, Calvinists opposed charging excessive rates of interest for capital loans and disapproved of businessmen who took advantage of the laws of supply and demand to gouge their neighbors. However, a modest gain on one's investment was considered good business sense and commendable in the eyes of God, who expected his stewards to increase their wealth. God required men to labor diligently in their callings and to improve the earth. The increasing wealth of individuals increased the common-wealth and honored God's commands. Puritan social theory, in short, was in harmony with social change; it dignified and sancti-fied trade and commerce, while Anglican social theory sought to regulate and impede its progress.

Consequently, Puritan beliefs and values began to gain a wider hearing among the gentry and middle class after 1610. Anglicans caught in the intellectual and religious confusion between experien-tial necessities and outmoded norms looked about for new light on their problems. Honest men simply could not engage in trade without borrowing and lending capital at interest; they could not grow wool without enclosing common land and abridging some of the traditional privileges of the peasantry; they could not engage in competitive trade without making up by high profits the losses they sustained in bad ventures. Nor did it seem fair to them that the king should arbitrarily take away their profits by high taxes and forced loans or appoint his favorites to head monopolistic trading companies, which prevented other (and better) businessmen from running them more profitably. Puritanism was a revitalization movement within English society. It urged English tradition in church and state to yield to changes beyond the comprehension of the old institutional structure. It offered a new code of beliefs and values more harmonious with experiential needs. The Calvinistic ethic, as Tawney noted, was the necessary complement to the rise of bourgeois capitalism:

The pioneers of the modern economic order were . . . *parvenus* who

elbowed their way to success in the teeth of the established aristocracy
of land and commerce. The tonic that braced them for the conflict was
a new conception of religion which taught them to regard the pursuit of
wealth as not merely an advantage but a duty. This conception welded
into a disciplined force the still feeble bourgeoisie, heightened its
energies, and cast a halo of sanctification round its convenient virtues.

Thus, Tawney concludes, Puritanism's new light worked with the
forces of social change, while Anglican old light worked against
them. Tawney and Weber may have overemphasized the extent of
capitalistic individualism and the power of the bourgeoisie in
seventeenth-century England, but they clearly delineated the
general nature of the cultural distortion at the beginning of the
century and the cultural transformation at work in the thrust of the
Puritan rebellion.

Eventually, Puritan concepts spread among the common people
as well as the merchants and gentry, for they too were caught up in
the disjunction of norms and experience. The commoners who
suffered most in this transition were attracted to the more radical
implications of Puritan theology. They took more literally the
concept of direct communion with divinity, the power of God's
grace to transform the hearts of individuals, the possibilities of total
social reformation, and the creation of God's Kingdom on Earth.
The Puritan appeals for the rights of the bourgeoisie in Parliament
could be extended downward to suggest republicanism; their
appeals for the rights of conscientious dissent against Anglican
persecution of Puritans could be taken to mean that every man had
the right to his own religious views and practices. The attacks on
bishops could be extended to an attack on all religious establish-
ments. George Fox, the founder of Quakerism, even claimed in
1647 the right to refuse to make war or to swear a civil oath or to
take his hat off to any man. Ultimately the necessities of revolution
forced Cromwell to tolerate a wide range of religious dissent, and
the rights claimed by the bourgeoisie were extended by radical
theorists in the New Model Army to commoners; some even argued
for total leveling, equality, and common ownership of the land.

Like all revitalization movements, Puritanism could not be
confined within the bounds of moderate reform. Once the crust of
custom was broken, a whole host of blackbirds flew out to sing their

own songs of spiritual and political freedom. Conservative Puritans (like the Scottish Presbyterians or those who settled New England) had never denied that the Church of England was a true church of God; they sought to reform it from within and were horrified when more radical reformers declared it the church of Anti-Christ, broke away from it, and set up their own churches on Anabaptist, Quaker, or Leveler principles. When James I harried the first Separatists from the land in 1608 (the Pilgrims, who went to Holland to escape jail), conservative Puritans had applauded. But not long afterward they were themselves faced with the same choice of flight or persecution under Charles I. Between 1630 and 1640 almost 30,000 Englishmen of varying degrees of Puritan commitment went to New England alone; as many more went to other colonies in North America, where, though Puritans constituted a smaller proportion of the settlers, they nonetheless had a significant impact, even in Virginia.

## The Puritan World View

Historians are still arguing over the precise definition of Puritanism. Perry Miller tried to limit its definition to those who held the views of New England's founders. Since Roger Williams and Anne Hutchinson were banished from Massachusetts for heresy, Miller excluded them from the Puritan fold. More recent interpretations, however, have not only included Williams and Hutchinson within the broad framework of this new-light movement but have extended the definition to include the Anabaptists, the Quakers, the Seekers, the Ranters, and the Levelers on the left and the Presbyterians on the right. Similarly, a reexamination of the Anglican movement (the old lights) reveals that it too was badly divided between an Anglo-Catholic (or high church) right wing and a Presbyterian left.

To examine the distinctions among the proliferating varieties of religious opinion in the Puritan movement (as in other awakenings) is less important to our sociological viewpoint here than it may be to historians of church history. Theologically and ecclesiastically it is possible to make distinctions between the views of John Cotton and

Anne Hutchinson, Thomas Shepard and Roger Williams, Roger
Williams and John Clarke, John Clarke and Mary Dyer, and so on.
But to a social anthropologist these particularist distinctions do not
alter the basic contours of the revitalization movement of which
they were a part. Various groups within every new-light movement
adopt different strategies suited to various social, regional, or class
needs in coping with the cultural distortions they face. Nevertheless, each belongs to the counterculture opposing the older world
view. We are less interested here in the shape of the trees
than in the configuration of the forest, less concerned for the
varieties of dissent than in what they share in each awakening.
What was the overarching world view of the new-light revitalization
movement we call Puritanism? And how did its beliefs and values
come together to form the early subculture of the British colonies of
America?

Perhaps the most important belief they all shared was a conviction that the Bible contained absolutely authoritative answers to all
questions of human and social action. Miller has stated that the
Puritans of Massachusetts Bay were "radical" in their opposition to
the Anglican concept of traditionalism, i.e., the view that the Bible
is not a complete code of ecclesiastical and civil practice and that
reliance on customs and the wisdom of the past may supplement
(though not replace) biblical authority. The Puritans' reliance on
biblical authority, interpreted through the reason of those enlightened (or "newly lighted") by God's grace, made them extremely
dangerous to a social order that rested so much authority on custom
and tradition. To the Puritans every action of man (including both
church leaders and civil rulers) was subject to scrupulous conformity
to biblical law. This quarrel over "authority" or the source of truth,
Miller said,

> involved very important elements in the state and society; conservatives,
> satisfied with things as they were, saw in Puritan radicalism a serious
> threat to the vested interests; those dissatisfied with the *status quo*
> welcomed, for social as well as for religious reasons, the Puritan
> condemnation of the episcopal hierarchy with its wealth, its monopoly of
> advantages, and its alliance with the Court and aristocracy. Political
> passions and economic grievances increased the tension. In the 1640s
> both sides appealed to the sword and the God of battles.

Other common features of the Puritan world view included its belief in appeal to a higher law, its millennialism, its covenant ideal, and its theory of separation of church and state. All of these took firmer root in America than in England. Because of selective immigration, the weakness of the Church of England, and the complex confrontation with the wilderness, the Puritan world view found the New World more congenial. Anglicanism never attained the power in the colonies that it had in England. Even the so-called Anglican colonies distrusted bishops and fought vigorously against efforts to send a bishop to America. More radical sects in all the colonies held strong views about the rights of private conscience and the spiritually inspired individual's right to interpret God's will for himself. In some places this radical element in Puritanism was held in check by the conservative view that only a learned ministry could fathom the subtle metaphysics and ancient linguistic meanings involved in biblical exegesis. But in the New World, where colleges were few and the population widely dispersed, this tradition could not long prevail.

The defeat of Puritanism as a political movement in England and the amalgamation of its world view there, after 1688, with the new Anglican-dominated synthesis curtailed the radical aspects of the English revitalization movement. However, the more important political and economic ends of the movement were accomplished. In America, far from the scene of Puritan warfare, the colonists continued to follow their own ways, despite sporadic efforts by the Crown and Parliament to assert controls. Among the pietistic settlers who came to the various colonies, the Puritan way of reliance upon the Bible, the higher law, and inalienable God-given rights persisted and grew, in part because these settlers lacked the institutions to sustain Anglican ways and in part because adjustment to the frontier broke down the traditions they brought with them.

Because the New England Puritans established in their colonies a very conservative social order (a patriarchal system with closed, corporate towns rather than the individualistic system associated with modern capitalist society), recent social historians have argued that Puritanism (in England and America) might more properly be understood as a backward-looking, traditionalist, nativist movement rather than (as Tawney and Weber implied) a forward-looking, revolutionary movement. This is a chicken-and-egg controversy. Perry Miller, in *The New England Mind: The Seventeenth Century* (1939), long ago noted the traditionalist aspect: "Springing from the traditions of the past, from the deep and wordless sense of the tribe, of the organic community, came a desire to intensify the social bond, to strengthen the cohesion of the folk." New Englanders (and Englishmen in the other colonies as well) naturally brought with them customary ways of organizing their relationships—in families, in towns, in farming, in crafts. A host of local and town histories have demonstrated how the first settlers laid out their towns, chose their officers, and ordered their local regulations according to the time-honored practices of the rural villages they had left behind. All immigrants have demonstrated nostalgia for the old world and have done their best to recreate as much of its order as they could.

Recently the works of Peter Laslett, Christopher Hill, and Lawrence Stone have reemphasized this aspect of colonial settlement, and a new school of social historians has emphasized "the conservative peasant mentality," the "staunch country morality," and the "folk memory" of the early settlers. It is beyond denial. But it has been further argued that it was this conservatism that lay behind the appeal of the Puritan movement and the desire to emigrate. Puritan ministers preached sermons of apocalyptic doom in the early seventeenth century because England was departing from the customs and traditions of the past and God would punish the nation for its corruptions, for the wickedness of its king, the licentiousness of the aristocrats, and the heresies of the bishops. Hence simple country folk, who made up the vast majority of the early colonists, were eager to fly from this wrath. In America they sought shelter and a hiding place, hoping to appease God's anger by reestablishing, there, the good old ways of their forefathers.

In effect this school of social history has simply stood Weber's and Tawney's analysis on its head. Puritanism was a ghost-dance religion, a nativist reaction to social change, a fearful return to the past rather than the herald of a more glorious future, the vanguard of social revolution. These social historians have educed considerable evidence to support this view. Puritans did fear God's wrath and, like Jeremiah, denounced the corruption of the nation's leaders. Peasants did come to the New World and recreate many aspects of their old ways of life, a way of life that, as Laslett shows, had been thoroughly disrupted in the sixteenth century, leaving that social chaos and confusion among the rural villagers that provided such fertile ground for the more radical movements of Cromwell's day. Nevertheless, it seems perverse to portray America as a backwater of English culture and to imply that the Puritans wanted to reestablish the past. The whole thrust of their world view, however premillennial its sermonizing in the years 1590 to 1630, was toward perfecting the world; its goal was reformation, purification. And its social ethic (the economic virtues, the doctrines of the calling and stewardship, the sense of manifest destiny inherent in the predestination of the elect) was much more harmonious with the new socioeconomic trend of the times than to the peasant life of the medieval past.

Miller's argument is correct, that 90 percent of Puritan social thought and practice was shared with Anglicanism, but he is also correct that the other 10 percent completely altered its temper. There were traditionalist or nativist aspects to the early stages of the movement, when future reformation seemed hopeless; but the drive that produced the revolutions of 1642 and 1688 was not backward-looking, even when arguments were made in terms of Magna Charta and common law. As for the conservative peasant villages established in the American colonies, their conservative elements were thoroughly mixed with new ideological elements. And how long did they last as peasant communities? The Puritan world view may have achieved only partial success in the new consensus that emerged in England after the Glorious Revolution, but in America, I would contend, its ideology found continued implementation in each new awakening.

The townspeople of Puritan New England were not huddled together in fear of God's wrath but in the conviction of his favor and their assurance that they were the vanguards of a better world order. They established church covenants and town covenants (as John Demos and Kenneth Lockridge have shown) on principles of religious fellowship and perfectionism totally at odds with the

territorial parish system and feudal theory of old English villages.
Their churches were organized, led, and upheld on new principles.
Any examination of the Cambridge Platform of 1648 indicates that
it was written to demonstrate that "the New England way" of
church government was to be a model for restructuring the Church
of England. It was common sense and not "conservative peasant
mentality" that led New Englangers to face the Indians and the
wilderness in organized townships.

It is true that Puritans believed that society should be arranged in
hierarchical ranks; they even arranged the seating in their churches
on the basis of social status. They also believed that only "saints"
(the predestined elect) should vote and hold office. It is true that
the Puritan magistrates were authoritarian and regulated every
aspect of dress and behavior, but it is also true that they specifically
excluded ministers from holding office and churches from inflicting
civil penalties and that they struggled to maintain a distinct line
between civil and ecclesiastical authority. Despite the emphasis in
the Puritan ideology upon organic order, community, and obedience to authority, it is important to keep in mind Miller's
statement that "there was a strong element of individualism in the
Puritan creed." It is this tension between individual freedom and
social order that Edmund S. Morgan describes as "the Puritan
dilemma." "They had themselves been rebels," Morgan writes,
"in order to put into practice their ideas of a new society. But to do
so they had to restrain the rebellion of others"—like Antinomians,
Baptists, and Quakers. "The result was a long conflict between the
demands of authority and the permissiveness of freedom." In this
polar tension lies much of the dynamism of the American culture
core. "To a considerable degree," writes Oscar Handlin, in his
introduction to Morgan's book, "the American pattern of constitutional and responsible liberty emerged from more than three
centuries of such conflict."

## Puritanism in the American Colonies

We can see these tensions most clearly in terms of the Puritan ideal
of the covenant, which bound each individual to obey God first and
foremost and at the same time bound him to submit himself to the

will of the group for the common good (whether that group was the brethren of the church, the majority in the town or colony, or, later, the will of the electorate in the nation). This is the substance of our earliest and most important social documents, the sacred symbols of our culture: the Mayflower Compact of the Pilgrims in 1620, the first code of laws adopted in Virginia in 1610, the famous sermon of John Winthrop on board the *Arabella* in 1630, and the Cambridge Platform of Massachusetts of 1648.

Early Virginians also considered themselves chosen of God for a special mission in the New World. John Rolfe expressed this in his well-known statement describing the settlers in the South as "a peculiar people, marked and chosen by the finger of God, to possess it, for undoubtedly He is with us." Virginia's *Laws, Divine, Moral, and Martial* (1610) provides good evidence of the Puritan temper in that colony. These laws prescribed severe penalties against cursing, speaking against the Christian religion, and failure to attend church on the Sabbath. The first House of Burgesses in 1619 immediately enacted laws against idleness, gambling, drunkenness, and excess in apparel. Every town and borough in Virginia was required to collect tithes for the poor and set aside 100 acres of land to support ministers and churches. Virginia's magistrates appointed days of fasting, humiliation, thanksgiving, and prayer. While E. S. Morgan has shown how strong a hold the Protestant ethic (with its individualistic drive for profit and success) had upon early Virginians, these religious laws indicate that even in a colony not closely identified with the Puritan movement the tension between communal piety and individual freedom was strong.

John Winthrop's sermon in 1630, calling upon the settlers of Massachusetts to establish a utopian city upon a hill, is probably the classic formulation of this tension within the culture core:

> Thus stands the cause betweene God and vs. Wee are entered into a Covenant with him for this worke. . . . Now if the Lord shall please to heare vs, and bring vs in peace to the place wee desire, then hath hee ratified this Covenant and sealed our Commission [and] will expect a strickt performance of the Articles contained in it, but if wee shall neglect the observacion of these Articles . . . seekeing great things for our selues and our posterity, the Lord will surely breake out in wrathe against vs [and] be revenged. . . . For this end wee must be knitt

together as one man, wee must entertaine each other in brotherly
Affeccion, wee must be willing to abridge our selues of our superfluities
for the supply of others necessities.

The implication here is clearly toward a voluntary ideal of self-
sacrifice for the common good. And John Cotton, the Aaron to
Winthrop's Moses in the Bible Commonwealth, stressed the
importance of drawing a proper line between church and state (one
of the more radical departures of Puritanism from Anglicanism):

> It is necessary therefore, that all power that is on earth be limited,
> Church-power or other. . . . It is counted a matter of danger to the State
> [by anti-Puritan royalists] to limit Prerogatives [of the king]; but it is a
> further danger not to have them limited. . . . It is therefore fit for every
> man to be studious of the bounds which the Lord hath set: and for the
> People, in whom fundamentally all power lyes, to give as much power
> as God in his word gives to men: And it is meet that Magistrates in the
> Commonwealth, and so Officers in Churches, should desire to know
> the utmost bounds of their own power.

This was still a far cry from the view of separation that Thomas
Jefferson or the eighteenth-century Baptists were to espouse (and
that the First Amendment to the Constitution would include
within the supreme law of the new nation); yet Roger Williams
came out of the same Puritan tradition as Cotton, and in the colony
of Rhode Island he came close to establishing in 1636 what the rest
of America finally evolved to after 1776. The seeds of later
revitalization movements were thus embedded in this earliest
awakening. That the Puritan Awakening started America on a
different road from England can be seen in the facts that England
still has a Crown, its church is still established, and its bishops still
sit in the House of Lords.

Embedded also in the Puritan movement were the ideals of a
congregational church polity, a voluntary church membership, a
justification for the priesthood of all believers (the right of the laity
to prophesy), and an evangelistic concept of soul-winning. The
Cambridge Platform, designed to point the way forward to old
England, gave church members the right to choose their own
ministers and to remove them. While these powers were hedged in
among the conservative Puritan communities of New England, they

were not so hedged eleswhere in the colonies, among the Baptists and Quakers.

Not only did the Pilgrim Separatists argue that God had yet further light to shed upon his Word, but the Congregational Puritans of New England told the more conservative Presbyterian Puritans in England in 1648 that their light on what God had ordained as the true form of church government was better than the light John Knox and the Presbyterians had: "wee conceiv a different apprehension of the mind of Christ" than you and proceed "(as in the spirit wee are bound) to follow the Lamb withersoever he goeth and (after the Apostles example) as wee believe, so wee speake." This readiness to follow their own apprehension of God's higher laws became ingrained in American culture. The individual is responsible first and foremost to that higher law, as he apprehends it. And having justified their own schism from the Church of England, Puritans laid the basis for countless other schismatics, separatists, and "come-outers" in later generations.

These central themes of the Puritan Awakening pervaded all of the British colonies in North America. If we accept the fact that Puritanism in some form influenced most of the denominations that broke off from the Church of England in the seventeenth century, and if we acknowledge that, even within Anglicanism, Puritanism had its exponents, we will have a better understanding of the importance of the Puritan Awakening on the nascent ideology of Americans. It is sometimes forgotten that in Anglican Virginia there were Puritans and Quakers who upheld this ideology, and Puritan views in sectarian form were widely diffused in Maryland and Rhode Island, which tolerated all sects. Quakers espoused their form of Puritanism widely, but especially in the colonies of Pennsylvania and New Jersey. In fact, most of the churches in the colonies were decidedly Calvinistic in their theology; Congregationalists, Presbyterians, and Baptists were of course the most orthodox, but Calvinism tinctured even many Anglican pulpits. In New York, the Dutch Reformed churches were strict Calvinists, and their views spread out to Long Island, where they met the expanding Congregational Calvinism from Connecticut. The Presbyterian form of Puritanism received a great boost from the migration from Scotland and northern Ireland to all the colonies after 1660. Presbyterian Puritanism was particularly strong in the Middle Colonies, whence it spread southward and westward along the Appalachian valleys and passes. In addition, there were close relationships between Puritan pietism and most of the German sects attracted to Pennsylvania in the late seventeenth and early eighteenth centuries. In short, a broad Calvinistic Puritan base was the common feature of the colonial world view, and it grew stronger rather than weaker as the years went by. In this respect, Puritanism was the prevalent ideology in the colonial period.

The New England colonies, however, possessed a cohesive and organizational power that gave their institutions and ideas pre-eminence. Its learned clergy used the printing press to spread their views everywhere; its public school system (supported by compulsory taxation at the township level) was widely imitated; its concept of town-meeting democracy and its aggressive economic theory set the tone for much of the rest of the colonial system. And these practices moved westward as the population moved.

Perhaps the most important Puritan legacy, though the hardest to measure, was its toughness of temper, its strenuous, self-disciplined sense of commitment, its soul-searching and self-testing, its seriousness of purpose, its intensity of will, its determination. While these qualities had their harsh and cruel side, they were particularly appropriate for the conquest of a howling wilderness. They are not far from the "Spirit of '76." Michael Walzer has admirably described the political features of this driving, unquenchable spirit in *The Revolution of the Saints* (1969).

Walzer's thesis is important also for the light it throws on the important link between religious awakenings and social reform in American culture. The Puritan movement, Walzer argues, developed for the first time in modern history "a politics of party organization and methodical activity, opposition and reform, radical ideology and revolution . . . detached appraisal of a going system, the programmatic expression of discontent and aspiration, the organization of zealous men for sustained political activity." These elements still lie within the American political tradition, as the frequent creation of third parties and other voluntary political groups attests. Behind this political commitment to perfect the world lay an intense religious conviction; we owe to Puritanism, Walzer states, the "idea that specially designated and organized bands of men might play a creative part in the political world." This is the basis for much of what is called the American liberal tradition—a tradition based on voluntary, lay-directed, participatory political activism. "What Calvinists said of the saint," Walzer concludes, "other men would later say of the citizen." Edmund Burke did say precisely that in 1775, when he noted that the patriots of the North American colonies (and not only of New England) constituted "the dissidence of dissent and the Protestantism of the Protestant religion." Walzer says that

> the same sense of civic virtue, of discipline and duty, lies behind the two names. Saint and citizen together suggest a new integration of private men (or rather of *chosen* groups of private men, of proven holiness and virtue) in the political order, an integration based upon a novel view of politics as a kind of conscientious and continuous labor.

When later foreign commentators spoke of the United States as "a nation with the soul of a church," they were taking cognizance of this moral view of politics, which still tends to see all official acts (or omissions) as matters of right or wrong and all officeholders as men of morality or corruption.

Walzer has also pointed out the strong Puritan emphasis on consent or voluntary action in nonpolitical activities. Just as men must voluntarily sacrifice time, energy, and wealth for the public good in political affairs, so must individuals act with each other in terms of consent or persuasion. Marriage in the Puritan ideology was not a holy sacrament and not to be arranged by parents but a civil covenant requiring mutual consent of husband and wife. The basis of this covenant was to be love, not convenience. Likewise, Puritan children obeyed their parents by consent; church members joined in mutual brotherhood by consent; the local community and the colony's inhabitants submitted to magistrates, clergy, and the majority of their elected representatives by consent. "Radical politics was dependent upon the breaking up of the traditional family," Walzer notes; "it also had a part in the reconstruction of the family in more modern form."

This is not to say that the Puritans were not patriarchal, did not

believe in obedience to duly constituted authority, or were egalitarian in social relations. But they held in their social theory, as in
their church polity, a radically different principle of human
relationships from that of the Anglican old lights (or the medieval
social theory), whose ideology they challenged in the early seventeenth century. And just as they expected the king to govern by the
consent of his subjects, so in the "little commonwealths," the
towns of New England, each member of the community voluntarily
assented to participate in self-government and be governed by the
consensus of their fellow townsmen. The history of the New
England town, writes Kenneth Lockridge, is above all "the story of
the implementation of the politics of perfection written into the
[town and church] covenant." So, eventually, did the citizens of
the new nation, after 1787, establish a new government on the basis
of a pledge, in the name of "We, the people" to form "a more
perfect Union."

There is one more dualism that the Puritans bequeathed to
American culture: the conflict between reason and intuition,
between the head and the heart, between realism and idealism.
Certain elements in Puritanism, Perry Miller wrote, "were carried
into the creeds and practices of the evangelical religious revivals"—
the mystical experience of conversion, the ecstasy of a direct
spiritual confrontation with God—"but others were perpetuated
by the rationalists and the forerunners of Unitarianism"—the
tendency toward skepticism, the preference for scientific explanations. In rebelling against the formalism and sacerdotalism of the
Church of England, the Puritan theology "brought every man to a
direct experience of the spirit and removed intermediaries between
himself and the deity." Yet, at the same time, the Puritans were
heirs of humanism, and their faith in human reason led them "to
accentuate the element of rationalism." On the one hand the
Puritans distrusted "the affections," emotions, passions, "enthusiasm"; but on the other they urged men to "strive for an
inward communication with the force that controls the world." The
Puritan longed for the mystical wonder and beauty of communion
with God's Spirit and at the same time checked himself against
visions, arguing that God gave man reason in order to distinguish
truth from hallucination. In short, the Puritans managed to hold in

delicate but firm balance the idealism of Platonic thought (or the mysticism of the saints) and the realism of Aristotelian thought (or the skepticism of the humanist). When Anne Hutchinson claimed that she governed her thought and actions by direct revelations from God and that the Holy Spirit dwelt in her heart, so that she did not need learning or the Bible to understand God's will, the Puritans of Massachusetts banished her for losing her balance. They treated even more harshly the Quakers, who claimed to receive "leadings" from the Holy Spirit and to be guided by the "inner light" of God's divinity that dwells in all men. Yet the Antinomians and the Quakers were part of that same rebellion against Anglican formalism and sacerdotalism; they simply placed too much weight on the evidence of the heart and too little on the evidence of the head to suit New England Puritans. Some generations later, Jonathan Edwards was to accuse the proto-Unitarians of erring on the other side.

American culture has tried to sustain this same balance but has constantly shifted its emphasis from one side to the other. If the seventeenth century was the Age of Faith, the eighteenth was the Age of Reason; if the nineteenth century was the Era of Romanticism, the twentieth became the Era of Scientism. In times of awakening, the antinomian tendency is more prominent than in times of homeostasis, but the two elements are never far apart.

The Puritan awakening in which American culture was born revitalized English society by facilitating the transition from a medieval to a capitalist economy, by transforming the divine right of monarchy into a constitutional monarchy, by emphasizing the individualistic ethic of Calvinism over the corporate ethic of feudalism, and by establishing the principle of religious toleration as opposed to uniformity of faith and practice. It was these beliefs and values, predominantly expressed in the world view of Calvinism, that were established firmly by the first settlers in America. Puritanism, in all its various forms, and Calvinism, expressed in various denominational formulas, permeated the American colonies, while Anglicanism remained weak and unstable.

The Calvinistic world view needs only a brief summary here. It started from the assumption that God, having created the world, rules directly but mysteriously over everthing that takes place in it.

He has revealed much of his will in the Bible, which is the supreme authority for all human action. But God's will can be accurately ascertained only by men of learning, infused by God's grace, and even they are fallible; man can never fathom all of God's ways. Human nature, since Adam's fall, has been totally corrupt and selfish, ruled more by passion than reason, though susceptible to appeals to fear, authority, and self-interest. Life is a constant struggle with Satan, both in the life of the individual and among groups of people, and only by the most intense effort, self-discipline, and self-control can man hope to keep Satan at bay; church ritual is of no help in this, but the mutual support of other saints is. God has, however, promised to help those who accept the Christian faith as revealed in the Gospel and has, through Christ's atonement, arbitrarily predestined some for salvation, though all deserve hell. By constant piety and soul-searching men may come to entertain a hope that they are among the elect and may experience an infusion of God's grace, enabling them to see the world through different eyes from those who are reprobate, not among the predestined elect. In the best form of government the magistrates will always be "saints"—those who have obtained inner knowledge of God's grace through a conversion experience (conversion from selfish depravity to regenerate love of God). But for most of mankind the only way even minimal order and social prosperity can be preserved is through strict laws, hard work, self-control, and dedication to one's vocation or calling. Men must help each other (be charitable), show respect to their betters (the clergy, the magistrates, the learned, the gentry and upper orders), and observe all of God's laws (especially regarding prayer, church attendance, Bible-reading, temperance, and morality). Good or bad, whatever happens is God's will, and men must graciously accept it. Ultimately, in God's own good time, Christ will return and a millennium of peace and plenty will take place, after which God will judge the quick and the dead and the world will come to an end.

This harsh ideology, combined with the social customs of English life, came to America and proved well adapted to the harsh environment of frontier life. It made sense to people, and, living according to its beliefs and values, the colonies first established the coastal towns, then conquered the Indians and began to move westward and to prosper. But the very prosperity of this way of life posed a problem. Free land was one of the prime causes of the difficulty, for it broke down the reliance upon the community and provided a source of wealth that brought corruption to everyone. The opportunities for gain led men to break the rules that poverty and necessity had enforced upon the first generations. With these opportunities came selfishness as opposed to charity, individualism as opposed to cooperation. As the seventeenth century ended, Perry Miller noted,

> the character of the people underwent a change; they moved further into the frontier, they became more absorbed in business and profits than in religion and salvation, their memories of English social stratification grew dim . . . ; the frontier conspired with the popular disposition to lessen the prestige of the cultured classes and to enhance the social power of those who wanted their religion in a more simple, downright, and ''democratic'' form. . . . [However,] not until the decade of the Great Awakening [1735–45] did the popular tendency receive distinct articulation through leaders who openly renounced the older conception.

What Miller was describing was an accumulated series of social, political, and economic changes that brought about a disjunction between the older norms and the new frontier experience. Early in the eighteenth century, signs of individual stress and cultural distortion began to appear. (Some argue that the witchcraft trials in Salem were an early symptom of this.) The synthesis that had emerged following the Puritan Awakening began to disintegrate; men began to question their institutions and authority figures. A new awakening was in the making.

# 3

# *The First Great Awakening, 1730–60*

## *Sinners against the Fathers*

When Jonathan Edwards described the outbreak of revivalistic fervor in his parish in 1734 as "a surprising work of God," he spoke for most Americans. Well aware of the social and psychic crisis that had been building among the people for some time, he had preached frequently on the problems upsetting New England. What surprised him (and them) was not the intensity of the emotional outburst but the mercy of a stern and angry God, who suddenly, inexplicably, offered peace and hope to so many whom, in justice, he might have destroyed. Calvinistically oriented Americans (probably three-fourths of the colonists) fully believed that they deserved to be "cast into hell" for their refusal to obey God's commands. Yet, beginning in 1734 (in some colonies earlier, in others later), God mercifully extended forgiveness and salvation to thousands (the best estimates are thirty to forty thousand in the years 1740–43 out of a total population of one million). Edwards was astonished. Look, he said, at "the people of Suffield, where they are flocking from day to day to Christ"; see how many reborn souls around the colonies are "rejoicing and singing for joy of heart." Sinners should take hope "in the present remarkable and wonderful dispensation of God's mercy." Why remain dejected, despairing, tormented, and despondent "when so many other children in the land are converted and become holy and happy children of the King of kings?" (It is worth noting this infantilization of the congregation, called "children" by their minister.)

Readers of this sermon, "Sinners in the Hands of an Angry God," sometimes neglect Edwards' conclusion that the gates of heaven were wide open:

> And now you have an extraordinary opportunity, a day wherein Christ has flung the door of mercy wide open and stands in the door calling and crying with a loud voice to poor sinners; a day wherein many are flocking to him and pressing into the Kingdom of God . . . ; many, that were very likely in the same miserable condition that you are in, are now in a happy state, with their hearts filled with love to him that has loved them and washed them from their sins.

We miss the whole spirit of this Calvinist awakening if we fail to recognize it as one of extraordinary hope, joy, ecstasy, and release. Edwards was only one of many new-light prophets in the years 1730 to 1760 telling distressed individuals in a time of cultural distortion that God still loved them and was ready to help them out of their confusion.

Of course, like all revivalists, Edwards also warned that those so confirmed in their guilt, so smug in their complacency, so "given up to hardness of heart and blindness of mind" as to resist or refuse to "wake thoroughly out of sleep" and hearken to "the loud calls" might have "to bear the dreadful wrath of that God" who was trying so hard to help them. The fault, however, and the responsibility were not God's but theirs; it was their stubborn, willful refusal to yield to his will and accept his loving concern for their welfare that prevented their salvation. Obviously, Edwards dearly wanted his people to "strive to enter in at the gate" of heaven, where he saw Christ beckoning. Although, like most of the revivalists in this awakening, Edwards believed in predestination and felt that men were so innately selfish that they had an overwhelming propensity to sinful disobedience, nevertheless he preached that if they would simply yield their wills to the higher authority of their Father in heaven, he would guide and reward them.

Despite the dangers in applying psychological theory to the past, there are so many aspects of this and subsequent awakenings that relate to the changing patterns of child-rearing, and specifically to the breakdown of the patriarchal family structure brought from England, that it would be a grave omission to avoid speculation

about this subject in this essay. One need not be a Freudian to
recognize the connotations of the deep emotional relationship in
the Judeo-Christian religion between God's power over his "children" and a parent's power over his children. God's fatherhood is
one of the most powerful symbols or metaphors in that tradition. In
the Calvinist use of the metaphor, God is further defined as
omniscient, stern, strict, and usually angry. Furthermore, Western
culture has identified all authority figures in paternal and godlike
terms. In New England the selectmen who ruled over the towns
were called "the town fathers"; the pastor was a father to his
parish; the colonial magistrates were described as "nursing fathers
to the church" and fathers of the colony; the king was a "father to
his loyal subjects." When dissenters in New England were brought
to court for breaking the laws of church or state, they were told they
had dishonored the Fifth Commandment: "Honor thy father and
thy mother." Lawgiving and law-enforcing officials were father
surrogates and viceregents of God, who had "ordained the powers
that be." To understand this First Great Awakening—and also the
revolution against the king, which followed it—we should take a
closer look at how psychic conflicts within the family contributed to
it.

   In the midst of all the demographic, economic, and intellectual
changes that produced increasing tensions within the colonial
system in the years preceding the awakening, the family structure
remained the basic bulwark of social order and control. This was
particularly true on the isolated, expanding frontier, where village
and church controls were weakest and the authority of the colonial
legislatures most distant. But as old institutional restraints weakened after 1700, the family everywhere bore the brunt of the strain.
The Calvinistic theology, which predominated in the colonies,
magnified the father's role over the "little commonwealth" that
was the family. To sustain order in the household, the father was
required to bring up his children in strict obedience to his will.
Child-rearing meant teaching self-discipline. Submission of the
stubborn will of mankind was the essential feature of the prevailing
Christian world view, even among incipient Arminians and Enlightened rationalists. Since all children, as a result of Adam's sin
(or their animal nature), were born rebels against authority, the

first necessary step in child-rearing was to subdue the rebellious will of the infant.

Parental (usually "paternal") child-rearing practices in the eighteenth century were fair but firm. Fathers and mothers took very seriously their duty to exact obedience even from infants—for their own sake, not simply for that of the parent. God commanded parents to break their children's wills: Spare the rod and spoil the child. Spoil the child, and one had sinned in one's duty to God, the child, and the community. Philip Greven, in *Child-rearing Concepts, 1620-1861*, has compiled numerous statements from many different sources which indicate that subduing the wills of stubborn children took place in most families immediately following weaning, often as early as six months after birth, almost always within the first year. Infants were not even allowed the pleasure of wailing protests against discomfort in their cradles but were taught to cry softly if at all. John Robinson, spiritual leader of the Scrooby Pilgrims, wrote in 1628:

> for the beating and keeping down of this stubbornness [of will in children] parents must provide carefully for two things: first that children's wills and wilfulness be restrained and repressed, and that in time, lest sooner than they imagine, the tender sprigs grow to stiffness. . . . Children should not know, if it could be kept from them, that they have a will of their own.

John Locke, himself the son of Puritan parents but more famous as a progenitor of Enlightenment rationalism, wrote in 1690 that the great mistake most parents made was not in "due season" to have taken care that the minds and wills of their children were "made obedient to discipline and pliant to reason when first it was most tender and most easy to be bowed. He that is not used to submit his will to the reason of others when he is young, will scarce hearken or submit to his own reason" when he is of age.

Susanna Wesley, Anglican mother of John Wesley, wrote that in raising her children, "When turned a year old (and some before) they were taught to fear the rod and to cry softly, by which means they escaped abundance of correction which they might otherwise have had." John Wesley himself lamented, as the leader of the great evangelical revival in eighteenth-century England, that so few parents understood the importance of curing the self-will of children: "A wise parent, on the other hand, should begin to break their will the first moment it appears," and that would be within their first or second year. It required, he said, "incredible firmness and resolution," but without it we cannot "cure the Atheism of our children"—atheism being the logical result of disobedience to parents.

These precepts were doubtless followed religiously by most pietistic parents in the colonies, as well as by many who did not belong to any church. Yet it seems obvious that if children not yet able to talk, scarcely able to walk, and in the midst of the trauma of weaning were subjected to such severe discipline by supposedly loving parents from whom they expected succor and comfort, they might be permanently marked. Freudians maintain that a severe "reaction formation" will inevitably result. The child, feeling at first outrage, fear, and hatred toward this exercise of parental authority, can come to terms with it only by reversing his feelings and assuming total submissiveness. Unconsciously repressing his fear and hatred, his dangerous desire to strike back, he adopts an attitude of reverence and love. He thus grows up desiring to please the parent in all things, constantly seeking approbation and affection. Expressions of parental disapproval for later acts offensive to family or social propriety further exacerbate this internalized guilt. The connection between parental punishment and God's eternal punishment was also inculcated from infancy. Colonial families commonly practiced daily Bible reading and prayer; the laws in all colonies required regular church attendance; school-children were compelled to learn their lessons from biblical stories (if not from the Bible itself) and were catechized regularly by pastors of the established church. In all these rituals, obedience to the authorities and to God was stressed. The two words "obey God" virtually encapsulate American culture.

Nevertheless, by both training and necessity, colonial children were also required to become increasingly independent and autonomous as they grew older. They had to learn a trade, prepare themselves to become church members, fathers, voting members in ecclesiastical and town affairs. Under stable conditions the growing child learned that submission worked to his benefit. Parental love

and social approval sustained his own obedience and provided
psychological security and self-esteem. During adolescence, when
the child was faced with moving from a dependent to an autonomous role in the community, he was expected to have a crisis
conversion experience, during which he replaced dependence on his
father with dependence on God. If he felt anxiety about his
ultimate reconciliation with God, nevertheless it was an anxiety
shared with his fellows and even his parents. Enculturating institutions provided release from stress in regular rituals, ordinances,
and symbolic functions.

However, as the fervor of the Puritan Awakening waned after
1660, a steady formalization and routinization of church ordinances
gradually took place. The voluntary covenant broke down in the
church and the township. Church membership in almost all
denominations was open to those who had had no conversion
experience; birthright membership replaced committed voluntary
membership. Voting rights were equated with property-holding,
not covenant-signing. The abundance of cheap land made office-
holding and the full privileges of adulthood available to every
able-bodied white male. It became difficult to tell saints from
reprobates, the upper social orders from the lower. This formalism
may have helped to sustain outward relations with the church and
the state, but it undermined the emotional ties and sense of
common purpose uniting the community. It also weakened the
means of establishing forgiveness and close communion between
brethren and with God.

While this falling-off in conversions worried the clergy, it did not
at first appear to trouble the laity. Times were generally prosperous,
and those who worked hard were able to make their way in the
world. Material success was taken as a sign that one's behavior was
acceptable to God; the rewards of prestige and power demonstrated
approval by one's neighbors. Since so few in any town or parish
experienced "saving grace," the majority felt they were no worse
than the next. Ministers, while regretting the lack of conversions,
preached that ultimately God, in his own way and his own good
time, would save the souls of his elect. God would display the same
kind of paternal approval that parents gave to children who did
their duty and obeyed the rules. After 1662 baptism was extended

in Puritan churches to many whose parents had not been church members; some ministers baptized all children of respectable parents. The Reverend Solomon Stoddard of Massachusetts set a precedent followed by many ministers after 1700 when he allowed all respectable persons who "owned the covenant" (i.e., who formally assented to the doctrines of the parish church) to participate in communion, hitherto a sacred ordinance reserved for the elect. He did so on the ground that the Lord's Supper was a means of grace through which God's spirit might work upon the souls of men. Cotton Mather urged after 1710 the importance of "doing good" to the poor and needy as a means of demonstrating one's concern to be a worthy servant of God (though he denied that good works could lead to salvation). By 1720 the vast majority of ministers were telling their parishioners that regular prayer, church attendance, upright behavior, and responsible citizenship were all means of preparation for the salvation God would send when the time was ripe. Outwardly even the most sincere Calvinist began to feel secure in his own rectitude. But inward malaise spread.

Although times were generally prosperous in the colonies after 1690, they were far from stable; institutions strained to maintain order as expansion, mobility, economic opportunity, and political friction produced growing tensions. The ministers no longer elicited deeply felt responses but rather a vague and undefinable discomfort. Men and women in every colony recognized that their efforts to succeed in this world were compelling departures from older behavior patterns and values. Businessmen had to cut corners to compete with their rivals. Farmers had to charge high prices to pay off mortgages on new land. Political leaders distorted the truth to win votes or gain influence. Town fathers enriched themselves and slighted the needs of the community. Lawyers and judges seemed unable to reach verdicts recognizably just to both parties. Legislators seemed to yield to special interests instead of serving the general welfare. On the frontier, where institutional restraints were weakest, men increasingly took the law into their own hands —against Indians, horse thieves, or an interloper overreaching himself. The westerners began to resent the power of easterners, who controlled the land sales, the lumber operations, the Indian trade, the roads, and the taxes. In poorer communities there was resentment against the high taxes required to support the church and its ministers; sometimes the ministerial graduates of Yale and Harvard requested higher salaries than the towns thought they were worth. Similar tensions over salaries and church discipline wracked Anglican parishes in the South. Occasionally, when a parish fell behind in paying the minister's salary, he went to court to sue for it. But who was more to blame? The people, for not joining the church and giving freely to support it? Or the pastor, for preaching too formally and relying on the courts for his pay?

As the social order lost its old cohesion, guilt and anxiety increased. Men became angry with their neighbors, with the authorities, with themselves and their families. Quarrels and lawsuits become more common than obedience to authority or subjugation of self to commonweal. The rapid pace of social change made it impossible for the existing institutional structure to sustain what A. F. C. Wallace calls "a minimally fluctuating, life-supporting matrix for individual members of the social organism." Individual stress increased to the point of cultural distortion. Historians have explained this growing incongruence between prescriptive norms and prevailing circumstances in a number of ways. Some of their explanations apply specifically to one part of the colonies, some to all parts equally. But friction increased everywhere.

Explanations of the cause of what we call the First Great Awakening in America may be divided into five broad categories: first, those that stress rapid social change, arguing that after several generations of fairly stable communal life, based on the patriarchal social order carried over from Europe, a variety of demographic and psychosocial factors made this system inadequate to the needs of the expanding population; second, explanations that argue that the Calvinistic world view, always a delicate balance of polar concepts, faced such grave challenges from the new ideological thrust of the European Enlightenment that it burst apart; third, environmental explanations, which emphasize the importance of the frontier in dispersing the population, in providing new opportunities for individual enterprise, in breaking down law and order, and in creating sociopolitical divisions between East and West; fourth, those explanations that stress the changed relationship with the

mother country after the Glorious Revolution of 1688, since
the increasing presence of royal authority led the more well-to-do
Americans to abandon their simple life-style and pietism in order to
imitate courtly manners and to share power, and bask in the
prestige of closer alliance, with those close to the king. A Marxist
interpretation provides the fifth line of argument, to the effect that
between 1650 and 1750, as the Industrial Revolution advanced, the
old feudal, patriarchal agrarian system was replaced by a new
bourgeois capitalist system; consequently, Americans became
colonial pawns of English imperial interests, and, within the
colonies themselves, elements of class conflict arose between the
rich and the poor, the merchant-bankers and the artisan-farmers,
the power-brokers of English capitalists and the proletariat (white,
red, and black) that supplied them with raw materials and markets.

We could subsume all of these arguments under the general
heading of "changing structures of authority and power." Or we
could speak of them all in terms of the continuing shift from a
medieval, corporate, organic ideal of social order to a modern,
individualistic, contractual, atomistic social order (what Ferdinand
Tönnies described as the transformation from *Gemeinschaft* to
*Gesellschaft* that accompanies modernization). English settlers,
whether Calvinistic or Anglican, brought with them to America in
the early seventeenth century a world view that stressed the ideal of
a collectivist, hierarchical social structure of mutual rights and
obligations among the class ranks. By 1720 individualism had
advanced so far that this older order was under severe stress.

Most historians seem to agree that personal economic ambition
was at the root of much of this social tension. The Protestant ethic,
as Max Weber said, urged men to work hard at their callings in
order to get ahead in the world. Ministers urged upon their
congregations the norms of diligence, frugality, honesty, and
persistence. At the same time, however, they worried that people
were becoming too eager for material wealth and luxury, too
centered on the goods of this life rather than on the good of eternal
life. "Restraint of ambition," as Richard Bushman writes in *From
Puritan to Yankee* (1967), "was a vulnerable spot among the
interlocking institutions and beliefs that contained man through
most of the seventeenth century, for Puritan preachers could not

clearly distinguish laudable industry from reprehensible worldliness." The tension was inherent in Calvinism, but, as Perry Miller wrote, "It was only as the seventeenth century came to a close that the imported structure began to show the strain." The rapidly expanding economy in America after 1690 simply provided too many easy opportunities for men to get rich quick, too many ways to improve their status, and they saw no reason not to take advantage of them.

But laudable diligence frequently bordered on sinful acquisitiveness. "As, in the expanding economy of the eighteenth century," Bushman writes, "merchants and farmers felt free to pursue wealth with an avidity dangerously close to avarice, the energies released asserted irresistible pressure against traditional bounds." Others, like Perry Miller, place much of the blame for this upon the leveling forces of frontier life, where respect for learning and culture gave way to "more simple, downright, democratic feelings." To attribute the cultural distortion of this era to environmental causes requires more than a discussion of the opportunities of self-reliance on the wilderness edge of the frontier. The whole colonial region was the frontier of Europe, the ragged edge of civilized order. To the rugged individualism of the western pioneer we would have to add the capitalist enterprise of the seacoast entrepreneur. Environmental factors in the broadest sense include the increasing self-confidence of the people, the restless desire to escape old restraints, the willingness to experiment.

But the price of boldness was criticism, especially in the form of what Perry Miller called "the jeremiads" of clerical upholders of tradition. Ministers everywhere in the colonies berated parishioners for growing rich, and yet the parishioners could not see that their exercise of business acumen was a sin against the community if the whole community was prospering. R. H. Tawney pointed out that, from the earliest days of Plymouth Colony, Governor Bradford observed "how men grew 'in their outward estates' " and predicted that "the increase in material prosperity 'will be the ruin of New England, at least of the churches of God there.' " But as the economy flourished "the desire to prosper" Bushman notes, simply "precipitated clashes with law and authority, adding to accumulating guilt":

After 1690, in their ambition to prosper, people disregarded the
demands of the social order. Nonproprietors contested the control of
town lands with proprietors, and outlivers struggled with the leaders in
the town center to obtain an independent parish. In the civil government settlers fought for a clear title to their lands and new traders for
currency. Church members resisted the enlargement of the minister's
power or demanded greater piety in his preaching. All these controversies pitted the common men against rulers and the laws. Under these
circumstances, the social order became a menace to peace of mind rather
than a shield against divine wrath.

By 1730, Bushman concludes, "estrangement" between the ordinary people and their leaders in church and state had created
unbearable stress. While there was still, especially among the rising
bourgeoisie, a general religious conformity, the more pious pastors
and laymen saw it as a mere façade. Yet, the more the law punished
(or winked at) offenders, and the more the clergy berated (or
placated) them, the more confusion grew and the greater became
the loss of credibility in "the standing order":

> When the Great Awakening added its measure of opposition, the old
> institutions began to crumble. By 1765, while the [old Puritan] structure
> still stood, the most perceptive leaders were looking for new methods of
> ordering society in an age when human loyalties would be forthcoming
> voluntarily or not at all.

By "voluntarily," he means outside the compulsions of traditional
beliefs and customs.

A very similar scenario is presented if the breakdown of the old
order is analyzed from the viewpoint of the new social history.
Although the studies of Greven, Lockridge, Rutman, and Demos
find Miller's analysis of the jeremiads too literary, the Weber-
Tawney thesis too reductionist, and Turner's frontier thesis too
simplistic, their general conclusions supplement rather than contradict these earlier explanations of the decline of Puritanism.
Concerned less with the internal tensions within Puritan ideology
than with the folkways of peasant villagers, they argue that, after
an initially successful reconstruction of sixteenth-century communal order in the New World, the expected stability or homeostasis failed to sustain itself. The availability of cheap land and
the increasing autonomy of the younger generation led, by the

beginning of the eighteenth century (if not earlier), to a serious disruption of the patriarchal peasant order. "Sublimation of self to society," Rutman says in *American Puritanism* (1970), "was matched by exaltation of self in pursuit of personal gain." And "the same urge which brought them to abandon what they had in England could lead them to abandon what they were creating in New England," i.e., the urge to better their condition. "Even those motivated to cross the ocean less by profit and more by religion (and hence more wedded to the traditional by the preachers' rhetoric) could be tempted away from the village by the promise of profit."

Greven stresses, in *Four Generations* (1970), the desire of young adults for independence from parental authority. In the seventeenth century this independence was often not achieved until the age of thirty-five, after marriage. The effort to sustain the European patriarchal system, with its closed organic community of extended kinship, had succeeded initially because the first three generations of fathers and sons stayed within the original township boundaries. By deeding their property to their children only in their wills, the fathers sustained authority over the sons even after these had families of their own, for sons did not obtain fee-simple ownership over their own farms on their father's land until the father died. However, when the original townships became crowded (by an increasing birthrate and longevity), parents no longer had enough land nearby to be divided; nor could they purchase more nearby except at high prices. Then the sons, seeking status as heads of their own patriarchy, were forced to move away. At first they left reluctantly, uneasy at breaking loose from family ties and paternal protection. In new western townships (as close as possible to the old family) they tried to reestablish the same patriarchal, extended-kinship pattern for their sons and grandsons. But their effort was less successful. Land in the West was too plentiful. Paternal authority became steadily more tenuous with each new settlement. After 1720, Greven discovered, the younger sons were far more individualistic, while the fathers (themselves having broken loose) were more willing to grant early autonomy to the succeeding generation. The nuclear family was cutting itself loose from the extended family and the older sources of order and conformity. But the nuclear, self-reliant family did not always find life easier; socially and psychologically its resources were diminished, its self-doubts increased.

John Demos found, in *A Little Commonwealth* (1970), that in the more loosely controlled Plymouth Colony, with its Separatist background, the closely knit communal order broke down within a single generation. Kenneth Lockridge, studying the town of Dedham, Massachusetts, in *A New England Town, the First Hundred Years* (1970), described 1686 as the critical turning point in village life. In his chapter entitled "Toward a New Society," Lockridge presents a model for the whole disruptive process:

> The ironies of the town's evolution had now become inescapable. From the day the policies of perfection had fallen into disuse [1686], the townsmen had begun to cast off the old collective passivity [subjugation of self]. They went freely into court to assert their individual claims against neighbors. Each showed up at the town meeting to defend the concept of the community which he thought ought to prevail, and so together they remade the meeting into the arena of new politics based on their contending interests. They came to expect the right to attend or even to form a church whose minister voiced their particular convictions. They were gradually turning Dedham into an open society where diversity prevailed and the majority ruled. More, they were moving toward an age in which the free individual would move among a vast array of choices—legal, political, religious, occupational, geographic—and would be enshrined as a new kind of god. The logical next step in this process was for men to begin breaking free of the last ties of the old community.

But in order to break free of the last ties, the individual villagers had to break free of the picture they carried in their heads of the ideal social order and its relationship to God.

The tremendous cultural reorientation that this required—Bushman calls it "a psychological earthquake"—is the movement historians have called the First Great Awakening. We may see it in part as the breakdown of the inner tensions between pietistic radicalism and collectivist authority. "The tensions between tradition and counter-tradition," writes Darrett Rutman, "could be accommodated nowhere. The traditional gave way—social unity to the institutionalization of diversity and conflict (the politics of representative democracy) and to geographic mobility ('frontier'

restlessness or more apt, if less exciting, urban restlessness . . . )."
In short, by 1720 the old ideological framework had lost its cultural
legitimacy and the people needed new light from God by which to
guide their behavior, measure their goals, and establish new sources
of communal authority in church and state. The awakening was a
search for new loyalties.

Yet, when this process began, so unexpected was the "awakening," so buried in the unconscious was the smoldering revolt
against the fathers, that people could comprehend it only as a
miraculous, "surprising work of God." No other explanation
seemed to account for the transition from pain to ecstasy, from
confusion to confidence. A contemporary, commenting on the
revival outburst in Jonathan Edwards' parish in 1734-35, wrote:

> 'Tis worthy of our Observation that this great and surprising Work does
> not seem to have taken rise from any sudden and distressing Calamity
> or publick Terror that might universally impress the Minds of a People:
> Here was no Storm, no Earthquake, no Inundation of Water, no Desola-
> tion by Fire, no Pestilence or any other sweeping Distemper, nor any
> cruel Invasion by their Indian Neighbours, that might force the
> Inhabitants into a serious Thoughtfulness and a religious Temper by
> Fears of Approaching Death and Judgment.

However, fear of death and judgment was preached by Edwards
and most other revivalists. What people feared, and why they
welcomed the release of a crisis conversion experience, was their
own rebellious tempers (as the revivalists rightly told them) and,
beneath that, their expectation of deserved paternal punishment
(God's wrath for their continued disobedience to their fathers'
ways). By calling it "a work of God," they excused this rebellion
against traditional authority; it was out of their hands. What joy,
then, to find that God loved and forgave them, once they had
confessed their willfulness. During the trauma of conversion they
received new light on their place in the universe, a light that
reinstated them in paternal grace. They awakened as from a
nightmare to discover that they had been living under a false
consciousness of their sinfulness. They had felt guilt because they
were not following the ways of their fathers, but they now saw, and
were stunned at the wonder of it, that it was their fathers' ways that

had been false. The church and the state had been living by a dim, distorted light and by that light had led the people astray.

Once the individual broke out of his old darkness, he longed to share his joy and tell his experience to others; he sought spiritual communion with his brethren. Out of the awakening emerged new churches and new sects, new forms of Christian fellowship. Individual freedom and fraternal union went hand in hand. The new sense of brotherhood and sisterhood was expressed in new church covenants. Out of the ecstasy of many regenerated souls came the union of all in service to God. More slowly, a new, overarching sense of intercolonial unity emerged.

At first the awakening was a spontaneous, undirected, individualistic breaking-out from the dead skin of the past that had inhibited personal freedom and social energy. It began with private explosions of the personality in emotional conversion experiences; these occurred in scattered local revivals in the 1720s and 1730s throughout the colonies. Then, after 1739, when the experience had taken common shape and been given general articulation, the whole of British North America, from Georgia to Nova Scotia, seemed to explode like a string of firecrackers. Massive and continuous revival meetings were kept in motion by traveling preachers from 1740 to 1745. In some places the established authorities tried to quench the riotous behavior of the awakened. In others the local authorities were themselves caught up in it and supported it. There were also examples of nativist reaction among old-light opponents of the awakening, who saw it as the work of the devil or of popular demagogues intent on arousing the rabble against their rulers.

During the generation in which this revitalization movement worked itself out, the colonists came to see that acculturation to the New World had opened an enormous gap between them and the mother country. They felt a new and semiautonomous identity as a people; and when the king, their royal father, refused to acknowledge this, they turned against him as a wicked, unnatural parent, unwilling to grant freedom to his mature and self-reliant sons of liberty. However, during that awakening generation, an immense amount of new experience and new ideas had to be accommodated to the new world view in order to give it shape and coherence.

Because the various colonies were in different stages of acculturation, because their experiences and leadership differed, the awakening progressed unevenly and took different forms in different
regions. Different denominations devised different strategies to
meet local exigencies. However, by 1765 the majority of members
of the leading denominations were all at approximately the same
point in the new ideological consensus and were thus ready to move
on together into political reformation. Still, it will be easier to
follow the course of this movement if we consider separately its New
England, Middle Colonies, and southern phases. While the timing
varied and different denominations took the major roles in each
region, a common pattern of meaning and events prevailed
everywhere. Before we look at the three regional variations within
the awkening, it is important first to describe what they shared: a
new preaching style, itinerant evangelists, and a new morphology
of conversion.

## The New Light and Its Itinerant Prophets

Throughout the colonies the awakening began when itinerant,
though ordained, ministers offered new styles of preaching and a
new rhetoric that ostensibly called people back to God but in effect
redefined their relationship to him. The enthusiasm aroused by
these itinerant men of God inspired imitators, sometimes local
pastors, sometimes persons who were not ordained but who felt an
internal call to preach in a new way out of their own experiential
confrontation with God. This call led them from place to place,
seeking an audience for their new message. Soon itinerant exhorters
and revivalists were swarming through the countryside, arousing
such disorder that parish ministers became alarmed and sought aid
from the civil authorities to suppress them. At first this call for law
and order simply increased the disorder by stimulating true believers in the new-light message to denounce both the established
clergy and the established authority that backed them. Schisms and
separations followed, with increasing denunciations on both sides.
A few disturbed souls concluded that the world was coming to an
end, that only withdrawal into communities of the perfected saints

could preserve a "saving remnant" from God's wrath. A few charismatic figures assumed messianic roles and were treated by their followers as God incarnate. To the new lights the old order seemed insanely disordered; to the old lights the new fanatics seemed out of their minds.

Perhaps the major contributing force to the general outbreak of the itinerant aspect of the awakening was the Reverend George Whitefield, who had already established a reputation as a sensational preacher in England. He had the advantage of coming from outside the prevailing colonial society yet of bearing with him the authority of his Anglican ordination; he also had an appealing youthfulness (he was twenty-three) and a striking new style in the pulpit. His sermons, when read today, seem banal, but contemporary accounts confirm the striking charisma of an approach that both startled and enthralled his audiences. Whitefield allowed full range to his flair for histrionics. He would sing hymns, wave his arms, tell stories in colloquial language, employ vivid imagery, weep profusely over his own melodramatic appeals, and pray extemporaneously and directly to God, as though he were talking to him. On provincial Americans who had never seen anything like it, the effect was electric. No one supposed that preachers were to appeal so directly and powerfully to the emotions of their audience (it had not been done since the 1630s). Moralizing and doctrinal sermons had for several generations become the accepted formula for colonial preaching. Whitefield deemphasized the institutional side of religion and emphasized the personal responsibility of the individual.

Apart from his flamboyance, the most characteristic features of Whitefield's rhetoric were his assumption (despite his alleged Calvinism) that sinners could repent and be saved if they really wanted to, his effort to arouse individuals by repeatedly using the word "you" in his imperative commands (looking directly at some person in the crowd), and his emphasis on the joy of salvation:

> "Rejoice in the Lord always; again I say, rejoice." Christ is made to you of God's righteousness, what then should you fear? You are made the righteousness of God in him; you may be called "The Lord our righteousness." Of what then should you be afraid? What shall separate you henceforward from the love of Christ? Shall tribulation, or distress, or

persecution, or famine, or nakedness, or peril, or sword? No: I am
persuaded neither death nor life nor angels, nor principalities nor
powers, nor things present, nor things to come, nor height, nor depth,
nor any other creature, shall be able to separate you from the love of
God, which is in Christ Jesus our Lord, who of God is made unto you
righteousness.

Whitefield was here addressing those already converted, but he
made that state seem so ecstatic that all his hearers clamored to
attain it: "What shall *I* do to be saved?" How could they attain
that blessed love, assurance, and personal security that Whitefield
promised to all who believed in God on faith?

Nor did it hurt Whitefield's popularity among the Calvinists that
he was opposed by most of the Anglican clergy in the colonies for
his flamboyance and for his willingness to preach in non-Anglican
churches or to address large throngs in public squares or open
fields. His refusal to be cowed by his superiors' threats to bring him
to trial in ecclesiastical courts made him a hero to other rebels for
God.

Whitefield's first itinerant tour of the colonies in 1739–40 is
generally described as his most successful, but his many later tours,
from Maine to Georgia, always drew large crowds wherever he
spoke. He set a new style, which impressed people as different as
Jonathan Edwards and Benjamin Franklin. Edwards' wife marveled
at his "deep-toned, yet clear and melodious voice" and declared it
"wonderful to see what a spell he casts over an audience. . . . I
have seen upwards of a thousand people hang on his words with
breathless silence, broken only by an occasional half-suppressed
sob." One ordinary farmer, who saddled his horse, hoisted his wife
behind him, and rode madly into town when he heard Whitefield
had arrived, said that when Whitefield mounted the scaffold
erected for him on the village green,

he looked almost angellical, a young slim, slender youth before some
thousands of people & with a bold undainted [undaunted] countenance
& my hearing how god was with him every where as he came along it
solumnized my mind & put me in a trembling fear before he began to
preach, for he looked as if he was Cloathed with authority from ye great
god.

Not all the itinerant revivalists spoke in the same way, but

Whitefield set a pattern; and in their various styles, Jonathan
Edwards, Gilbert Tennent, Samuel Davies, Eleazar Wheelock, and
Samuel Finley aroused the same awesome respect as messengers of
God. Consequently, when these prophets told anxious sinners that
their deplorable spiritual condition was not entirely their own fault,
they believed it. The reason they had lost touch with God and
could not understand what they must do to be saved was because
they had had such poor spiritual guidance from their regular
pastors. "The generality of preachers," Whitefield said, even of
the respected Massachusetts clergy, "talk of an unknown, unfelt
Christ. The reason why congregations have been so dead is because
they had dead men preaching to them."

Tennent told them of "the dangers of an unconverted ministry"
and left no doubt that most opponents of the revival were
unconverted preachers who, having no knowledge in their own
hearts of spiritual rebirth, naturally could not convey such knowledge to others. God did not, and could not, work through such
"dumb dogs." No one who did not "experimentally" (i.e.,
experientially) "know Christ" could convey the new light to
anxious souls. Tennent, and others after him, told the people on
his revival tours that if a man could not receive spiritual nourish-
ment in his parish church, he might "lawfully go, and that
frequently, where he gets most good to his precious soul." The
awakening made it clear that the private spiritual needs of the
individual came before any loyalty to his parish church or pastor
and that each man knew best where to find what he needed for his
own good.

Among features of the First Great Awakening that were shared
throughout the colonies, the conversion experience was even more
important than itinerant preachers. There is no typical conversion,
but it is possible to select an example that conveys its most
important aspects. This account was written after the event by a
young man who was converted in 1741 in the town of Norwich,
Connecticut. Born into a family of prosperous farmers, he led the
ordinary life of a farmboy, attended church regularly, learned the
catechism in the public schools, participated in family prayers, and
expected to find his way into church membership when he married.
His parents had been admitted to the local Congregational church

without conversion, and the minister did not require it. "I lived a careless and secure life," wrote young Isaac Backus, "for more than seventeen years, though in all this time I did never think that I was converted but flattered myself with this, that I would turn by and by" from sin and receive God's grace. But suddenly, shortly after Whitefield had stormed through New England, a revival broke out in his town. Many friends and neighbors were converted, and Backus heard many exciting itinerant revivalists preach. He was seventeen years old and wanted to be saved but did not know how to go about it.

> Although I was often warned and Exorted (especially by my godly mother), to fly from the Wrath to come, yet I never was under any powerful conviction [of my sinfulness] till the year 1741. When it pleased the Lord to cause a very general awakening thro' the land. . . . Before these times I never thought myself in a safe [i.e., elect] state yet eased my self with purposes of turning [to God] by and by when I should have a more convenient season . . . ; in May and June 1741, God by his Spirit was pleased in infinite mercy to bring eternal things near to my soul and to show me the dredful danger of delays.

Though Backus does not mention it, his father had died suddenly in November 1740, and we may suspect that this had a profound psychological effect upon the adolescent boy (as we know it did on his mother). His father had not been converted, and Backus had not yet made his own adjustment to adult autonomy. His urgent desire "to go and hear the most powerful preaching that I could" may have stemmed from a personal combination of fear and guilt, but it was one shared in other ways by countless members of his generation.

> Nothing now distressed me more than to find that hearing the most powerful preaching and also the shrieks and cries of souls under concern did not affect me as I desired, but my heart felt hard notwithstanding. But in truth the Lord was then letting me see something of the plague of my heart and the fountain of corruption that was there . . . ; thus I worried for some weeks.

It is commonly thought that all conversions during revivals of religion take place during preaching services, when large groups of people are under the immediate influence of the preacher's rhetoric and personality. But Backus's experience was typical of many who

were converted in solitude at a moment when they least expected it.
His defenses were down and his guilt welled up:

> On August 29, 1741, . . . I was mowing in the field alone. . . . It
> appeared clear to me that I had tried every way that possibly I could
> [for salvation] and if I perished forever I could do no more—and the
> justice of God shined so clear before my eyes in condemning such a
> guilty Rebel that I could say no more—but fell at his feet. I saw that I
> was in his hands and he had a right to do with me just as he pleased.
> And I lay like a dead, vile creature before him.

The rebel submitted—not to established authority, but to a new,
more powerful source of paternal authority—to God himself. The
confrontation was a direct, felt, visualized experience of the senses
(perhaps a reenactment of his childish submission of his will to his
father). It had a unique and unforgettable reality, like a blinding
light piercing his innermost being:

> And just in that critical moment, God, who caused the light to shine out
> of darkness—shined into my heart with such a discovery of that glorious
> righteousness which fully satisfied the law that I had broke, and of the
> infinite fullness that there is in Christ to satisfie the wants of such a
> helpless creature as I was . . . that my whole heart was attracted and
> drawn after God and swallowed up in admiration in view of his divine
> glories.

The experience was overwhelming in its power, transforming in its
result, and ecstatic in the sense of relief that it provided. "And now
my Burden (that was so dreadful heavey before) was gone: that
tormenting fear that I had was taken away, and I felt a sweet peace
and rejoicing in my soul." Backus does not state precisely what his
burden was or what sins he felt had made him a rebel. Few
conversion experiences do. The guilt is not specific but unconscious, repressed. It is felt as an inexplicable burden, bearing down,
which none of the ordinary stress-release mechanisms can relieve.
The wonder of the experience is part of its success. Feeling reborn,
his slate wiped clean, his burden gone, Backus dated his Christian
birth from that afternoon.

The intensely personal relationship of God to the convert, the
fact that no intermediary (no minister, no congregation, no ritual)
participates, constitutes the most vital part of the experience. "The
Lord God is a Sun," Backus later wrote, and "when any Soul is

brought to behold his Glories, them [*sic*] eternal rays of Light and Love shine down particularly upon him to remove his darkness.'' So personal is this light that ''its rays appear to point as directly to us as if there was not another person in the world for it to shine upon.'' Thereafter the whole world looked different to the convert. He had a new consciousness of his place in the sun. The individual became his own church, and he yearned to share his experience, to make converts to his new way of seeing.

Backus joined his parish church but found no comfort from the preaching of its minister and no reinforcement from a congregation that included so many unconverted persons. When he and other new-light converts asked the minister to exclude from membership those who did not experimentally know Christ, he refused; so they left the parish church and formed a new-light or ''Separate'' church. Meeting in a private home, they exhorted each other for a while until they discovered that one of their members had a special gift from God—the gift of preaching the Word. He was not a college graduate and had no ministerial training, but when he spoke about a ''felt Christ'' in terms his fellow converts understood, they ordained him as their pastor. Refusing any longer to pay religious taxes to support the established parish church and its minister, many of these new lights in Norwich were taken to jail or had their household goods sold at auction by the local sheriff. Some of them began to talk of the need of separating the church from the state, for God did not want people taxed to support false religion when they were supporting true religion voluntarily.

Backus then followed the next step taken by many new lights. He discovered that he had an internal call from the Holy Spirit to preach. He became an itinerant exhorter in Connecticut, Rhode Island, and Massachusetts. In 1748 he formed a Separate church in Middleborough, Massachusetts, which chose him as its pastor. In the following years he and many other itinerant new lights helped to found scores of these churches throughout New England. In 1756 Backus left the Separates to become a Separate Baptist, thereby adding another denomination to the proliferating sectarianism of the colonies.

## The New England Phase of the Awakening

E. S. Gaustad has rightly called the founding of these two new denominations (the Separates and the Separate Baptists) "the most conspicuous institutional effect of the Great Awakening in New England." They "destroyed the traditional parish system, weakened the structure of the establishment, and undermined the Saybrook Platform" (a plan uniting church and state in Connecticut). The English Toleration Act of 1689 had forced some tolerance for tiny groups of dissenters in Anglican and Puritan colonies in New England, but they had made little headway against the entrenched power of the established Congregational church system. After the First Great Awakening began, it became impossible to hold dissent in check. By 1755 there were 125 Separate (or Strict Congregational) churches in New England, and by 1776 there were 70 Separate Baptist churches (excluding those in Rhode Island). The Anglican churches, too, gained an enlarged following in New England after 1740 by attracting many conservative upper-class folk who found the enthusiasm of the awakening too disorderly and the new evangelical Calvinism of the new-light preachers too pietistic. Later, the Universalists, Free Will Baptists, and Shakers added further religious pluralism to the once uniform religious life of New England. The established ecclesiastical system lingered in a formal sense until 1833, but after 1755 it was constantly on the defensive and divided in its counsels.

From the rise of religious pluralism naturally flowed the long effort to disestablish the Congregational churches. At first the Separate and Separate Baptist dissenters struggled simply to attain legal exemption from religious taxes. This had been granted to Quakers and Anglicans in 1727–29 and to old-light (pre-Awakening) Baptists. But when these new-light radicals were denied exemption and defined as "schismatics" or "tax-dodgers," they developed a more concerted program to end the whole concept of tax support for religion. They started petitioning the towns and legislatures for changes in the tax laws. When this proved ineffective, they petitioned the King in Council. After 1774 they petitioned the Continental Congress.

Thus an awakening that had started simply as an effort to save souls and revive church piety moved by logical degrees toward a fundamental restructuring of one of New England's most basic institutions. Some of the Separates, facing what they considered political persecution, demonstrated aspects of social revolt. They practiced civil disobedience; they published tracts denouncing the magistrates and clergy as a tyrannical upper class. Ebenezer Frothingham, a Connecticut Separate leader, wrote a book in 1767 to show that the people of New England were as "priest-ridden" by their establishment as their forefathers in England had been by Anglican bishops during the Puritan Awakening. Isaac Backus became a student of history and wrote a stunning three-volume analysis of New England Puritanism from the dissenting viewpoint that finally resurrected the all-but-forgotten Roger Williams as a hero of religious liberty. But not until the Second Great Awakening were New Englanders sufficiently enlightened to abandon their established ecclesiastical practices.

At the opposite extreme from the new-light rebels were the old-light reactionaries, led by Samuel Niles and Timothy Clap. Clap, the president of Yale College, became so alarmed by the intensity of the religious dissent following Whitefield's itinerancy that he published a statement in 1743 accusing him of a "Design to turn the generality of the Ministers in the Country [New England] out of their Places and resettle them with Ministers from England, Scotland and Ireland." Niles reinforced this conspiracy theory two years later when he claimed that Whitefield's purpose in arousing "illiterate and enthusiastick Exhorters" to attack the spiritual deadness of the New England churches was to make "a Push at our Constitution . . . with a Design to overthrow it . . . the Sooner the better." Whitefield, in short, was making dupes of the new lights as part of a secret plot by the Church of England to subvert the Puritan established system in New England. Twenty years later Clap was to make peace with the new lights and, in the pre-Revolutionary era, to find them a bulwark of resistance to the tyranny of Parliament. But, as in all awakenings, the initial stages of revitalization aroused excessive fear among those in positions of authority.

The principal contribution of New England to the First Great

Awakening was its articulation of the new-light theology later
known as "Edwardsianism," "Hopkinsianism," "Consistent
Calvinism," or Evangelical Calvinism. Basically, the First Great
Awakening split the New England clergy into four factions. One of
the two old-light factions (the Arians, Socinians, or "Arminians")
was in fact responding to the influence of the Enlightenment in
Europe rather than to the new lights in America. This faction
included the incipient rationalists, deists, Unitarians, and Universalists. Though differing widely among themselves, they generally
opposed the doctrines of predestination and innate depravity,
arguing for freedom of the will and universal salvation. However,
this faction was small in New England prior to 1775. The Arians
(who denied the doctrine of the Trinity and claimed that Christ was
not of the same substance as God) remained within the state
churches as "liberal" or "rational" Christians and did not openly
avow their Unitarian principles until after 1800; they were generally
called Arminians by the new lights because they denied the
necessity of a conversion experience and believed that all men could
attain salvation by leading moral, honest, respectable lives.

The second, and by far the greatest bulk of the old-light group,
was the faction that upheld the covenant theology, along with the
various modifications in church practice that had been adopted
since 1662 (like the halfway covenant, Stoddardianism, the Saybrook Platform). Theologically they were moderate Calvinists, and
many of them were sympathetic to the awakening until its enthusiasm began to cause schisms in the churches. After the furor had
cooled and a new theological consensus had emerged, many of
these moderates joined hands with the moderate new lights to
sustain the old ecclesiastical order against the schismatics and
Anglicans.

The new-light or pietistic reformers were also divided into two
factions. The leading figures in the larger of the two were ordained
ministers who supported the theological and ecclesiastical position
represented by Jonathan Edwards. The smaller faction was a more
vehement, uncompromisingly radical group that demanded
immediate and drastic reform in the ecclesiastical system and, when
this was not forthcoming, broke away to become Separates and
Separate Baptists. (At the far end of this radical spectrum were

extreme perfectionists like Shadrach Ireland, Jemima Wilkinson, and Ann Lee, who formed their own charismatic sects.) However, the great majority of the new lights remained within the established churches and sought to reform them from within.

Best described as Evangelical Calvinists in theology, the new lights placed great emphasis on spiritual regeneration or a crisis conversion as the criterion for church membership and worked to return church practice to the original Puritan congregationalism of the Cambridge Platform of 1648. It was the revitalization of Calvinism by these new lights that constituted the heart of the awakening in New England. Through their close association with Presbyterianism, their influence was also important in the Middle Colonies. The revised world view of this new-light group was more optimistic, progressive, individualistic, and democratic in its spiritual and social outlook; ultimately it converged at certain points with the new world view in European thought that we call the Enlightenment. One such point of ultimate agreement was separation of church and state (though Edwards himself did not share this). More important were agreements about postmillennialism, the concept of a higher natural law, belief in the special mission of America, and belief in the free and morally responsible individual. In political outlook the Enlightened rationalist and the new-light pietist came also to agreement on the Lockean theories of government by the consent of the governed, on no taxation without representation, and on the necessity for separation from the mother country. But it required more than a generation to work through to these common grounds. At the start of the awakening, the new lights saw the rationalism of the Enlightenment as the real threat to Calvinistic pietism. It was against its Arminianizing tendencies (i.e., its exaltation of man's reason and free will) that Edwards directed his primary effort.

Edwards is generally considered the leading theologian of the First Great Awakening and consequently might be called its chief prophet. However, the process was far too complex to be summed up in the career of any one person. Moreover, Edwards died in 1758 before the awakening had yet worked out its final consensus. In many respects he did not understand the full extent of the transformation in which he played so large a part. He criticized those radical new lights who separated from their old-light parish churches; he always defended the necessity for religious taxation and an established church system; there is scarcely a word in all his writings to justify social reform, and nothing on politics. Edwards carefully explained to ecclesiastical and theological moderates of his day that he could not defend the foolishness of the pietistic perfectionists, Separates, or Separate Baptists, and thus he helped lead the way to the new consensus. The beauty of God's universe for him, as for John Winthrop, lay in its hierarchical order and harmony, not in arrant individualism and social mobility, diversity, or equality. "There is a beauty of order in society," he wrote, "as when the different members of a society have all their appointed office, place and station, according to their several capacities and talents and everyone keeps his place and continues in his proper business." Social disorder, leveling, was not only rebellion against duly constituted authority but a disruption of God's rank-ordering of the universe.

Edwards did his best to interpret the new light to meet the objections of moderates. Though his Arian opponents failed to appreciate it, his writings endeavored to integrate the epistemology of John Locke into a revitalized Calvinist theology. He should be seen as a Janus-faced figure, looking back as well as forward. The most forward-looking aspects of his new vision were the "sensational" (sensory perception) psychology upon which he based his analysis of conversion, his postmillennial view of the rising glory of America, and his concept of disinterested benevolence. To understand the democratic thrust in Edwardsian or Evangelical Calvinism, we first have to understand the position of the old lights in this awakening.

Because those who held to the Arian and Arminian theological positions in New England (represented by the incipient Unitarians in Boston and Harvard, as well as by the Anglican ministry) were committed to the concept of salvation by education, by traditional church ordinances, and by moralistic self-discipline (which was not likely to be evident among the poor and ignorant), they can be seen as the most socially conservative wing of the awakening, despite their "liberal" or rationalist theology. The Arians (sometimes called "supernatural rationalists") do not deserve to be called old

lights in the sense of intellectual reactionaries. They were on the
forward edge of the Enlightenment's revitalization of Western
culture. But to pietists they seemed a throwback to the pre-Puritan,
pre-Reformation view of salvation by works. They were also old
lights in their staunch defense of the established order, with its
elitism, its social conformity, and its ecclesiastical formalism. The
revival to them was a despicable example of the aroused "animal
affections" or emotions; it was spiritually unrefined, lacking in
gentility. Intelligent men knew that harmony, good order, and
social prosperity depended on prudence, moderation, and balance
—on exalting the rational side of human nature, not the irrational.
As the Reverend Charles Chauncy of Boston put it, in his famous
denunciation of the awakening, "an enlightened mind, not raised
affections" must always be the way to truth and "a saving
knowledge" of God. When an old light spoke about "knowledge
of God," he meant knowing intellectually how God's universe
operated, not feeling the presence of God in his heart.

The rationalistic Christians of New England, who shared much
with the liberal or latitudinarian Anglicans in the South and with
deists like Benjamin Franklin in the Middle Colonies, found God
through scientific study of the laws of nature. "Natural theology"
was for them a more trustworthy guide to the higher moral law of
God than a hysterical revival experience. They were shocked that
educated ministers like Edwards still clung to the old doctrines of
Calvinism in their starkest form, portraying God as a mysterious,
angry, vengeful deity who had nothing but contempt for his
creatures. They failed to understand Edwards' emphasis on God's
grace, mercy, and beauty. The rational, "enlightened" outlook of
the liberal was in many respects as paternalistic or elitist as the new
evangelical Calvinism was democratic. Though many of the "liberal Christians" became ardent patriots, they were never ardent
democrats. God may have given reason to all men, but he did not
give it to all in the same amount. Birth, intelligence, and education
distinguished the *aristoi*, the best and the wisest, from *hoi polloi*.
In a well-ordered society the common folk must still defer to their
betters. (Even Jefferson's advocacy of a common school system was
democratic only to the extent of raising the natural aristocrat from
the rubbish of the common herd.) Alan Heimert, in *Religion and*

*the American Mind* (1966), quotes the "liberal" Jonathan Mayhew
(whose sermon against unlimited submission to kings made him a
hero to pietists and proto-Unitarians alike in 1750) on the limited
abilities of the common people: "It is not intended," he said, in
claiming that all men are reasonable, to argue "that all men have
equal abilities for judging what is true and right. . . . Those of the
lower class can get but a little ways in their inquiries into the natural
and moral constitutions of the world." They would always have to
rely on those of superior education and talent to govern them in
worldly and religious affairs if they wished to avoid anarchy and
chaos.

Nevertheless, the rationalists believed that men are far from
totally depraved. On the contrary, men have the ability to comprehend the Bible, to know right from wrong (through God-given
conscience or "the moral sense"). Furthermore, the evils of this
world are not the result of Adam's Fall and original sin but of
ignorance, lack of information, lack of care, forethought, and self-
discipline. It is true that most men are motivated by self-love, but
self-love can be manipulated or directed by ministers and educators
toward virtuous behavior. Men are bright enough to see that it is to
their own best interest to obey the law, act honestly, and treat their
neighbor as they wished to be treated. Punishing the incorrigibly
vicious and rewarding the morally good is God's way of leading
men toward heaven. Any reasonable man can see that this is more
realistic or practical than counting on irrational revival experiences
to turn men toward true virtue.

In opposition to these views, Evangelical Calvinism as preached
by the new lights of all denominations offered a far less elitist view
of human nature and a more benevolent view of God's will: God is
no respecter of persons. He sheds his light on rich and poor alike—
in fact, more commonly on the poor, since the rich are unwilling or
afraid to bend their pride. The role of the preacher in the new-light
ideology is to bring the word of God to his hearer with such power
that it literally bowls them over.

To preach "a felt Christ" was more than a figure of speech. All
religion is concerned with power. Evangelical Calvinism was concerned with the power that changes depraved, selfish men from
rebels against God to loving servants of God. Such power cannot

derive from education, worldly experience, prudence, or moral self-discipline. True holiness or benevolence toward God is so ineffable, so indescribably different from anything we can know from worldly, sensual experience that it cannot come to us through the intellect and understanding. The link between man and God is not the reason, the head, but the heart.

The heart is "moved," transformed, regenerated through the religious affections or religious feelings. These feelings resemble the ordinary feelings of men, but they operate on a different, higher plane of existence. While John Locke was right to say that men gain knowledge only through sense impressions, he failed to describe how the soul receives impression of (or from) God. To have spiritual "feelings" we must assume that God operates through religious stimuli working upon spiritual sensibilities lodged in the soul. Theologically this is termed "infusion with grace." God's sensational operations upon the human heart, through the felt but unseen agency of the Holy Spirit, parallel on the spiritual plane of man's being those mundane impressions made on man's animal nature by the sensation of light, heat, sound, taste, or odor. "Our people," said Edwards in 1742, "do not so much need to have their heads stored as to have their hearts touched." Conversion is, symbolically, the touch of God's finger on the heart, a perception of his glory upon the mind's eye, a divine illumination.

Depraved men are stonyhearted. As Edwards put it, "by a Hard heart is plainly meant an unaffected heart, or a heart not easy to be moved with virtuous affections, like a stone, insensible, stupid, unmoved, and hard to be impressed." Revival sermons consequently speak constantly of breaking, crushing, storming, shattering, and cracking the stony hearts of the unconverted. The revivalists' words (conveying the divine "Word") are said to stab, wound, shock, pierce, and cut the hearts of their hearers. This is not simply metaphor. The revivalists were using the precise, technical, scientific terminology of the psychology of their time—Lockean empiricism. They were describing as accurately as they could the physical laws of divine force, a force so great, so overpowering, that those who are hit by it cannot forbear sometimes to cry out, to groan, to shriek, to jump up from their pews or fall off their seats in a faint. The impact of God's power, as Edwards said, is too much for frail human affection to bear. The essence of the shock, however, is not physical but spiritual. The physical manifestations are side effects, symptomatic of an inner change of heart. The function of grace is not to harm but to heal. The revivalist says of the fainted convert, "He is slain and made alive by the power of the truth." The old Adam, the old man, the devil who ruled the depraved heart is dead from the blow; the saint, the new Adam, is reborn, "a new man in Christ." Metaphorically, the grace of God strikes off the chains that have bound the soul in slavery to Satan (or self), and the captive cannot help shouting, "Lord God Almighty, free at last!"

It is significant that the new-light revivalists throughout the awakening found that their liberating theology had a profound effect upon the powerless and the poor of society—upon black slaves, upon women, upon Indians, upon children. These suffered more tensions and suppressed rage than most in society and felt the release of conversion (the reaction formation) more deeply. They could not, however, actualize the new freedom and power they felt except in religious activity—in preaching, saving souls, becoming missionaries (or missionaries' wives). Yet even this form of sublimated freedom produced a surprising number of black, Indian, and women preachers and exhorters in the years after 1740. Heimert has argued persuasively that in the First Great Awakening, God was democratized.

Revitalization of the individual led to efforts to revitalize society. Having a new sense of harmony with God, the new-light convert was impelled to work in conjunction with God's power to help his fellow men have it likewise. The regenerate could not rest content with the world as it was; they wished to make it what it ought to be. Where the old lights saw human progress as slow and gradual, limited by hereditary and environmental contingencies, the new light found the world open to the miraculous—unconditioned, full of new possibilities and unrealized potentials. Religious revivalism, saving souls, is in this respect a political activity, a way of producing a reborn majority to remodel society according to God's will and with his help. Despite Edwards' arguments against freedom of the will, despite the continued belief in man's innate depravity and God's predestined election, the awakening raised hopes that the whole continent might be converted. God might have elected all Americans to sainthood.

Although millennialism in various forms had been prevalent during the Puritan Awakening, the majority of those who came to America had adopted a premillennial interpretation; namely, that God would have to send Christ back a second time to bring order to the world. Increase Mather, appalled at the barbarism of the frontier and the provincialism of the colonies, concluded that ''in the glorious times promised to the Church on Earth, America will be Hell.'' Eighteenth-century rationalists, though slightly more optimistic about progress because of advances in scientific knowledge, nevertheless were cautious about it and clung to the classical view that history moves in cycles. The British Empire might be in its ascendancy at the moment, but, like Greece and Rome, it too would fall in time. Unitarians like John Adams and deistic Episcopalians like Thomas Jefferson held to this cyclical view even for the United States of America.

But the new lights caught a glimpse of another possibility. They found evidence from the surprising work of God in the awakening and from a careful rereading of biblical prophecies that the premillennial interpretation might be wrong. To them it seemed entirely possible that God might create a millennial order without some cataclysmic holocaust compelling Christ's return. In fact, Christ might not return until *after* the millennium (hence ''postmillennialism''). History might not be moving ever downward or in cycles but in a straight line of ascension from Adam's Fall to the redemption of mankind. ''We are sure this day will come,'' said Edwards in 1742, ''and we have many reasons to think that it is approaching; from the fulfilment of almost everything that the prophecies speak of as preceding it . . . and the late extraordinary things that have appeared in the church of God and appertaining to the [present] state of religion.'' According to Alan Heimert and Clarence C. Goen, this postmillennial note in the new-light movement was the most striking feature of the whole awakening and its clearest claim to being a cultural watershed in American history.

Edwards said that the New Jerusalem would not be ''accomplished at once, as by some miracle'' but would be ''gradually

brought to pass," presumably through human effort in cooperation
with God's grace. Furthermore, Increase Mather notwithstanding,
it would very likely begin "in the wilderness"—in America—for
there men were not yet so corrupted by the Old World's decadence.
The mighty outpouring of God's grace during the awakening
seemed clearly to presage the approach of that glorious time when
"all the world [shall] be united in one amiable society. All nations,
in all parts of the world, on every side of the globe, shall then be
knit together in sweet harmony." Explaining the meaning of the
awakening to his parish in 1742, Edwards said,

> It is not unlikely that this work of God's Spirit, so extraordinary and
> wonderful, is the dawning, or at least a prelude, of that glorious work
> of God so often foretold in scripture, which, in the progress and issue
> of it, shall renew the world of mankind. . . . And there are many things
> that make it probable that this work will begin in America.

In the years that lay ahead, more and more Americans came to
share Edwards' view that America had been discovered and popu-
lated by Calvinistic, English-speaking Protestants so that "God
might in it begin a new world in a spiritual respect." American
success in the French and Indian Wars gave further proof that God
might have predestined the rising glory of America. John Adams
said that the Revolution commenced after 1765 "in the minds and
hearts of the people; a change in their religious sentiments." But in
fact it had its beginning a quarter of a century earlier.

Finally, the New England phase of the First Great Awakening
and the ideological reorientation that Edwards and his followers
effected in the old Calvinistic world view helped to bring about a
new social ethic—the pietistic contribution to late eighteenth-
century humanitarian reform. While in some respects this ethic can
be seen as complementary to the benevolent sentiment among
Enlightenment rationalists and Christian liberals, it was in fact
based on a totally different rationale. Paradoxically, the rationalists
and Arians based their social ethic on a more pessimistic reading of
human nature than the Evangelical Calvinists. Reason and historical experience taught the rationalists that men are fundamentally
motivated by self-interest and that few would ever have the moral
self-discipline to overcome this. The Calvinist argued that men are

born innately depraved but can be reborn (as more and more of them were, every day) with a totally different nature. God's grace having infused new benevolent or "gracious affections" in their hearts, the converted no longer acted from self-love or self-interest but from "disinterested benevolence." When Edwards taught that true virtue or true holiness meant "disinterested benevolence toward Being in general," he meant by "Being in general" the total mystical beauty of God's pervading power and love, animating the universe; his followers, however, noting that men, too, are beings, suggested that true holiness meant serving one's fellow man from disinterested concern for both his eternal and this-worldly well-being.

Joseph Conforti has pointed out that Edwards' rather mystical view of disinterested benevolence led to a quietistic view of Christian ethics: "Edwards always felt more comfortable dilating on the subjective fruits of regeneration than upholding or making manifest its social and political consequences." He placed "holy action" last in the list of twelve distinguishing signs of conversion that he discussed in *The Religious Affections*. However, Samuel Hopkins, Edwards' most prestigious pupil, wrote a work to confute (or, as he said, "improve on") Edwards' doctrine. In it he redefined Being in general, Conforti notes, "and put earthly flesh on what in Edwards' thought was an abstract metaphysical concept. . . . Where Edwards located true virtue in exalted consciousness, Hopkins placed it in elevated social behavior. Consequently evangelical activism superseded mystical quietism."

Hopkins did this by two means. First, he redefined Being in general so as to give it a this-worldly component. Regeneration, he said, creates in man a universal benevolence or "love to God and our neighbors . . . or friendly affection to all intelligent beings." Second, he argued that rationalist followers of Shaftesbury and Hutcheson in social ethics were wrong to argue that moral virtue can be derived from self-love or enlightened self-interest, because these are in fact nothing but selfishness. Selfishness can never be a means of attaining true holiness or true virtue: "Selfishness is the source of all the profaneness and impiety in the world, and of all pride and ambition." Hence regeneration is in fact the transformation of human selfishness into human self-sacrifice or self-denial for

the good of Being in general and our neighbors. Hopkins made the
new Evangelical Calvinism more than closet piety or soul-winning.
He moved it into the world of social reform and set the example by
attacking the sin of slavery in his own slaveholding community—
Newport, Rhode Island—in 1770.

Yet even before this, as Richard Bushman has pointed out, the
Reverend Jonathan Lee delivered a new-light election sermon in
Connecticut (in 1766) in which he denounced the rationalist ethic
of self-interest and urged evangelical Calvinists to a higher concept
of public service: "Irregular and inordinate self-love and private
interest," said Lee, "have so much dominion in the heart that
unless true benevolence and public spirit prevent, there is eminent
danger that private interest will be pursued at the expence, or built
on the ruins, of the public weal." Self-interest might corrupt, and
mere rationality or education was no guarantee of honesty. Lee's
concept of "public spirit" and Hopkins' ideal of "self-sacrifice"
were eventually to merge with the neoclassical view of "civic
virtue" or "public service" during the Revolutionary era. But the
two men came to this common position from very different starting
points.

Bushman notes that out of the First Great Awakening came a
new concept of government and public good based on the recip-
rocal interest of the governed and the governing. Under the older
Puritan theory, the social ethic stressed subjugation of private
interest to the covenanted society. The duty of government was to
restrain the selfishness of the individual for the sake of the
commonwealth. But "Whereas public good at the beginning of the
century had implied the denial of private interests for the sake of
more transcendent values," Bushman writes, "it now [as of 1765]
contained the promise also that government would serve private
interests. The civil authority was to act as the public's agent and not
merely as its disciplinarian." Thus the kind of institutional restraint
that had frustrated and confused rising American individualism
from 1690 to 1740 disappeared. The government was to help the
individual to fulfill himself, and the individual in turn was in times
of crisis to sacrifice himself, out of disinterested benevolence (or
civic virtue), for the general welfare. Voluntarism replaced coercion, and a new kind of fraternity replaced the old covenant ideal

or, rather, gave it a revitalized form. As Jonathan Lee put it, "the happy tendency of vital piety to heal the maladies and rectify the disorders of the church of Christ" would expand, under the continuing power of the revival, to a "blessed tendency of vital piety to happify the civil state."

## The Awakening as an Acculturation Movement in the Middle Colonies

In the Middle Colonies the religious life in the early eighteenth century was more diverse, fragmented, and unstable than in the other two regions. Not only did it lack an established church system (outside the feeble Anglican establishment in four New York counties); it lacked even firm denominational organizations. The very atmosphere of toleration in New Jersey, Pennsylvania, Maryland, and Delaware contributed to the instability. Small religious groups, persecuted and deprived in Europe and the British Isles, flocked into these colonies as a haven. Their members, however, were usually poor, uneducated, and traditionally conservative farmers or villagers who tended to cluster together for security, since they were often isolated from their neighbors by language as well as religious barriers. Most frustrating for them was their lack of learned ministers, who in the old country had given order and cohesion to their communities. As they struggled to gain a livelihood from the soil, they were overwhelmed by a steady stream of newcomers, seeking assistance. Tension and anxiety arose in part from the newness of their settlements and in part from their indecision over how much of their cultural baggage they needed or wanted to retain. Whether to be clannish ethnic nationalists or new Americans was the crux of a very emotional dilemma.

Although Dutch settlers had been in New York City and along the Hudson since the early seventeenth century, their culture had been disrupted by the British conquest of their colony and the effort of royal governors to supplant their Calvinistic Dutch Reformed churches with an Anglican establishment. Faced with increasing religious restrictions, many of them moved southwestward to New Jersey, but they still looked to traditional leadership from their conservative New York pastors and from the "classis" (the governing religious body) of the established church in the Netherlands. In 1719 several groups of these settlers along the Raritan River near New Brunswick, New Jersey, sent a request to Amsterdam for a learned minister. The classis of Dutch Reformed ministers and elders sent Theodore J. Frelinghuysen to act as a missionary to these outposts of the mother church. Frelinghuysen, though German by birth, had been educated in Holland at the University of Lingen, where he was influenced by the remnants of the old Puritan and Pilgrim pietism. He thus came to New Jersey eager to arouse the fervor of the conservative Dutch farmers, not realizing that the traditional order was what they expected and thought necessary for their spiritual and psychological comfort.

When Frelinghuysen began demanding more rigorous moral discipline from his Raritan Valley congregations and required a spiritual-crisis experience for admission to church membership (unknown in Holland), he roused a hornet's nest of opposition. Conservative parishioners in the four rural churches he served complained first to the New York pastors (who sympathized with their position) and then to the classis in Holland. Other parishioners, however, found his spiritual zeal stimulating and through the conversion experiences that followed his pietistic preaching attained a greater security and assurance than they had known before. In the turmoil over this conflict between conservatism (formalism) and pietistic fervor a revival spirit arose in the years 1720–28 which some historians have seen as the first symptom of the First Great Awakening in the colonies.

A similar and more far-reaching clash between conservative and pietistic elements occurred among the foreign-born or first-generation immigrants in the Presbyterian churches. Presbyterianism was not new to America in the eighteenth century; but as a result of both English oppression of the Scotch-Irish in Northern Ireland and various schisms arising from theological changes among the Presbyterians in Scotland at the start of the eighteenth century, a tremendous new influx of Presbyterian immigrants occurred. They were not especially welcome in New England. Many were shunted to the Blue Ridge Mountains to act as buffers against the Indians in the southern Anglican colonies, but most of these Scotch-Irish settled in the Middle Colonies, where, by the time of the Revolution, they were the dominant religious group. However, these immigrants, like the Dutch, Scandinavian, and German groups, were intensely conservative. They sought psychological security by trying to maintain their old ways as peasant farmers and devout Calvinists. They wanted their church life in America to be as much as possible like the one they had left behind. Like the Dutch, they had been used to a state establishment whose civil authorities, through taxes, sustained the religious and educational life of the community. But in the New World they had few ministers and fewer schools.

Many of these Presbyterian settlers were twice uprooted within a single generation: from Scotland to Ireland and from there to the New World. The stresses of resettlement were great. They looked to their synods in Ireland and Scotland for guidance and missionary help. But most of the Presbyterian ministers who came to America (where congregations were poor and scattered and salaries—because not guaranteed by taxes—were scanty) were, like those in the Anglican churches, the dregs of the established system at home. Many were doctrinally unsound, badly educated, morally corrupt, intemperate, and psychologically unstable. They caused tension instead of alleviating it. Furthermore, the Enlightenment and the waning Calvinistic fervor in Great Britain were producing Arian, Arminian, and deistic inroads among the Presbyterians; this produced a spiritual crisis in Scotland, where there were intense ecclesiastical problems over the maintenance of orthodoxy. The new immigrants brought these fears and problems with them to America; Old World fears sometimes dominated New World needs.

After the founding of the first Presbyterian synod in America, in Philadelphia in 1717, the denomination faced a series of controversies; these had produced a serious schism just at the time George Whitefield was quickening the revivalistic fervor throughout the colonies (1740). The first of these controversies concerned doctrinal orthodoxy and church discipline. Called "the subscription controversy," it resulted from the conservatives' attempt to require all ministers to subscribe to the standard (Westminster) Calvinistic confession of faith before they could be licensed and ordained. The conservatives passed a rule in 1738 that all ministers must be educated at a university in the British Isles or at Yale or Harvard. This rule arose from the effort of the Reverend William Tennent

and his four sons to educate a native Presbyterian ministry at an
academy called the Log College in Neshaminy, Pennsylvania
(twenty miles north of Philadelphia). Founded in 1726, the college
(or academy) graduated sixteen to eighteen young men before it
closed, following Tennent's death, in 1746.

Though William Tennent was a graduate of the University of
Edinburgh, some conservatives disliked the pietistic tone of his
young seminary graduates. Furthermore, his most talented son,
Gilbert, had formed a friendship with Theodore Frelinghuysen,
whose churches were near his at New Brunswick. Gilbert Tennent
and his brother John had engaged in fervent preaching for
conversion in the late 1720s (probably influenced by Frelinghuysen)
and had produced a series of local revivals, between 1728 and 1738,
similar to those in Frelinghuysen's congregations (and to Edwards'
in Massachusetts). Some of the Scotch-Irish immigrants praised
these as works of God, while others considered them disruptive
works of the devil and contrary to traditional Presbyterian practice.
The Presbyterian churches in Britain did not require crisis conversion as a test of membership, and the imposition of this test as a
requirement for membership in the New World was disturbing.

In 1740 the issue reached a crisis. The synod of Philadelphia
refused to ordain a recent graduate of the Log College, John
Rowland. Rowland had been licensed to preach by the presbytery of
New Brunswick, which was dominated by the Tennents and other
pietists. They argued that the synod had no right to overrule their
presbytery. But the issue was not ecclesiastical order; it was the
Americanization of the Presbyterian church. The ecclesiastical
quarrel was in fact a power struggle between traditionalists, who
wanted to adhere rigidly to the old ways, and pietistic progressives,
who wanted to acculturate their congregations to new circumstances
to meet new needs. Hard upon the controversy over educational
standards came the issue of itinerant revivalism, the "intrusion" of
outside ministers into the parishes. Again the conservatives argued
that the progressives (soon to be known as "the New Sides") were
trying to arouse the people against their own pastors by resorting to
emotional appeals cloaked as religious revivals.

Gilbert Tennent seized upon the arrival of George Whitefield to
press the case for a revitalization of Presbyterianism by means of

itinerant preaching, crisis conversion, and an internal call to preach. The latter point, frequently raised by new lights in New England, was a defensive thrust against the conservatives. It held that no minister who had not undergone a conversion experience and then been "called by the Spirit" was capable of preaching God's truth with power to save souls. However highly regarded they might be in the British Isles, mere learning and orthodoxy were, in America, insufficient standards for the ministry. In the spring of 1740 Tennent delivered the most vehement blast against the "Old Side" conservatives that was to appear anywhere in the colonies during the whole awakening. He delivered it while he was "intruding" in the Old Side parish of Nottingham, Pennsylvania, on the border of Maryland. He was there, he said, because pietistic ministers had a duty to preach to the spiritually starved people whom the Old Side preachers were neglecting.

Tennent's sermon "The Danger of an Unconverted Ministry," indicates that there were some elements of class antagonism embedded in the controversy, as well as a generation gap and an acculturation gap. He implied that some antirevival ministers were more interested in their own social status and the "trade" of preaching than in saving the souls of common folk. Comparing the Old Sides to the Pharisees, who opposed the itinerant revival preaching of Jesus and his disciples, he said, "these Orthodox, Letter-learned . . . old Pharisees were very proud and conceited; they loved the uppermost seats in the Synagogues and to be called Rabbi . . . ; they were masterly and positive in their assertions, as if, forsooth, knowledge must die with them; they look'd upon others that differed from them, and the common People, with an Air of Disdain."

Not only anticlericalism but anti-intellectualism and demagoguery were evident in Tennent's sermon. The antirevivalists "came into the Priest's Office for a Piece of Bread; they took it up as a Trade, and therefore endeavoured to make the best Market of it they could. O Shame! . . . Credit [status] and Money may draw them," but, "being greedy of filthy lucre," they are guided by "the Devil"; they are "wicked [and] natural men," untouched by the supernatural power of conversion. Consequently, "their Discourses are cold and sapless . . . ; they want [lack] divine Author-

ity.'' Seeking prestige, favor, and wealth, the Old Sides spoke only
platitudes to keep the support of rich and complacent members
who paid their high salaries. ''They had not the Courage or
Honesty to thrust the Nail of Terror into sleeping Souls'' but only
told them to perform the rituals, mouth the creeds, and do their
''duty, duty'' to church and civil authority. ''O sad!'' These
''moral Negroes'' are white on the outside but black as sin within.
Tennent concluded this attack by urging the common people to
find relief for their pent-up frustration where they got the most
help: ''If the great Ends of Hearing [the gospel] may be attained as
well and better by Hearing of another Minister than our own, then I
see not why we should be under a fatal Necessity of hearing him, I
mean our Parish-minister, perpetually.''

L. J. Trinterud, the historian of this awakening among the
Presbyterians, entitled his study *The Forming of an American
Tradition* (1949)—the tradition of appealing over the heads of duly
constituted authority to a higher law and asking the people to judge
and act in terms of their own experiential needs and satisfactions.
The Log College men, Trinterud wrote,

> defeated by this controlled Church organization, appealed to the laity.
> They stated the issue as being for or against any revival of spiritual and
> ethical life in the Presbyterian Church. They struck so hard and loosed
> such a force in turning a spiritually aroused, but not spiritually
> disciplined, laity against an apathetic and in some instances morally
> corrupt clergy, that they well-nigh lost control of the situation . . . ; the
> war was in the open now, no longer behind the shelter of Church laws,
> educational requirements, and the like.

The year after Tennent's blast, the synod expelled the New
Brunswick Presbytery from the denomination. Attempts by New
Englanders in the denomination (Jonathan Dickinson and Aaron
Burr) to end the dispute failed. For seventeen years ''the Truth''
was put to the test of experience. The Log College men, joined by
other prorevival Presbyterians from other presbyteries, formed a
new synod, the New York Synod, in 1745, consisting of presbyteries with ministers from Long Island, New Jersey, Pennsylvania,
and Delaware. This synod ordained graduates from the Log College
and its affiliated academies, founded by young men trained by
William Tennent. It sent its itinerants into every hamlet where

Scotch-Irish congregations were looking for assistance (between 1738 and 1741 it received eighty requests for ministerial supplies). Its evangelists went even to Virginia and the Blue Ridge Mountains to carry the revival to the dispersing Scotch-Irish on the frontier. In 1746 they obtained a charter for the College of New Jersey (first located at Elizabeth, then at Princeton). Three of its first five presidents were Yale graduates (including Jonathan Edwards), and two were graduates of the Log College, including Samuel Finley, who had been expelled from Connecticut in 1742 for breaking the law against itinerancy.

If conversion was the fundamental personal experience of the First Great Awakening, itinerant preaching was the fundamental social phenomenon. Harry Stout has recently pointed out the importance of itinerant revivalism to the emergence of intercolonial unity and the forming of a single American identity. Far more than colonial newspapers, printed sermons, or letters of correspondence, itinerant preaching constituted a new form of mass communication in America. Itinerants not only spread the word of God's new-light ideology but delivered that message in a new medium—the spoken word of the common man. Oral communication by laymen without formal education (as many itinerant new lights were, especially among the Separates, Baptists, and Methodists) meant that ordinary people were speaking to each other with new authority. Their power did not come from their learned academic degree, their ordination by some clerical body, their role as members of the established upper class, but simply from the Spirit of God. What was more, they did not speak by leave of any local authority or relate their message to local circumstances and institutions. They did not even bother to seek admission to local pulpits but delivered their messages in private homes, to small groups in the market-place, or to large groups in barns, schoolhouses, or open fields. They democratized religion; they broke down colony and class lines, denominational and regional differences.

If the medium was the message of itinerancy, it was a message fraught with importance for the creation of America's identity. If God spoke through the common man, the voice of the people was the voice of God. If he spoke everywhere in the same way, then mobility to the West was part of God's plan for perfecting the world. Preaching, formerly confined within meetinghouses, parish boundaries, and specific local regulations, was now boundless. Furthermore, these preachers emphasized not doctrinal creeds, theological dogmas, or specific rituals and ordinances; their first and primary interest was to convey their own spiritual experience of rebirth. This experience, conveyed in the words and accents of men of their own social rank, conveyed dramatically the view that God was no respecter of persons. God's power could manifest itself through the mouths of the most ordinary person. He did indeed choose the weak and ignorant to confound the learned and powerful. Not rank, education, and political power but the persuasive power of the spoken word was the message of revivalism. "The revivals [and revivalists] of this awakening," as Sidney Mead has said, "demonstrated the spectacular effectiveness of persuasion alone to churches rapidly being shorn of coercive power." And respect for the message, acknowledgment of its power, meant respect for those who bore it and those who accepted it. "The revivalists," Mead also notes, "stressed religious experience and results—namely conversion—more than correctness of belief, adherence to creedal statements, and proper observances of traditional forms." All of this was to have a marked effect when, after 1765, the revitalization movement entered its period of political reformation and institutional restructuring.

Ultimately the New Side Presbyterians demonstrated that their method of revitalization (or acculturation) through itinerancy was superior to that of the Old Sides. When the two factions reunited in 1758, the number of Old Side ministers in the Philadelphia synod had decreased from 24 to 23, while the New Sides in the New York Synod had increased from 22 to 72. The congregations and churches of the New Sides had likewise grown to more than three times the size of the Old Sides. While Tennent accommodated to the conservatives by dropping the requirement that a crisis conversion was fundamental to church membership, the reunited denomination adhered to his rule that no ministers could be licensed or ordained without evidence of an "inward call" from God to preach. A new kind of religious leadership began to emerge.

The success of Frelinghuysen among the Dutch Calvinists in New Jersey and of the New Sides among the Scotch and Scotch-Irish immigrants throughout the Middle Colonies was not matched by the efforts of Count Zinzendorf to unite and revitalize the many small German groups in this region: Moravians, Lutherans, German Reformed, Schwenkfelders, Siebentagers, Dunkers, Mennonites. A Moravian who assumed the role of a Lutheran bishop, Zinzendorf came to Pennsylvania in 1741 to bring the pietistic movement in Germany to his countrymen in the New World. He tried also to extend his ecumenism to the Scotch-Irish, but language barriers, heightened by the fact that most of the Germans were not Calvinists, prevented this. Nor would the Calvinists of the German Reformed churches accept his overtures. The small German sects proved too tenacious of their own pietistic, tightly knit, peasant communitarian patterns. Somewhat better off than the Scotch-Irish, more committed to living and working in cohesive groups, and kept united by the animosity of English-speaking neighbors, these groups resisted acculturation. But as a result they did not grow. Or, rather, they grew inward, so intent on perfecting their own communion that they remained outside the mainstream of American religious and social development.

The absence of state churches in the Middle Colonies left the New Side pietists with no particular political focus for their rebellion. Their anticlerical diatribes against the denominational fathers must not be taken as parallels to the anticlericalism of deists. If there were bad clergymen and laymen interested only in power and wealth, there were also good clergymen and laymen interested in saving souls. There are no significant overtones of social revolt or political reform in the Middle Colonies' revivals other than opening the ranks of the clergy to talented new men and giving the laity a larger role in church affairs. The acculturation process served primarily to give self-confidence and American identity to the recent immigrants. With the formation of a college to supply an educated native ministry, the Scotch-Irish (and later, with the forming of Queens College in New Brunswick in 1766, the Dutch) entered the American mainstream. The Reverend John Witherspoon, though brought from Scotland to head Princeton College in 1768, saw no reason not to serve in the Continental Congress, sign the Declaration of Independence, and work in every way he could for

the patriot cause. The Scotch-Irish were doughty supporters of the
Revolution everywhere.

## Aspects of Social Revolt in the Southern Awakening

In the southern colonies the failure of the Anglican church to
achieve significant autonomy and political leverage left the ecclesiastical system in the hands of the same lay gentry who dominated
the political establishment. These gentry opposed the creation of an
episcopate in America, preferring to keep the vestries, the clergy,
and ecclesiastical taxes under their own control. The royal governors
and a series of ''commissaries'' to represent the bishop of London
constituted only a limited counterforce to the plantation gentry's
domination of parish life. For nominal Anglicans the social tensions
between rich and poor were alleviated by economic opportunities
that allowed easy access to power and wealth. But for non-Angli-
cans the social order was all but closed. The weakness of the
Anglican church, however, left a spiritual vacuum. There was in
effect no ecclesiastical stress-relief mechanism available for even the
ordinary anxieties of frontier life. Violence in military activities,
problems in controlling the slaves, warfare with Indians, and
hunting and dueling provided outlets for some kinds of tensions
but doubtless exacerbated others. The revelry of social life provided
occasional means of psychic catharsis (gambling, horse racing,
shooting matches, cock-fighting, card games). But none of these
replaced the spiritual solace of a church in cases of sickness or death,
and after 1740, when widespread social dislocations led to deep-
seated personal stress and cultural distortion, the common people
became eager to hear the words of invading itinerant revivalists
from the Middle Colonies and New England. The spiritual message
of these men of God brought extensive emotional responses from
the poorer sort, but it also aroused the antagonism of those in
authority.

Emotional dissatisfaction with the spiritual inadequacies of
Anglicanism at the bottom of society was matched by intellectual
alienation at the top. Men of education, wealth, and leisure, many
of whom had traveled in Europe and were widely read, came under

the influence of Enlightenment ideas that challenged their formal allegiance to Anglican doctrines. Arianism and Arminianism, which in New England led to the Unitarian movement among the upper class, produced in the South a broad-church or latitudinarian movement within Anglicanism. Men like Jefferson, Madison, and Washington emerged from their reading in science, the classics, and rationalist philosophy with deistic views that reduced their religious activism to merely formal participation. Washington's minister said that he never once saw him kneel to God. Jefferson and Madison later took the lead in disestablishing their own denomination. This apathy toward the preferred status of the Church of England did not at first prevent most of the gentry from opposing the social disturbances that resulted from the fervent revivalism of itinerant dissenters.

The dedicated new-light missionaries from New England and new-side itinerants from the Middle Colonies who went south after 1740 in response to manifold calls for their services found a social order rife with confusion and discontent. Not only a religious but an institutional vacuum had developed in many areas where there was no church, no school, no ministerial leadership to provide a sense of order and guidance in the competitive struggle for existence and success. The first calls came after Whitefield had aroused widespread interest in the new theology of Evangelical Calvinism. But Whitefield had been repudiated by most of the clergy in his own denomination, and there were few able to answer the questions about new spiritual sources of power. Many poor and middling folk, nominally Anglican, who agreed with Whitefield's condemnation of the established clergy as unconcerned with the spiritual needs of their flocks (and interested primarily in hob-nobbing with the gentry at their dances, foxhunts, and card games) did not know where to turn for a different kind of ministry.

When a group of pious laymen in Hanover County, Virginia, led by Samuel Morris, an ironmonger, began holding meetings to read aloud the printed sermons of Whitefield, they were arrested and fined for failing to attend the parish church on the Sabbath. When they invited a Presbyterian minister, named John Roan, from Gilbert Tennent's presbytery in New Jersey to come to preach to them in 1744, he neglected to obtain permission to preach from the local justice of the peace and was cited by the grand jury for breach of the ecclesiastical laws. Governor Gooch had agreed to tolerate Presbyterianism after 1720 in the unsettled areas west of the Blue Ridge Mountains, but he did not want to tolerate dissenting churches east of the mountains. During the prosecution of Roan in April 1745, Gooch denounced those "false teachers that are lately crept into this government who, without orders [i.e., Anglican ordination] or licenses or producing any testimonial of their education or sect, professing themselves ministers under the pretended influence of *new light* or extraordinary impulse and such like fanatical and enthusiastic notions, led the innocent and ignorant people into all kinds of delusions." Roan soon returned north, but he was followed by William Robinson and other New Side Presbyterians, some of whom roundly attacked the Anglican clergy for their spiritual deadness, declaring their parish churches to be "the synagogues of Satan."

In the spring of 1747 the governor of Virginia ordered all justices of the peace and other magistrates "to suppress and prohibit . . . all itinerant preachers." For some reason, that same spring, the governor and council were willing to grant a license to preach to Samuel Davies, a colleague of Tennent's, perhaps because he carried documents from the New York synod ordaining him as an evangelist. Davies was allowed in 1748 to preach to four dissenting congregations in Hanover County, but when he requested a license for an assistant pastor to relieve him of part of this burden, he was turned down. He was told first that the Toleration Act of 1689 did not apply in the colonies; second, that it was improper for pastors to be itinerant; and third, that the schism among the Presbyterians in the Middle Colonies made it impossible to tell which ministers were legitimate, orthodox Presbyterians and which were not. After considerable effort Davies finally convinced the governor that the Toleration Act did apply and that the New Side Presbyterians were orthodox. This broke a very important barrier to the spread of dissent in Virginia. Thereafter the Presbyterians were able to obtain licenses to preach, though their itinerancy was restricted.

But when the Separate Baptist new lights came down from New England (led by Shubal Stearns and Daniel Marshall in 1754), they disdained asking for licenses. They argued that the Word of God could not be limited by the power of civil authorities—a position they had been forced into by the laws outlawing itinerancy in Connecticut, after they had separated from the Congregational churches. Not only would they not abide by the licensing and anti-itinerant regulations in Virginia and the Carolinas, but they brought to the South the movement for total separation of church and state. Their congregations were poor, scattered, and subject to constant persecution by the authorities in the South until after the Revolution began.

Rhys Isaac, who has done the most intensive research into the Separate Baptist movement in Virginia, argues that it was not only an "evangelical revolt" and a "challenge to the traditional order in Virginia" but was, in its more violent phase, between 1765 and 1775, "a radical social revolt, indicative of real strains within the society." Mobs led by upper-class Anglicans encouraged attacks on the meetings of these revivalists and boarded up their churches. Many were beaten, jailed, and fined. Isaac says that the success of the new-light and new-side movements in the South caused "a crisis of self-confidence . . . in the Virginia gentry." Some magistrates charged the Baptists with "carrying on a mutiny against the authority of the land." (This was not unlike the charges raised by New England justices of the peace against the Separates and Separate Baptists from 1745 to 1760.)

The new-light Baptists denied that their movement was political. "We concern not ourselves with the government, we form no intrigues . . . nor make any attempts to alter the constitution of the kingdom to which as men we belong." They contended, they said, only for the spiritual and moral purification of the social order. Yet, as Isaac correctly notes, to change the norms and values of a society, to say nothing of its religious ideology, was rightly perceived by those in power as an attack on their legitimacy. In effect it asserted that the rulers were not entitled to respect because they lacked proper moral and spiritual qualifications. Isaac lists the contrasting values of the lower-class pietists and the upper-class Anglicans: where the gentry were arrogant and haughty, the Baptists tried to be humble and long-suffering; where the gentry sought violent challenges (man-to-man) and courted tests of skill and daring through violent confrontations (in duels, horse races, and cockfights), the Baptists honored reconciliation and harmony among men; where the gentry were self-centered and willful individualists, the Baptists emphasized brotherhood, mutual consideration, and caring; where the gentry flouted law and order by mobbing the preachers of God, the Baptists encouraged self-discipline and group discipline for the preservation of order. It was as though the new lights found the gentry responsible for the continued barbarity of frontier life and consciously sought to restore a sense of social responsibility. The gentry were setting a bad example by continuing the worst aspects of man's combative nature; the Baptists tried to set an example of man's peaceable and supportive character. The southern planter used his leisure and talent for competitive self-display; the poor, hard-working pietist preferred cooperation and mutual respect. Thus in the norms and values for which the new-light movement stood in the South, Isaac concludes, "The beginnings of a cultural disjunction between gentry and sections of the lower orders, where hitherto there had been a continuum, posed a serious threat to traditional leaders of the community." These leaders reacted by repression and ridicule. They laughed at the emotionalism of Baptist revival meetings, disdained their moral puritanism, and abused their preachers as ignorant, illiterate fools who had pretensions beyond their class. Only learned men of the better sort were considered fit for the ministry. In the Western world at that time, it was everywhere an upper-class vocation.

Isaac's description of the awakening in Virginia corresponds in many respects to Bushman's description of it in Connecticut, though in New England towns the differences in wealth and rank were less conspicuous and the clergy closer to the people. The awakening in Virginia, he says, was an effort to reorganize society on different principles. It was "a popular response to mounting social disorder"; the conversion experience "was at the heart of the popular evangelical movement." Through that experience, no matter under what denominational preacher, "a great burden of guilt" was lifted from those who knew they were antagonistic toward their fathers and father surrogates. Isaac's summary of the awakening's meaning among Virginia's Baptists can stand for its essence everwhere:

> When the Baptist movement is understood as a rejection of the style of life for which the gentry set the pattern and as a search for more powerful popular models of proper conduct, it can be seen why the grounds on which the battle was mainly fought was not the [big planta-tion] estate or the great house but the neighborhood, the farmstead, and the slave quarter. . . . The struggle for allegiance in the homesteads between a style of life modeled on that of the leisured gentry and that embodied in evangelicalism was intense. . . . The Baptists did not make a bid for control of the political system—still less did they seek a level-ling or redistribution of the worldly wealth. . . . Yet the Baptists' salva-tionism and sabbatarianism effectively redefined morality and human relationships; their church leaders and organization established new and more popular foci for authority and sought to impose a radically different and more inclusive model for the maintenance of order in society.

The same may be said for the Methodist movement, though it started much later and was not nearly so widespread before the Revolution. As of 1776 there were only 3,000 Methodists through-out the colonies, and all of them were ostensibly within the Anglican church. If the Baptists attacked the gentry life-style from outside the establishment, the Methodists tried to do it from within.

The Methodist movement began within the Church of England in the 1730s, when John Wesley and George Whitefield were both members of "The Holy Club" at Oxford. Wesley, like Whitefield, went to the colony of Georgia in 1736 to strengthen Anglicanism, but Whitefield proved a far more successful revivalist in the American colonies. Wesley, on the other hand, was far more successful in England. For a time the two worked closely together, but in 1739 they split after a bitter theological dispute over Calvinism. Wesley attacked the doctrines of predestination and irresistible grace, while Whitefield defended them. Whitefield could never have played so important a part in the First Great Awakening in the colonies had he not been a Calvinist. Wesley took the view that Christ died for the salvation of all men (not just for the predestined elect) and that men have an important role to play in obtaining their own salvation. Theologically these views

were called "Arminianism," and to most Calvinists they were
grievous doctrinal errors. But they were not incompatible with
Anglicanism.

Wesley's efforts to revive piety among Anglicans in the British
Isles were successful not only because of his charismatic preaching
and the marvelous hymns of his brother Charles, embodying his
views, but also because he created a magnificent organizational
structure for his movement. Of particular importance were his use
of itinerant evangelists, lay preaching, and the formation of small
"classes" or groups of converts to form pietistic nuclei within each
parish. After 1769 he sent a number of his followers to the colonies,
where they proved highly popular in many Anglican communities.
Because Methodist preaching did not openly challenge Anglican
tradition or authority but simply urged a great evangelical piety and
a stricter ethical morality, it was supported by a number of ordained
Anglican priests, among them Devereux Jarratt in Virginia.

Methodist itinerants, like Separate and Separate Baptist preachers, were popular among the poorer members of the community,
who felt estranged from a church that catered to the upper classes.
Consequently, the Methodists tapped the same revitalization spirit
as the Baptists in the South, but they were less successful in New
England. Their lay preachers organized "circuits" in the scattered
backwoods settlements, where ordained Anglicans seldom bothered
to preach. In each community they formed "classes" of ten or
twelve converts, who strengthened each other in spiritual activity
and watched over each other's moral discipline. And, like the
Baptist congregations, these Methodist groups were despised by the
gentry for the countercultural values they espoused.

Unfortunately, Wesley, like most Anglican ministers, took the
king's side in the Revolution. Hence the revival spirit that his
movement had so successfully begun in the late 1760s collapsed
after 1776. It did not begin to revive until after 1784, when Wesley
took the dramatic step of separating the Methodist movement in
America from the Anglican (by then the Protestant Episcopal)
church and created the Methodist Episcopal Church in America. Its
doctrines of experiential conversion, moral purity, and growing in
grace (which Wesley formalized as "perfectionism" or "sanctification" through a "second blessing") were in harmony with the

spirit (if not with the Calvinist theology) of the First Great
Awakening. It was to become even more popular in the Second
Great Awakening, when the Methodists reaped the advantage of
the reaction against "Consistent Calvinism" and when their
circuit-riding itinerant system proved tremendously effective on the
trans-Appalachian frontier.

## National Liberation and Evangelical Calvinist Ideology

In the decade after 1765, the concept of political independence,
Gordon Wood notes in *The Creation of the American Republic*
(1969), "became not only political but moral. Revolution, republicanism, and regeneration all blended in American thinking." The
awakening had regenerated not only thousands of individuals but
the spiritual core of the whole people. Such evils as remained were
considered more the result of British corruption than American sin;
or, rather, it was America's sin only so long as Americans tolerated
British corruption. In one sense, as Wood notes, the clergy saw
"British tyranny as a divine punishment for the abomination of the
American people." In another sense, God had clearly expressed his
great faith and hope for America by sending it such a revival of true
virtue. God had therefore renewed his covenant with his New
Israel. And, with God's help, they could build a harmonious new
social order of "comprehensive benevolence" and fulfill their
millennial dream of being "the eminent example of every divine
and social virtue" to a perishing world. Wood's conclusion to his
chapter "Republican Regeneration" makes explicit the fundamental link between the First Great Awakening and the Revolution:

> The traditional covenant theology of Puritanism combined with the
> political science of the eighteenth century into an imperatively persua-
> sive argument for revolution. Liberal rationalist sensibility blended with
> Calvinist Christian love to create an essentially common emphasis on the
> usefulness and goodness of devotion to the general welfare of the
> community. Religion and republicanism would work hand in hand to
> create frugality, honesty, self-denial, and benevolence among the
> people. The Americans would then "shew the nations of the earth" . . .
> that they had "virtue enough to think of and to practice these things."

The city upon the hill assumed a new republican character. It would now
hopefully be, in Samuel Adams' revealing words, "the Christian
Sparta."

The interval between 1760 and 1789 can hardly be seen, then, as a
"declension" from the fervor of the awakening but rather as an
extension of it. The Revolution, implementing the new republican
ideology, was in fact the secular fulfillment of the religious ideals of
the First Great Awakening. In liberating *their* country from British
tyranny, the colonists were both freeing their consciences from a
rebellion against the authority of their fathers and asserting the
rising (postmillennial) glory of America.

# 4

# The Second Great Awakening, 1800–1830

## The Search for National Unity

The cultural consensus that emerged from the First Great Awakening was theologically Calvinistic, but it emphasized the willingness of God to save those who truly repented of their sins, and it stressed God's continued favor toward America as the potential scene of the millennium. The success of the Revolution and the consolidation of the thirteen states into a republic based on a written constitution (a federal covenant) seemed to confirm the optimistic world view that had carried the nation through its epochal birth. But by 1800 new fears and doubts began to mount.

The new nation, struggling to develop its own institutions and sense of direction, seemed to be losing its revolutionary fervor and commitment. There was general agreement on the nation's achievements and its potential but considerable disagreement about how to proceed, especially after President Washington passed away in 1799. What, after all, did it mean to be "an American"? Which of the two political parties, which leaders, had the best program for national development? The rise of the Jeffersonian and Hamiltonian factions, with widely different programs, had brought doubt, division, and confusion to the young nation. In 1793 there was even a small rebellion in Pennsylvania against the federal government's excise tax on whiskey. The compromises that had been necessary to attain the Constitution were beginning to show signs of strain. In his last years as president, even the revered Washington had been bitterly attacked in the partisan press.

Adams faced the same fate. The French Revolution, originally hailed as the fair offspring of America's, had ugly consequences, threatening America's safety. Despite Washington's Farewell Address, warning against "foreign entanglements," the Hamiltonians wanted to ally the country with England against Napoleon, while the Jeffersonians argued that the revolutionary alliance with France committed the nation to war against England. Some saw Jacobinical or Jesuitical conspirators at work, trying to subvert the new republic from within, while others noted that the English were not living up to the treaty of 1783 in Maine and the Northwest.

At another level the nation was divided not so much between Federalists and Democratic-Republicans as between those who continued to believe in rule by the elite (the educated, the rich, the well-born) and those who thought the common man should dominate and control his representatives. Economically there was bitter controversy between the Jeffersonian program for an empire of fee-simple yeoman farmers (which appealed to rural people, especially in the South and West) and Hamilton's program to develop a mercantile, commercial, and manufacturing nation, centered in the cities and with a strong army and navy to protect its interests abroad (which the northeastern states and those in the coastal ports favored). Geographically there were growing sectional cleavages between East and West, North and South; the Jeffersonians were eager for westward expansion, while the Federalists still looked toward Europe. Socially, there was a rising egalitarianism, in sharp conflict with the old hierarchical structure of society. Denominationally, the religious practices of the nation continued to fracture, with new sects rising everywhere.

Most unsettling of all was the philosophical conflict between the world view of the Calvinists and the new Enlightenment rationalists. The former stressed man's depravity and untrustworthiness; the latter (called deists) stressed his innate goodness, free will, and reasonableness. The heritage of piety gave traditional strength to the former, but recent experience lent credence to the latter. Had not Americans taken their fate into their own hands in 1775 and succeeded in defeating the greatest empire in the world? Had not God crowned their efforts with success? Was not the economy thriving? And, as for predestination, men who dared greatly seemed to prosper greatly. Did not God help those who helped themselves?

This was not, however, what most Americans heard from their pulpits or from the learned educators and scholars (most of them Calvinist ministers) who presided over the colleges. Calvinism still taught that the fate of men and nations lay in the mysterious and arbitrary will of God. God might become angry at any time with the nation because of its materialism, its engrossment in trade and speculation, its neglect of worship. To some, predestination seemed fatalistic; to others, it seemed to make God the author of sin and a cruel father to his children. The claims of the deists that God is benevolent, that he governs by reason, that his laws are regular and beneficent, that his aim is to promote the happiness and well-being of mankind seemed more in harmony with American experience. Scientists had made enormous strides since Newton in revealing the laws of physics, chemistry, geology, and mathematics that governed the universe. It appeared that God had made the universe to operate in a regular, orderly manner, not by miracles or arbitrary thunderbolts. If man's reason was God-given (as even the Calvinists allowed), then education of that reason would enable men to comprehend God's ways and act in accord with them, thus advancing the millennium by their increasing knowledge of God's will and laws.

This optimistic, self-reliant view (though Calvinists called it heretical or blasphemous) was suggested not only in the works of the French *philosophes* and English deists but also by some latitudinarian Anglicans and the new ''supernatural rationalists'' in New England who called themselves Unitarians and Universalists. Unitarians considered the doctrine of the trinity (a triune God) irrational and doubted that God still worked miracles. Universalists insisted that God was not so cruel as to roast innocent people forever in hell (including children who had died before conversion). Yet comparatively few Americans dared to identify themselves with these radical new positions. Their self-confidence and their expectancy of God's benevolence were not so great as to endorse a totally permissive God or a totally reasonable mankind. The belief in hell, the guilt over their own sins, their self-doubt over their own wisdom, all kept them close to the orthodox view of man's

weakness and the righteousness of God's justice in punishing
wickedness.

Still, the Calvinists seemed to have an overly severe conception of
the relationship between God and man. The harshest view of the
human condition was that taught by the followers of Jonathan
Edwards, the neo-Edwardsians or "Consistent Calvinists" led by
Samuel Hopkins. Their insistence on man's total dependence upon
God and total unworthiness in the sight of God, and particularly
their claim that absolutely nothing a sinner can do is pleasing in the
sight of God, caused intense frustration. Some who knew not which
way to turn to seek God's approval recited a popular jingle that
went

> You can and you can't,
> You shall and you shan't;
> You will and you won't.
> You're damned if you do,
> And damned if you don't.

Yet Consistent Calvinism had been the "new light" of the First
Great Awakening, and Edwards' followers in the years after 1740
were known as the "New Divinity Men." The doctrines that had
brought such fervor and had inspired such hope in Edwards'
generation had hardened into a discordant, unbelievable formula.
Some even called Hopkins' theology the "willingness-to-be-
damned" concept of conversion, for Hopkins implied that only
those so self-sacrificing as to be able to say honestly, "I would be
willing to be damned for the glory of God," could be worthy of
salvation. It was not a viewpoint that squared well with the rising
glory of America and the sense of self-worth generated by the
Revolution.

Somehow the "new light" of the First Great Awakening seemed
to have lost its spirit in the letter of the law. Warning men
constantly against the sin of pride and the hopelessness of human
effort just at the moment when the new nation needed all the
confidence it could muster brought anger and quiet desperation to
pious men. As their thoughts toyed with other alternatives,
ministers, worried about the inroads of deism and the declension of
church attendance, called fervently for a new awakening to revive

the spiritual life of the nation. Donald Mathews in his essay "The Second Great Awakening as an Organizing Process" (*American Quarterly*, 1969) sums up well the prevailing mood in 1800:

> The norms of the old life were changing; its stimuli were gone, its manners inapplicable, its conventions often incapable of being reinforced. . . . The Revolution had created great anticipation for the future; but the kind of future people wanted was not easily realized. The result was a vague uneasiness.

But that vague uneasiness grew from year to year. Mathews argues that the Second Great Awakening was "not in the first instance an intellectual movement" but rather "an organizing process that helped to give meaning and direction to people suffering in various degrees from the societal strains of a nation on the move into new political, economic and geographical areas."

Organization, however, can make sense only if people cohere around meaningful beliefs and values to achieve commonly accepted goals. Mathews is right in one sense: awakenings are nor properly conceivable as "intellectual movements." They are, in fact, often anti-intellectual in the sense that they rely more on intuitive or emotional responses (the religious affections) than on rational constructs. Nevertheless, they do combine those religious feelings with symbols, and symbols have meaning in the deepest sense of motivating and inspiring reverence, devotion, self-discipline, and self-sacrifice. Symbols give unity and direction to culture; they provide national identity and national ideals. Beliefs and values are not intellectual, but they are the sources of common understanding about private and public behavior.

It will help us here to ponder the complex relationships of symbols, culture, and religion which Clifford Geertz describes in his essay "Religion as a Cultural System." "Sacred symbols," Geertz says, "function to synthesize a people's ethos—the tone, character, and quality of their life, its moral and aesthetic mood—and their world view—the picture they have of the way things in sheer actuality are, their most comprehensive ideas of order." For most Americans these symbols have been those of Judeo-Christian philosophy, modified by Calvinism and suffused with Enlightenment concepts of natural law and natural rights. Culture, Geertz writes, "denotes an historically transmitted pattern of meanings

embodied in symbols, a system of inherited conceptions expressed
in symbolic forms by means of which men communicate, perpet-
uate, and develop their knowledge about and attitudes toward
life.'' American culture has at its core a congeries of conceptions
that we have already identified: the chosen nation; the convenant
with God; the millennial manifest destiny; the higher (biblical or
natural) law, against which private and social behavior is to be
judged; the moral law (the Ten Commandments, the Sermon on
the Mount); the laws of science, presumed to be from the Creator,
and evolutionary or progressive in their purpose; the free and moral
responsible individual, whose political liberty and liberty of conscience are inalienable; the work ethic (or ''Protestant ethic''),
which holds that equal opportunity and hard work will bring
economic success and public respect to all who assert and discipline
themselves; and the benevolence of nature under the exploitative or
controlling hand of man (i.e., nature was made for man).

Out of these basic concepts, whose definitions have altered with
each awakening, has come a wide variety of other cultural myths:
the rugged frontiersman or Daniel Boone myth; the yeoman farmer
or agrarian myth; the success or Horatio Alger myth (featuring the
captain of industry); the myth of white, Anglo-Saxon supremacy
and the *Herrenvolk* myth of the slave-owning South; the myth of
the moral superiority, spiritual superiority, and physical frailty of
women (which isolated her on a pedestal); and a host of others, all
of which at one time or another were able to fit conveniently within
our cultural concept of who Americans are and what their place is in
God's universe. Many of these myths rose to central importance
during the Second Great Awakening, when they served to unite the
new nation in its expansionist and nationalist rise to power. Ralph
H. Gabriel, in *The Course of American Democratic Thought*
(1940), first identified this cluster of ideals, which, taken together,
''made up a national faith which, although unrecognized as such,
had the power of a state religion.'' But Gabriel mistakenly found
their origin in the years 1825 to 1855; in fact, their roots were much
older. Gabriel simply identified them in the form in which they
emerged after the Second Great Awakening. One way to describe
an awakening is to call it a period during which old symbols are
clothed in new meanings.

Finally, we come to Geertz's definition of religion—a definition that is intrinsic to this essay: "Religion is a system of symbols which acts to establish powerful, pervasive, and long-lasting moods and motivations in men by formulating conceptions of a general order of existence and clothing these conceptions with such an aura of factuality that the moods and motivations seem uniquely real." It is the role of the revivalist, the prophet of revitalization, to sustain the reality of the culture myths, to reinterpret them to meet the needs of social change, and to clothe them with an aura of reality that grows from his own conviction that he is a messenger of God. To sustain that conviction, the revivalist must inspire in his hearers the same conviction; this occurs when those who hear him accept his sacred character and react by feeling the power of God as it emanates from his words. His words become for them God's Word, his emotional concern, God's Spirit at work, and the emotional experience of acceptance or submission becomes the work of God's grace in the hearts of the believers. What the observer sees and hears in the revivalist is what gives the aura of reality to the relationship between God and man; what we believe is what we are. After we have come to believe, we can act, can organize (according to the various personal, regional, or fortuitous contingencies of our region, age, or class) into churches, congregations, denominations, and associations in order to sustain the moods and motivations that have provided us with this "real" comprehension of the general order of existence. The power of revivals and of religious organizations (and, in America, our political or reform organizations frequently have all the qualities of religious denominations) is the power we feel and perceive in the recurring cycle of God's prophetic awakenings, carrying his power into our hearts (or affections). In the Second Great Awakening, American religious leaders of all denominations learned how to routinize this power; they discovered (and trusted in) the spiritual mechanics of God's power and canalized it into the organizing process the nation sorely needed in a time of enormous growth, when it was beset by the centrifugal forces of sectionalism and individualism.

Perry Miller grasped the essential organizing mood of the Second Awakening in *The Life of the Mind in America* (1965) when he said that "Anxiety over the future lies at the heart of the movement." Four million people in the youthful society "sought for solidarity, for a discovery of its [America's] meaning." What Donald Mathews means by "the organizing process" of this awakening is explained from the quotation he takes from T. Scott Miyakawa: through the revitalizing force of the awakening "the churches provided elementary 'disciplined formal organization,' which created a society accustomed to working through voluntary association for common goals." But before people would voluntarily join such organizations, they had to have a clear conception of what their common goals were—what steps were needed to advance the millennium. They also had to agree on the means. Were they to be organized by the state or the elite—from the top down? Or were they to organize themselves—from the bottom up? And were churches and reform societies to assert controls over weak-willed, sinning men, or were Americans to experiment in utopian groups, where the inherent goodness and creativity of each could have full self-expression? The organizing process included all these approaches, but the consensus that arose from this awakening emphasized self-help, and "That government is best which governs least" was its shibboleth.

This new consensus also included the belief that Americans are a peculiar race, chosen by God to perfect the world. That was clearly the nation's manifest destiny, and it was unique. In that respect the Second Awakening drastically reoriented the universal quality the patriots had seen in their Revolution and that the prophets of the First Great Awakening had expected from the outpouring of God's grace in the New World. "The Revolutionaries," as Gordon Wood has said, "were patriots, to be sure, but they were not obsessed, as were later generations, with the unique character of America or with separating America from the broad course of Western civilization which was grounded in the eighteenth century's image of classical antiquity." The patriots of '76 saw America as a city on a hill, a model for all mankind, the voice of humanity's future. It invited idealists and refugees from the Old World to join it and expected them, in the free atmosphere of republicanism, to be transformed into the vanguard for the millennium. But after the Second Awakening, Americans narrowed their vision. Their destiny was not Europe's or mankind's but their own. Their people were not reinvigorated immigrants but a new and special race. Their institutions were beyond the capacities of decadent Europeans, superstitious Roman Catholics, ignorant heathen, or "colored" races to imitate. God had created a unique people and elected them to establish these institutions throughout the world; they were to uplift inferior peoples who, lacking the innate capacity for republicanism, might at least be converted or adapted to it if they could learn to assimilate the ways of Christian America.

Perry Miller spoke of this new outlook as "Romantic nationalism" and its religious core as "romantic evangelicalism." It was inspired by patriotic Christianity and an organic, evolutionary racial theory of white, English-speaking, Protestant, Anglo-Saxon supremacy. The Reverend Heman Humphrey, president of Amherst College, spoke in 1831 for the new consensus that by that time had emerged when he said that the nation had at last achieved a sense of "the true American union, that sort of union which makes every patriot a Christian and every Christian a patriot." The more flamboyant versions of this evangelical patriotism appeared as "manifest destiny" in secular Jacksonian editorials. By 1885, Lord Bryce, the astute English commentator on American culture, could assert without contradiction that "Christianity [in its evangelical Protestant form] is in fact understood to be, though not the legally established religion, yet the national religion." In short, America had acquired, as any culture must, a civil religion.

Yet, at the same time, this civil religion was expressed in a wide variety of denominational forms. The Second Awakening, like the preceding one, must therefore be examined regionally. The South, the West, and the Northeast (led by New England) were still different in their institutional structures and needs. It took the Civil War to give political unity and the Industrial Revolution to provide social homogeneity to the country, although its overarching ideological unity was clearly formulated and expressed in the Second Awakening.

## The Conservative New England Phase of the Awakening

Chronologically, the Second Awakening began in the southern states (in the trans-Appalachian valleys of Kentucky and Tennessee), but it is easier to understand its development if we start with

New England. To New Englanders the camp-meeting revivals of
the years 1798–1808 were barbarous emotional outbreaks, as far
from true religious activities as Jacobinism was from true republicanism. The camp-meeting hysteria seemed to New England
divines to be the work of the devil trying to discredit true religion,
just as the insane ravings of James Davenport had almost discred-
ited the First Great Awakening. The revivalistic excesses of the
frontier (which later psychologists were also to attribute to the
primitive quality of wilderness life) were crude appeals to "the
animal emotions" of illiterate, half-educated, half-savage men and
women who had strayed too far from the institutional order of
decent society. That was one of the great dangers facing the
republic: it was expanding faster than civilized institutions could
keep up with the moving population. Missionary work was needed
on the frontier, but the uneducated frontier preachers among the
Baptists, Methodists, and Presbyterians (who had started the
southern revivals) were incapable of preaching true religion or
restraining the wild passions of the rough, unruly folk who
preferred frontier life to civilized refinement. Even in the South the
eastern, educated clergy agreed that the western revivals were too
boisterous and tended toward unorthodox beliefs and practices; the
Presbyterians soon divided over the issue, leaving the frontier
essentially to the Baptists and Methodists. Thus the Second Great
Awakening in New England was somewhat more sedate, but it was
no less bitter in its divisions.

New England had emerged from the First Great Awakening
firmly committed to the new divinity and to national unity. New
lights and old lights had reunited after 1765 (essentially on
new-light terms) and worked shoulder to shoulder in the Revolution. The majority had even concluded that there was no need to
abandon the principle of tax-supported Congregational churches in
each township so long as certified members of other denominations were exempted from these taxes. This certificate system
was written into the new constitutions of every New England
state except Rhode Island. Hence it was a great shock to New
England when Jefferson was elected and lent his support to the
"dissenting denominations" or "certificate men" in their efforts
to abolish compulsory religious taxes in New England. It was an

even greater shock when many former Congregationalists abandoned strict Calvinism for Unitarianism, badly splitting the established churches and the power elite (the Unitarians tended to be
strong among the graduates of Harvard and the wealthy merchants
and bankers of Boston and Salem).

Yet New England, by virtue of its history, its institutions, its
wealth, and its intellectual and political leadership was a powerful
force—probably the dominant one—in American culture. The
awakening, which reoriented its religious outlook and brought it
more into harmony with the South and West, was traumatic for the
region but healthy for the nation. When, later, the South called all
those who supported the Union against the Confederate states
"Yankees," it paid tribute to the influence of New England's
continuing leadership. However, New England was so profoundly
disoriented and disillusioned about the course of the new nation at
the turn of the century that it could scarcely restrain itself from
seceding between 1805 and 1815. The French Revolution, so
inspiring to Jeffersonians, was a devastating event to New England
Federalists, for Jefferson's embargoes on American shipping almost
wrecked the commercial prosperity of the region.

The first phase of the awakening in New England is best
characterized as a nativist movement—an effort to call America
back to the old-time religion and traditional way of life that were
inevitably fading. John Adams, New England's Federalist president, signed the Alien and Sedition Acts in 1798 to put down
seditious attacks from francophile conspirators bent on changing
the American life-style. The Congregationalist clergy denounced
Jefferson as an atheist and founder of subversive Jacobin clubs.
Richard Hofstadter has accurately labeled the famous Bavarian
Illuminati scare of 1798–1800 in New England as the first example
of "the paranoid style in American politics."

At the same time, however, the more flexible and younger
members of the region (particularly among the college youth) were
experimenting with new life-styles and world views. They were
intrigued with deism and the new rationalism. Like Jefferson, they
admired the political ideals of classical antiquity and the pagan
philosophy of the Stoics. Greek Revival architecture replaced the
old Georgian style, and the new French pantaloons replaced the

smallclothes of eighteenth-century society. In the rural areas young men read the deistic works of Ethan Allen and Thomas Paine and challenged the cruel doctrines of Calvinism and the scientific inconsistencies of the Bible.

While Jefferson was winning the votes of the Baptists and Universalists and egging them on in their assault on "the Standing Order," the Methodists launched a vigorous campaign to win those disaffected from Hopkinsian Calvinism to their Arminian theology and their egalitarian form of church order. The circuit riding of Francis Asbury, Jesse Lee, and other zealous Methodist revivalists brought itinerancy back into the settled parishes of New England, and their camp meetings won many converts in the rural areas. The Congregational clergy, threatened from all sides, rallied to restore vitality to their own churches. In Timothy Dwight, Lyman Beecher, and Nathaniel W. Taylor New England produced three of the most influential prophets of the awakening.

The Reverend Timothy Dwight, who became president of Yale in 1795, appointed himself the champion of the old order. He and the Reverend Jedidiah Morse became the leaders of the nativist phase of the awakening, arousing the populace to the dangers of a foreign conspiracy to subvert the republic and praising President Adams' repression of sedition. But Dwight achieved his most notable success by attacking the spread of deistic heresies among the younger generation. Being a college president and molder of youth, he saw at first hand the struggle in which the younger generation was engaged. They simply could respect no longer the world view of their forefathers. This was true not only of New England college students. Historians of education have documented a widespread student rebelliousness throughout the colonies in these years, many of them violent in their disruption and frequently put down with harsh, authoritarian measures.

The young were torn between an outmoded Calvinism and deistic infidelity. Calvinism was the voice of their fathers, the voice of law and order and conformity to the establishment. Deism, though attractive in its exciting revelations of the universal laws of "the benevolent architect of the universe," was too antibiblical and anticlerical to be easily adopted, especially when Dwight and his nativist friends linked it to the worst excesses of the French

Revolution and foreign conspiracy against the republic. Dwight made it clear to the rising generation that they were in danger of becoming the dupes of radicals who would destroy the very foundations of morality and stability:

> . . . let me solemnly warn you, that if you intend to accomplish anything, if you mean not to labour in vain and to spend your strength for nought, you must take your side. . . . Will you teach your children that death is an eternal sleap [rather than union with God and loved ones in heaven]? that the end sanctifies the means? that moral obligation is a dream? Religion [biblical truth] a farce? and your Savior the spurious offspring of pollution [rather than of a virgin birth]? Will you send your daughters abroad in the attire of a female Greek [with a gown cut so low as to expose half her breasts]? . . . Will you make marriage the mockery of a register's office [in a civil ceremony]? . . . Will you burn your Bibles? Will you crucify your Redeemer? Will you deny your God?

Put in these terms, the choice became embarrassing. Some returned at once to the fold, while others became increasingly frustrated. If the new way was too radical, the old way was too unreal. Like most nativist or traditionalist appeals, this one exacerbated rather than overcame the cultural distortions and the crisis of legitimacy.

Dwight was keen enough to see that for most of the rising generation the harsher aspects of "hyper-Calvinism" were the great stumbling blocks, and he did what he could to make Christianity appear reasonable. "God cannot be proved to be the efficient cause of sin," he said, and man is not an automaton, for every man recognizes himself as "a being, a substance, an agent, immediately the subject of his own thoughts and the cause and author of his volitions and actions." Deists, he said, maliciously distorted the doctrines of predestination and election to delude people. But try as he would, Dwight (born in 1752) was too close to the Edwardsian generation to reject their doctrines or assert the freedom of the will. He was better at denouncing the deists and Unitarians than at providing a viable alternative. That task fell to his pupils, Beecher and Taylor.

Perhaps because he was a generation younger than Dwight, or perhaps because he was by nature more pragmatic, Lyman Beecher proved a more helpful prophet to New Englanders (and many

others in the Northeast and the Northwest). He did not insist on
upholding every jot and tittle of the old consensus. He liked, no
better than Dwight, the tendencies of Jeffersonian democracy, the
ideas of the deists, the barbarism of the West, and the crude,
unorthodox religious behavior of the Methodists and Baptists and
the western offshoots of Presbyterianism (the Campbellites, Stoneites, and Disciples). But he saw better than Dwight did that some
accommodation would have to be made to the changing nature of
the times. He warned his colleagues that Americans were fast
becoming "another people."

The nativist phase of the New England awakening ended with
Dwight's death in 1817 if not before (C. R. Keller thinks that it
ended as early as 1808). Beecher recognized even before that that it
was impossible to hold back the tide of disestablishment. New
England Congregationalism would have to give up its privileged
tax-supported church system. It was out of step with the times.
Beecher was later to argue that disestablishment was the best thing
that ever happened to New England, but this was after the
revitalization movement had created new mechanisms and opened
old mazeways for religious growth and organization. Connecticut
lost its established church in 1818, and the other New England
states soon after. Beecher and his friend Taylor had already started
on the second phase of the awakening.

Beecher concluded that the best way to beat off the Methodist
and Baptist inroads into Congregationalism was to organize a
revival among the Congregational churches. To facilitate this, he
and Taylor, the best theologian in New England, began cautiously
to restate or reinterpret the doctrines of Calvinism. Their second
step was to organize the converts of their revivals into missionary
and reform societies to sustain the faith and order of the nation.

In developing a conservative form of revivalism among the
Congregationalists, Beecher was greatly aided by a charismatic
preacher named Asahel Nettleton, whose intense but controlled
style evoked the same sense of spiritual presence among the middle
class that the more lively emotional style of the Baptists and
Methodists evoked among the lower class. Moreover, Beecher kept
control of the revival process by enlisting the regular parish clergy as
itinerants (or pulpit exchanges), thereby adding variety to the

regular church life of each town. Sidney Mead and Charles R. Keller have ably documented the carefully organized techniques developed by Beecher and his colleagues over the years 1812 to 1828. "We agreed," Beecher wrote to a friend after one planning session with the Congregational clergy in 1812,

> upon an interchange of routine preaching between the Northwestern and Litchfield South monthly meetings. Mr. Harvey and myself took the first tour, to see the brethren and get the thing under way. We visited the two Canaans, Salisbury, and Sharon and should have visited Cornwall had weather permitted. . . . Messrs. Crossman and Prentiss are to take the southern tour, beginning at Litchfield [on] Tuesday.

Whatever the Methodists could do, the Congregationalists would do better. "Revivals now began to pervade the state," Beecher said, and soon spread from Connecticut to other parts of New England as the most gifted preachers in the denomination caught the spirit. Beecher even went to Boston in the 1820s to lead a revival crusade against Unitarianism in the very heart of its following.

As the new converts joined the churches and old members regained their sense of commitment to perfect the Union, Beecher and his friends organized them into voluntary associations (taking care to give laymen and women important parts to play). They organized missionary activities to New England's northern frontier (in Maine, New Hampshire, and Vermont); they worked for temperance, against dueling, to improve Sabbath observance. They urged the legislature to enforce the blue laws and local constables to arrest prostitutes and gamblers. Among the more important of the new benevolent associations were the Home and Foreign Mission Society (1812), the American Bible Society (1816), the American Education Society (to educate ministers) (1816), the African Colonization Society (1817), the American Tract Society (1825), and the American Temperance Society (1826). Although they claimed to be interdenominational, they were dominated by the Congregationalists and Presbyterians.

It has been said that through their missionary and educational activities they sought to make the nation over in the image of New England. Beecher implied as much when he said, in a sermon to raise funds for the education of more ministers for the West, "The integrity of the Union demands special exertions to produce in the

nation a more homogeneous character and bind us together in
firmer bonds. . . . The prevalence of pious, intelligent, enterprising ministers through the nation at the ratio of one for one
thousand would . . . produce a sameness of views and feeling and
interests which would lay the foundation of our empire upon a
rock.'' While these benevolent societies were basically conservative
in nature, seeking to assert ''social control'' over the depraved
nature of the undisciplined ''common man,'' they inaugurated a
spirit of reform that became more radically inclined as the revitalization movement increased the nation's self-confidence and
optimism. As John L. Thomas has pointed out in his essay
''Romantic Reform in America'' (*American Quarterly*, 1965),

> The initial thrust of religious reform was moral rather than social, preven-
> tive rather than curative. . . . But the moral reformers inherited a
> theological revolution which in undermining their conservative defenses
> completely reversed their expectations for a Christian America. The
> transformation of American theology in the first quarter of the nine-
> teenth century released the very forces of romantic perfectionism that
> conservatives most feared. . . . As it spread, perfectionism swept across
> denominational barriers and penetrated even secular thought.

The concept of voluntary reform societies fitted perfectly into the
republican ideals of a virtuous citizenry sacrificing itself for the
greater good of the community. After 1830 they became effective
agencies of social revolution. In the anti-Masonic movement, the
Know-Nothing movement, the Prohibition movement, the
women's-rights movement, and, above all, in the antislavery
movement these societies entered into major aspects of institutional
restructuring. They stimulated third-party movements and ultimately generated the climate for civil war.

Underlying this profound national transformation, as Thomas
notes, was a reorientation in the ideological or religious world view
of the American people. Beecher and Taylor again provided much
of the impetus. Sometimes described as ''the decline of Calvinism''
or ''the rise of romantic evangelicalism,'' it would better be called
the transformation of Evangelical Calvinism into Evangelical
Arminianism or, perhaps, the interaction between the Age of
Reason and the Age of Romanticism. At the heart of the transformation lay the question of the freedom of the will.

Evangelical Calvinism, as the term is applied to the theology of the First Great Awakening, taught God's sovereignty and man's dependence, but it preached that man's repentance wins God's mercy. The First Awakening therefore weakened the old doctrine of predestination, and the Second Awakening finally subverted it entirely. The key issues became the role of man and the means he might use (or that God used) to effect the regenerations of the soul. The Wesleyan Methodists had accepted the freedom of the will much earlier, but the other denominations, especially New England Congregationalists and Middle States Presbyterians, went through a tortuous struggle over it. In practice the debate concerned the immediacy of conversion and the agency of the preacher. In philosophical terms it meant that if immediate conversion is available by an act of the human will, then, through God's miraculous grace, all things are possible: human nature is open to total renovation in the twinkling of an eye and so, then, is the nature of society. The world is unfettered from tradition, custom, institutions, is unconditioned by history or environment. Society is totally malleable to the power that works in harmony with God's will. It was from this assumption, pervasive in the nation after 1830, that perfectionism and millennial optimism grew to such importance.

Beecher's approach to the question of revising Calvinism was pragmatic. "I believe," he said, "that both the doctrines of dependence [man's total dependence on God for salvation] and moral accountability must be admitted. . . . I also believe that greater or less prominence should be given to the one or the other of these doctrines according to the prevailing state of public opinion." Hence in Boston, where he was trying to combat the appeal of Unitarianism, he found that the people "did not need high-toned Calvinism on the point of dependence; they needed a long and vigorous prescription of free-agency to produce an alternative." By giving them that, he got a revival.

Nathaniel W. Taylor, however, being a theologian rather than a revivalist, approached the problem more systematically. The prime error in Unitarianism, in Taylor's view, was not so much its denial of the doctrine of the Trinity as its overestimation of human reason, goodness, and educability. And, though Taylor did not say so, its prime weakness in the new republic was that it was elitist. It assumed that only men of superior intelligence and will power could really master their animal nature, perfect their intellect, and fathom the laws of political economy well enough to set public policy. Its appeal to the Boston upper class lay in its social conservatism and self-congratulation. It took a supercilious or pitying attitude toward the common run of mankind. Thomas Jefferson, who sometimes called himself a Unitarian, shared this elitist philosophy, which went down to defeat in this awakening; and the Boston Unitarians shared Jefferson's horror at the spread of revivalism and his disillusionment at Andrew Jackson's rise to power.

The new-light theology of New England after 1818 was known as Taylorism or Beecherism before it pervaded the Middle States and Midwest as "the New School." Its first revision of Edwardsianism was to modify its doctrine of the total inability of man to do anything toward effecting his own salvation (a view that deists, Methodists, and Unitarians frankly called "fatalistic"). Edwardsian old lights had serious doubts about the easy and "immediate" conversions that took place at enthusiastic revival meetings. Many such converts did not last. The hyper-Calvinists frowned on emotional displays and expected conversion to take place over a long, slow period of spiritual regeneration. God's grace could not be forced; heaven could not be taken by storm. Men must pray and wait for conversion. Yet the experiences in revival meetings conveyed a very different relationship between man's needs and God's mercy.

If we knew more about the child-rearing practices of Americans during the early years of the republic, we might have more insight into the psychosocial factors underlying the new morphology of conversion that emerged then, and we also might better understand the shift to the belief in free will that accompanied it. Apparently the generations that came of age after 1800 felt less awe and fear of their parents, more love and respect. Parents evidently treated their children in a less arbitrary fashion, perhaps because nuclear families encouraged voluntary cooperation from their children lest they take off for the West or go to sea. Greater affluence, greater freedom and mobility, and frequent uprooting detracted from patriarchal authority. Foreign travelers in the first half of the nineteenth century commented extensively upon the indulgence with which American parents treated their children, the freedom allowed to young adolescents, and the unquestioned assumption that couples married for love rather than family connections or money. The foreign observers also noted with dismay how self-willed American children were and how loath parents seemed to correct them. Mutual trust and self-sacrifice among equals were the accepted norms of republican ethics. Deference to authority had eroded everywhere, but rationalized beliefs for these new behavioral patterns had yet to be articulated and experienced.

The shift in child-rearing attitudes corresponds also with the Enlightenment view that the rights and worth of the individual are inherent and, subsequently, with the Romantic belief that children are closer to God than adults are—that there is a spark of divinity in all children that can and must be sustained. By 1830 educational theory and practice began to show the influence of Rousseau, Pestalozzi, and Froebel. Romantic poetry and Transcendentalist prose emphasized a pantheistic ''correspondence'' between God, nature, and man. After the awakening, a new genre of religious literature and prayers appeared, written especially for children. Professional revivalists even developed special techniques to deal with their tender minds and hearts. God became not an angry father in the new gospel hymns but a gentle shepherd and guide, protecting and guarding these ''buds'' from the hard blasts of the cruel world. Evangelical religion stressed Christ's words that men must become like little children if they would understand God's will, ''for of such is the kingdom of heaven.'' In 1835, when a Calvinist father wrote an article in a religious journal, explaining how he had followed the old practice of breaking his child's will at the age of fifteen months, instead of being praised he received letters rebuking him for heartless tyranny. Such unnatural ''brutality towards his own offspring,'' said one letter to the editor, ''should gain for him the anathema of the public and the indignation of every parent.''

The New School theology of the Second Great Awakening responded both directly and indirectly to these new feelings about enculturation. Both Beecher and Taylor denied the imputation of

Adam's guilt to all mankind. Although they aroused opposition from hyper-Calvinists for this, they insisted that the doctrine was not essential to Calvinism. In fact, through all the modifications and redefinitions of doctrine that they pursued, the New School Calvinists stoutly maintained that they were orthodox Calvinists, though of a new school of thought.

Taylor also denied that God condemns infants to hellfire if they die before conversion. He held that men are innately disposed toward sin but that there can be no sin until it is actually committed. To argue that nonsinning infants are punished by God would be to deny the free moral agency or responsibility of man and make God a sadist. Man is punished for knowingly sinning against God's will. Sin is a voluntary act. Of course, when asked at what age children might knowingly commit a sin, Taylor acknowledged that probably by the age of six months they could assert their stubborn willfulness against parental authority by refusing to cry quietly, by pushing a cup from their mouths, by throwing their porridge on the floor. The changes in child-rearing patterns may thus not have been very great. Still, the new doctrines gave parents pause; they must be sure that a child was consciously sinning before they punished him. They must explain the sin to the child as well as to themselves.

The central task for the new lights in this awakening was to assert the responsibility of men to choose right or wrong without limiting the power of God. As Sidney Mead says in his biography of Taylor, "if man is truly free, then God, by implication at least, must somehow be limited." Taylor accepted the task of explaining away this apparent inconsistency. Starting from the accepted premise that God's universe operates according to fixed moral laws, Taylor declared it only logical that moral law implies moral agents. From this it followed that "Moral agency implies free agency—the power of choice—the power to choose morally wrong as well as morally right under every possible influence to prevent such choice or action. Moral agency, and of course moral beings, can no more exist without this power than matter can exist without solidity and extension, or a triangle without sides and angles." (Taylor's method of argument was very "enlightened" and rational.) What Edwards and Dwight had defined as the "moral inability" of man to obey God's will, Taylor restated as "Man will not do what he can do." But his emphasis was less upon "will not" than upon "can do." Man *can do* what God wants, but, Taylor said, he needs God's help. Revivalism was a means used by God to help man. Beecher's revivals had demonstrated that. God's Word preached by "a man of God" is an offer from God of grace. We *can* believe on faith. We *can* strive to enter in at the gate. Man is a self-determining force in nature; that is the essence of his humanness and of his divinity.

Taylor became the Edwards of the Second Great Awakening—a new-light prophet whose influence extended far beyond his own region and denomination. As Williston Walker put it in his history of Congregationalism, Taylor "endeavored to explain it [Calvinism] in what he deemed a more positive and less objectionable way than the Edwardeans." In discussing Edwards' denial of free will, Taylor frankly said, "Edwards' mind was all confusion on the subject." Taylor allowed for the moral suasion of the preacher, assuming first that this suasion was God's Spirit at work and, second, that every soul had the ability to "choose aright." The help man needed came in the work of the Holy Spirit upon the religious affections. Choice "can be exercised by the sinner if he is aroused to action by appeal to the proper faculties of his mind." God arouses the heart, and man responds by a clear decision to accept God's offer. The key to conversion lay in the manipulation of human "sensibilities" or, as evangelical preachers preferred to say, "in an appeal to the heart." Walker has pointed out that "Taylor divided the mental powers into the intellect, sensibilities, and will, unlike the older Edwardeans, who made the twofold distinction of will and understanding. The feeling to which an appeal can be made is self-love."

Self-love is not selfishness, but neither is it, as the hyper-Calvinists said, "self-denial" or "willingness to be damned for the glory of God." Taylor was reverting to a position close to that of Shaftesbury and Hutcheson, which formed the basis for both the Unitarian moral philosophy and the Christian Scottish Philosophy of Thomas Reid and Dugald Stewart. To quote Walker again, "Taylor held that the highest form of self-love, the pursuit of happiness, could never be inconsistent with the best good of the universe, which is benevolence." It could not be inconsistent because God had implanted self-love in man so that it could be appealed to despite man's innate disposition toward evil. Appeals to the sensibilities can bring the will to an act of true repentance of sin because, through the instinct of self-love, God draws man ever upward to seek the greatest happiness of the greatest number (which is God's happiness as well). To clinch his argument for free moral agency, Taylor appealed ultimately to human experience or human consciousness: "Let a man look into his own breast, and he cannot but perceive inward freedom—*inward freedom*—for if freedom be not in the *mind* it is nowhere. And liberty in the mind implies self-determination." This consciousness of freedom within the self, plus the doctrine of self-love enlightened through the sensibilities under divine influence, was the center of the new Evangelical (New School, new light) ideology and the moral philosophy that emerged from the Second Awakening as a new consensus or world view. It became embedded in the textbooks of "moral science" that were used in schools and colleges for the remainder of the century. While some versions of the Scottish Philosophy tended toward Unitarian rationalism, the most common were simply apologies for Evangelical Christianity as Taylor and the other revival prophets of the awakening preached it.

Along with the redefinition of free moral agency, the New School world view revised the concept of a limited atonement. Obviously, if all men have free will, Christ did not die for only a few predestined elect but for "whosoever will" accept God's offer of salvation. Again, the Calvinist exponents of the New School did not repudiate the doctrine of election; they merely redefined it to meet the objections of those who claimed, unreasonably, that God had from the beginning of time excluded thousands upon thousands from the possibility of conversion. God of course knew from the beginning who would act upon their free will and who would not, but foreknowledge is not determinism.

Furthermore, the New School played down the idea that the atonement of Christ was a punishment he suffered for Adam's sin. Christ came to earth to suffer as a man because he wished to sacrifice himself for the love of mankind. It was a voluntary act of self-sacrifice and, as such, a stimulus or example to believers to sacrifice their own selfishness for their fellow men. The text that stressed this view of the crucifixion was John 3:16: "For God so loved the world that he gave his only begotten Son, that whosoever believeth in him should not perish but have everlasting life." This was a gospel of love; salvation was a gift from God; Christ was the Lamb of God, who sacrificed himself for rich and poor alike to bring them into harmony with God. Converts should sacrifice themselves to bring this message to others, whether as revivalists or by joining benevolent associations or by raising money for missions. There was work to be done in which all could join voluntarily according to their gifts.

Not only did this new exegesis emphasize the love of God and the humanity of Christ; it also tended to place the Son before the Father in Evangelical eyes. Christ became a personal savior, the mediator between God and his children. There is a relationship between this new theology and the changing role of women at this time. Some historians have spoken of the Evangelical movement as "the feminization of Christianity," not only because of its sentimentality (evidenced in the new concept of the sanctity of childhood and the emphasis on the sensibilities of "heart religion") but also because Christ became a female symbol, not unlike the Virgin Mary in Catholicism. The mother is the mediator between a stern father and the tender children in the family. The mother is the symbol of nurture, warmth, supportive love, mercy, tenderness, forgiveness. As urban industrialism sent men out of the family to work every day in the office, mill, shop, or factory, the mother became the head of the home, the goddess of "the cult of domesticity."

Women were put on a pedestal for many reasons, but one of them surely was the guilt of the father for abdicating his role of *paterfamilias* in the teaching and training of his children. If women were to be given this role, they would have to compensate the male ego in other ways. They would have to accept the fact not only that man was stronger and better able to cope with the rough-and-tumble of the world but that women were incapable of coping with the world outside the home and the church (as adjunct of the home). As goddesses of hearth and home women gave up equality for abstract enthronement. Children were tender rosebuds from God, and mothers must assume a sacrificial role in cultivating these

buds. The wife's sacrifices for husband and children paralleled in
symbolic ways the sacrifices of the Son of God to his Father.
Women were God's vicegerents in the home. Not even the minister
had such spiritual authority over the young. In urban, suburban,
industrial America, mother's love replaced father's discipline as the
central feature of the nuclear family. But in this new pattern of sex
roles, women's rights could have no place. Goddesses cannot be
equals. Only as a cultic goddess, as Father-Mother God or as female
incarnations of Jesus, could women have significant leadership roles
outside the home. This could not occur in the principal evangelical
denominations, where the ministry remained a masculine prerogative, but it occurred in Shakerism, in Christian Science, in Jemima
Wilkinson's Society of the Universal Friend, to some extent in
Quakerism, and above all in Spiritualism, where female "me-
diums" or mediators easily bridged the mystical gap between this
world and the next.

By 1823 the New School or New Haven theology (Taylor taught
theology at Yale), after ten years of careful evolution, was well
developed. Lyman Beecher gave it its first clear articulation in his
classic evangelical sermon "The Faith Once Delivered to the
Saints." The change that had been wrought in Calvinism from the
days of Edwards and Hopkins can be succinctly demonstrated in the
following view of this sermon, written for a Unitarian journal
(which Sidney Mead cites):

> What makes this statement of Christian doctrine remarkable, considered
> as coming from a reputed Calvinist, is its decidedly anti-Calvinist
> bearing; expressly denying some of the peculiarities of Calvinism,
> distinctly asserting none of them, nor even implying any one of them in
> such a manner as to make it obvious to a common reader . . . it begins
> with asserting, in as strong and unqualified language as was ever used by
> an Arminian or Unitarian, the doctrine of man's actual *ability* and *free
> agency* . . . ; on the subject of original sin and *native depravity*, our
> author is hardly less unsound in his orthodoxy . . . ; upon the difficult
> and much disputed question respecting the first motion in the conver-
> sion of the individual, Dr. Beecher advances the opinion, directly in the
> face of Calvinism . . . of pure Arminianism [free choice].

Beecher was later to be tried for heresy by Old School Calvinists,
and so were many other Evangelical ministers who took up this
Arminianized Calvinism after 1823. But the Old School, though it

expelled the members of the New School from the Presbyterian Church in 1837, was no more successful in stemming the cultural transformation than the Old Sides and old lights had been in the 1740s. Later the two Presbyterian groups reunited on essentially New School lines (as in Tennent's day). It is significant that many thought the schism of 1837 was part of the new antislavery impulse within the New School; the Old School represented those closer to the South's position (i.e., that slavery was a political, not a moral, issue). New School theology and the efforts to abolish slavery were to become increasingly related, though Beecher and the New England Evangelicals always remained moderates in their support of antislavery, opposing the perfectionist approach of the abolitionists.

## The Midwestern, Perfectionist Contribution to the Awakening

The principal contributions of the Midwest to the Second Great Awakening were a new definition of revivalism and a perfectionist theology. The leading prophet of these aspects of revitalization was Charles Grandison Finney, though he had many disciples who spread his views throughout the North. To the New Englanders, Finney seemed an enthusiast. Taylor and Beecher were so fearful that revivalism might become "enthusiastic" that they rigorously restrained the emotionalism of their auditors. Following a revival, they carefully tested those who claimed to have been converted, often keeping them "on probation" for four to six months before permitting them to join the church. This way they hoped to blunt old-light criticisms that their new-light theology led to false conversions. Although the transplanted Congregational Yankees of western New York, Ohio, and Indiana avoided the camp meetings of uneducated Baptist and Methodist preachers, they were not too proud to learn something from the "new measures" these sects found so effective in saving souls.

Under Finney the revivalism of the Midwest in the 1820s constituted the culmination of the northern phase of the awakening. After 1830 Finney brought his revival methods back East to

the major cities—Philadelphia, New York, Boston, Hartford—and
later reversed the precedent of Whitefield and the Wesleyans by
carrying the new American form of revivalism to the British Isles in
1849 and 1858.

Finney, after a profound conversion experience in Adams, New
York, in 1821, had been ordained (though he lacked a college
education) by the Presbyterians as an itinerant home missionary.
Tall, graceful, with a clear voice, hypnotic blazing eyes, and a
passionate conviction of his calling, he rode on horseback, preaching from town to town through western New York for the next
decade. Everywhere he drew throngs who reacted enthusiastically to
his demand that they do as he had done: make up their minds then
and there to give themselves to God. Their destiny lay in their own
hands, no matter what the old Calvinists told them. God gave men
the free will to effect their own salvation whenever they chose. So
successful were his meetings that a host of other revivalists sprang
up who imitated his style and message.

When this phase of the awakening began in western New York
under Finney's preaching in 1823, and when other revivalists joined
him in preaching the views of the New School theology, the
inhabitants became so thoroughly wrought up that they literally fell
off their seats in a state of shock and ecstasy. "If I had had a sword
in my hand," Finney said, "I could not have cut them off . . . as
fast as they fell." Reports in New England of these revivals
portrayed them as fanatical affairs, reminiscent of the worst frenzies
of Davenport's meetings in the First Awakening. Taylor, Beecher,
and Nettleton, fearing quite rightly that the Unitarians and other
rationalists would use these emotional excesses to ridicule their own
revivalism in New England, arranged to meet Finney and his
friends in New Lebanon, New York, in 1827. Their purpose was to
persuade the Finneyites to be more decorous. But the venerable
clergy from "back East" failed to convince the provincial revivalists
of the West that they were doing anything wrong. Why, they
asked, should they abandon what Beecher called dangerous "new
measures" when they were winning so many converts to God's
cause by using them? This pragmatic measure of success in terms of
statistical results was central to Finney's revisionist view of what a
revival was.

Among the "new measures" the Easterners complained of were all-night prayer meetings, praying for sinners by name, allowing women to pray and exhort when men were present, denouncing Old School ministers as "cold, stupid, or dead," speaking "with an irreverent familiarity with God," and employing an "anxious seat" or bench at the front of the congregation to which awakening sinners were asked to come for special prayers and exhortations by the revivalist. Finney, speaking for the westerners at New Lebanon, said they would agree to discourage "audible groaning," boisterous shouting, fainting, and other convulsions where possible, but in other respects there was no meeting of the minds. The westerners were determined to go their own way to meet the needs of their own people.

Finney's most famous sermon was entitled "Sinners Bound to Change Their Own Hearts," based on Ezekiel 18:31: "Make you a new heart and a new spirit: for why will ye die?" God, Finney said, could be taken at his word. If God commands men to change their own hearts, to give up selfishness and sin and attain a new heart, then he means that they had the power to do it. When people with Calvinist backgrounds said they wanted to do this but were "morally unable," he replied: "[To say] that we are under obligation to do what we have no power to do is absurd. . . . This is contrary to right reason. . . . As, therefore, God requires men to make themselves a new heart on pain of eternal death, it is the strongest possible evidence that they are able to do it." To drive this reasonable inference home, he said, in language they all understood, "A sinner under the influence of the Spirit of God is just as free as a jury under the arguments of an advocate." The revivalist was that advocate (Finney had been studying for the law when he was converted). He persuaded, cajoled, and browbeat people to live up to their own responsibility to change their hearts. He abandoned the metaphysical style of the old Calvinists: "I talked to them like a lawyer at the bar," he wrote; "I urged the people with such vehemence as if they might not have a moment to live." His strenuous, urgent style of argumentation suited the frontier temper. "I said 'you' instead of preaching [abstractly] about sin and sinners and saying 'they.' . . . I said 'hell' and with such an emphasis as often to shock the people." Shocking was of

course the kind of empirical, "sensational," style that Edwards had
favored in the frontier towns of the Connecticut Valley and that
Whitefield had employed in the colonial cities. But Finney was
considerably more colloquial than they, preaching man to man and
eyeball to eyeball, sometimes naming sinners from the pulpit:
"Oh, God, smite that wicked man, that hardened sinner. . . . Oh,
God, send trouble, anguish and affliction into his bed chamber this
night. . . . God Almighty, shake him over hell!" Naming sinners
in a small country town was bound to bring strong community
pressure to bear upon them, and the "anxious bench" was
designed to concentrate this pressure on those who wanted their
neighbors to "pray them through" the experience.

Unlike the Taylorite new lights of New England, Finney frankly
repudiated Calvinism, especially as formulated in the Westminster
Confession of Faith in 1648 (the formation to which the Old School
in this awakening adhered). "Reason was given us for the very
purpose of enabling us to justify the ways of God," Finney said.
Americans did not need to rely on the authority of English and
Scottish divines of two centuries before. Their doctrines were
incredible; Calvinism was nothing but an old "fiction." Finney
had not become a rationalist, of course; he merely believed that
"There is as much connection between means and ends in religion
as in nature." The sinner's "cannot is his will not. The will is free
and . . . sin and holiness are voluntary acts of mind." Man-made
creeds and confessions of faith must yield to common sense and
experience.

This doctrine led logically to a new conception of revivals, one
that denied their miraculous nature as mysterious showers of
blessing from heaven. Conversion, Finney declared, "is not a
miracle or dependent on a miracle in any sense. . . . It is purely a
philosophical result of the right use of constituted means."
Therefore, "a revival is not a miracle; it consists entirely in the right
exercise of the powers of nature. . . . The connection between the
right use of means for a revival and a revival is as philosophically
sure as between the right use of means to raise grain and a crop of
wheat." The laws governing revivals were so clear and simple that
anyone following them could obtain the desired results: "Mankind
will not act until they are excited," he pointed out. Hence,

> God has found it necessary to take advantage of the excitability there is
> in mankind to produce powerful excitements among them before he can
> lead them to obey him. Men are so sluggish, there are so many things
> to lead their minds off from religion and to oppose the influence of the
> gospel that it is necessary to raise an excitement among them till the
> tide rises so high as to sweep away the opposing obstacles.

Excitement rivets attention; the revivalist and the Holy Spirit,
working in tandem, then get the Word through to the people, loud
and clear.

Finney was not embarrassed to compare the work of the revivalist
to that of the Jacksonian politicians trying to gather votes for their
party: "What do the politicians do? They get up meetings,
circulate handbills and pamphlets, blaze away in the newspapers,
send coaches all over town with handbills . . . all to gain attention
to their cause and elect their candidates." The minister who wanted
a revival would have to use the same means to stir the wills of
sinners: "The object of the ministry is to get all the people to feel
that the devil has no right to rule this world but that they ought all
to give themselves to God and vote in the Lord Jesus Christ as the
governor of the Universe." This was the reason Finney's "new
measures" had worked so well. New times and circumstances
required novelty in advertising the Lord's party. "God has established no particular system of measures to be employed and
invariably adhered to in promoting revivals," Finney concluded.
"New measures are necessary from time to time to awaken
attention and bring the gospel to bear upon the public mind."
Better a full church with undignified preaching than an empty one
with it. "The results justify my methods," he said frankly. "Show
me the fruits of your ministry, and if they so far exceed mine as to
give me evidence that you have found a more excellent way, I will
adopt your views." Or, putting it more theologically, he wrote,
"When the blessing evidently follows the introduction of the
measure itself, the proof is unanswerable that the measure is wise."
Yet Finney was no advocate of emotionalism for its own sake.
Religion was to turn men's attention to higher things, to "the
reasonableness, fitness and propriety of their Maker's claims" upon
their lives, to "the hatefulness of sin" and the "stability" of God's
eternal truth in a world of flux.

In addition to his new scientific theory of revivalism, Finney
developed a new concept of professional mass evangelism and
demonstrated that it could be used as effectively in the cities as in
rural camp meetings. Except for the Methodists, no denomination
had created a permanent place for revival preaching within its
institutional structure. Home missionaries and itinerant preachers
usually found (after several years of moving about) a congregation
that invited them to settle down as its permanent pastor. During
the Second Great Awakening, however, the concept of a special
kind of preacher, a man with exceptional oratorical gifts, a man
particularly adept at using the spiritual means God had established
for working up revivals, became an accepted part of the Evangelical
Protestant ministry. In helping to make revivalism a profession,
Finney also popularized among non-Methodist (or formerly Calvinist) denominations the practice of "protracted meetings"—
usually three or four days of revivalistic meetings, morning,
afternoon, and evening, during which a whole town (or every
member of a particular denomination in a town) virtually ceased
secular activities. Finney sometimes held these meetings in tents,
sometimes in large churches or auditoriums or even theaters. Most
of the professional revivalists who conducted protracted meetings
did so for the particular denomination that had ordained them, but
a few superstars (like Finney) conducted interdenominational
meetings sponsored by all the churches in a town. Professional
revivalists served principally as supplements to the regular ministry,
appearing on call to provide a shot in the arm for a church,
denomination, or city when religious life was at a low ebb. Some
ministers, like Horace Bushnell, complained that they had a
disruptive effect on parish life, demeaning the regular pastors and
making anything less than revivalistic fervor in a church seem like
religious declension. By the end of the century the routinized
charisma of professional revivalism had become self-defeating;
associated primarily with small-town life in rural areas, it appeared
backward and out-of-date to city dwellers who had fled that way of
life. Through most of the century, however, revivalism was the
most powerful engine in the processes of American church growth,
frontier acculturation, and benevolent reform.

Finney's part in bringing frontier revival techniques to the rising cities of the East (and later to Great Britain) might be compared to the work of Whitefield and Wesley in England. Whitefield's many revival tours of America were largely city-centered, but his methods were focused almost entirely upon his own charismatic personality. By Finney's day cities were much larger and more cosmopolitan. Consequently, he developed a wide array of measures to reach the heterogeneous ranks of urban dwellers. He recruited lay workers in cooperating churches and organized prayer meetings in advance of his arrival; his lay workers posted placards, advertised in newspapers, and distributed notices of his meetings from door to door or to passersby in the streets. He trained the ministers and laity to work with awakened sinners after his sermons and to invite converts to join their churches (making them feel less lonely). He practiced house-to-house visitation and even hired a special musical assistant to direct the singing at his meetings, and his wife led special meetings for women. In the cities Finney extended his protracted meetings for many weeks, putting special emphasis on evening meetings, when clerks, shopgirls, and mechanics would be free to attend. The whole process was carefully planned and organized to reach out as widely as possible. Urban revivalism required extensive financing from the well-to-do lay leaders. In later years professional urban evangelists improved on Finney's techniques, but they did not fundamentally alter his approach.

Finally, something must be said about Finney's perfectionism. This developed logically out of his belief in free will, but he was to find that much of what he called "sanctification" or "the second blessing" had been anticipated by John Wesley. The wave of social reform that followed the Second Great Awakening owes much to this perfectionist zeal, as John L. Thomas, Gilbert Barnes, and Whitney Cross have pointed out. It was not originally part of Finney's revivalism to channel new converts into benevolent-reform associations, but, having "got right with God" themselves, new converts felt an almost uncontrollable urge to help others get right with him. They wanted to share their experience of liberation and bring the joy of salvation to others still in darkness.

Finney's view of salvation held that the reborn became totally unselfish or totally altruistic. "All sin," he said, "consists in selfishness; and all holiness or virtue in disinterested benevolence."

Regeneration was "a change from selfishness to benevolence, from having a supreme regard to one's own interest to an absorbing and controlling choice of the happiness and glory of God's Kingdom." This meant that the regenerate man was committed to sacrificing his own pleasure in order to advance God's Kingdom on earth. The reformed sinner "should set out with a determination to aim at being useful in the highest degree possible." He must make the world a fit place for the imminent return of Christ. "As saints supremely value the highest good of being, they will and must take a deep interest in whatever is promotive of that end. Hence their spirit is necessarily that of the reformer. To the universal reformation of the world they stand committed." "War, slavery, licentiousness and all such evils and abominations are necessarily regarded by the saint as great and sore evils, and he longs for their complete and final overthrow."

This view, called by John L. Thomas the spirit of "romantic perfectionism," was feared by the conservative New England revivalists; nevertheless, after 1830 it came to dominate American social thought. Thomas describes the nature of its radical social theory:

> In emphasizing the unfettered will as the proper vehicle for reform it
> provided a millenarian alternative to Jacksonian politics. Since social
> evils were simply individual acts of selfishness compounded, and since
> Americans could attempt the perfect society at any time they were so
> inclined, it followed that . . . deep and lasting reform . . . meant an
> educational crusade based on the assumption that when a sufficient
> number of individual Americans had seen the light, they would
> automatically solve the country's social problems.

Unlike the New England prophets, therefore, Finney did not support laws to restrain men or prohibit them from bad actions. Men must be reformed from within. No laws would ever produce a perfect society. In his Rochester revival in 1830-31 Finney identified drinking alcohol as a sin to be eradicated by conversion, not by temperance pledges or prohibition laws. A year later, in New York City, he concluded that slavery was a spiritual sin that must be eradicated by converting those who owned slaves or profited from slavery. He persuaded his church to admit no one to membership who had anything to do with slavery. In 1833, despite the mobs that threatened the effort, he allowed his church to be used to form the American Anti-Slavery Society under the leadership of William Lloyd Garrison (whom Beecher had refused to assist because his concept of immediate abolition was too radical). Finney's young convert, Theodore Weld, organized an abolition crusade in western New York and Ohio that may have been more effective than Garrison's efforts in the East.

Finney did not, however, approve of Weld's efforts to lobby in Congress to obtain a law abolishing slavery in the District of Columbia. Direct political action would only "roll a wave of blood over the land," he wrote to Weld. Finney instructed his students at Oberlin College, where he became a professor of theology after 1835, to avoid the abolition movement and dedicate themselves to converting the souls of those involved in slavery: "If abolition can be made an appendage of a general revival, all is well. I fear no other form of carrying this question will save our country or the liberty or soul of the slave." Finney also became deeply involved in the anti-Masonic movement in New York State, resigned his own membership in the movement after 1825, preached against its dangers, and said that Christians must dissociate themselves from such an undemocratic organization.

Optimistic about the progress of revivalism and the increase in church members across the nation, Finney predicted in 1835 that "the millennium can come in three years" if Americans and their churches would simply "do their duty." Human exertion in partnership with the Holy Spirit was the means, he said, for "the creation of a new heaven and a new earth." When William Miller, the founder of Adventism, predicted that the world would be destroyed in 1843 for its increasing wickedness, Finney pointed to the revivals and asked, "Are these evidences of the world's growing worse and worse? The world is not growing worse but better."

The new-light theology and moral-reform message articulated by Finney differed only in emphasis from the revival spirit of the South and New England. Together the three phases of the awakening created the most powerful reform era in American history. Ultimately the energies of this "radical democracy" coalesced around the effort to abolish human slavery. What is difficult to understand at first is how the South, where revivalism was equally strong in

these years, came to be so unequivocally divided from the North.
Why did revivalism in the South disdain social activism, and why
did it see the millennium from such a different perspective?

## Southern Camp Meetings and the Methodist Contribution to the Awakening

It is as difficult to give dates for the Second Great Awakening in the
South as for the First. John Boles, in a recent study of the
movement, dates it from 1787 to 1807, the period of the first camp
meetings. Wesley M. Gewehr's study of the First Great Awakening
in the South says that it began in 1740 and, except for a slump
during the Revolution, continued until 1790. Either the two
awakenings overlapped, or the First never ended. Methodist historians see the work of their denomination from 1766 to 1798 as the
connecting link between the two. Charles A. Johnson's book about
camp meetings indicates that, while camp meetings began in the
1790s, they continued through the nineteenth century, because the
Methodists incorporated them into their regular church life even
after the frontier had moved further West. There is no doubt that
the camp meeting under the trees was the preeminent symbol of
the awakening in the South; this highlights the fact that until the
Civil War a large part of the South was still virtually a frontier
region. The Cherokee Indians were not removed from north-
western Georgia until 1838, and the Seminoles were still fighting in
1842.

Because the old Southwest remained sparsely settled and had
poor transportation, little industrial or commercial life (outside
cotton), and only a crude school system, its religious institutions
came to play a much larger role than in the North as a civilizing or
acculturating force. Furthermore, to meet the psychological needs
and rugged life-style of its rude and dispersed settlements, the
revitalization movement here took on a more emotional and
dramatic form. Except for the blacks at the bottom and the very rich
at the top, there was generally an egalitarian and individualistic
social order in the South. Preeminently English and Scotch-Irish,
the population was also more homogeneous than in the North.
Comparatively few European immigrants found there way there. At

the time of the Civil War the South was 90 percent Protestant, and 90 percent of the Protestants were Baptists or Methodists.

The Separate Baptists had been generating revivals in the South since the 1750s. The Methodist movement began in the 1760s and, despite its Toryism, revived strongly in the 1790s. As the settlers moved across the Appalachians, they carried their religious zeal and their traveling preachers with them. Religion was both a form of social gathering (to see old friends, exchange news, and share experiences) and a way of finding relief from the anxieties of a hard and strenuous life. Here, particularly, Mathews' and Miyakawa's emphasis on the organizing process of the awakening makes sense. It needs to be emphasized that, in addition to seeking national unity, this awakening stressed localized unity—or, more appropriately, a sense of community. Camp meetings were communal in nature; churches became the centers of community life; and, above all, although a conversion was an individual confrontation of the soul with God, the sustaining fellowship of Christian brethren provided the continuity that routinized and canalized the fervor of the awakening into orderly social institutions.

Camp meetings, which had been known as "quarterly sacramental meetings" east of the Appalachians, were at first the only large-scale social activities in which men, women, and children joined together on the southern frontier. Without the time or money to establish churches in the early years of settlement, the frontier dwellers had nowhere else to get their children baptized, to pray and sing together, to have weddings performed by ministers, or to give vent to pent-up feelings. The great mass of people considered themselves good Christians in belief and desired salvation; they also wanted the regular services of a church and minister near their homes. The fact that people went to great effort to attend camp meetings, traveling miles by wagon over rough roads and camping out when they arrived, indicates a craving for human fellowship and spiritual consolation.

Women in particular were drawn to camp meetings, for they bore the heaviest burdens of pain, sickness, sorrow, unremitting labor, and old age. For their labors there were few social rewards and no public victories. Men at least had the satisfaction of public praise after winning a battle, building a cabin, or ploughing a straight furrow, and they could sublimate anger or fear in wrestling matches, shooting matches, horse races, and hunting. Women, toiling in the cabin, caring for the sick or aged, were excluded from most frontier pastimes. But with the coming of religious institutions to a community, women found a place outside the home where they could gather, express their fears and hopes, and join in song and prayer with other women. Christian fellowship also offered a different but equally important source of security for men and children. It gave regularity and order to life; it offered a source of strength beyond the self. John Boles rightly describes the evangelical religion that emerged during this awakening as "folk religion" (as opposed to churchly tradition). The churches were made for people rather than the people for churches. In sparsely settled places (as most of the South was) "folksiness" and "sociableness" were higher virtues than fine church buildings or sophisticated, learned ministers.

If demography and environment helped to make the difference between the awakening experience and church life North and South, it also goes far to explain the failure of southern revivalism to eventuate in political reform. What the southern churchgoer came to consider social reform (the only kind of reform appropriate to the Christian qua Christian) was the personal moral reform that brought order to the community by restraining violence, strengthening self-discipline, and encouraging familial and neighborly responsibilities for good behavior. Beyond personal behavior lay politics, and, according to the southern definition of the separation of church and state, the church was not to concern itself with politics. Among the Methodists the doctrines of perfectionism were especially strong in inculcating this emphasis on personal morality as the measure of Christian virtue, but Baptist church discipline also emphasized the need to subdue the unruly nature of self-assertion.

The most important result of revival meetings was the successful formation of new churches through which to sustain and routinize the socializing power of the camp meeting—to disperse its harmonizing power among the small crossroads hamlets from which the crowds had gathered. While Baptists and Methodists might attend and preach at the same camp meetings, they were constant rivals for the converts of such preaching. The Baptists had the advantage of the peculiar rite of baptism by total immersion to certify their adherents; they also had a more democratic congregational polity, in which the members of each local church chose their own minister and were subject to no higher ecclesiastical control or authority. This form of local self-government appealed to a wide segment of the population and had certain advantages in its flexibility. But the Methodists had other advantages. Though ruled by bishops, the bishops were elected. Though the bishops chose the circuit riders for each area to serve infant churches, the circuit riders were changed regularly to add variety to church life. The organizational strength of the Methodist system gave it a tensile strength the Baptist system lacked; it could resist strains that often fragmented Baptist churches. The advantage the two denominations shared was the fact that both gave the laity a prominent role to play in church affairs; both were open to new talent and made it easy for gifted laymen to enter the ministry; both encouraged ministers who were close to the people, who accepted low salaries, and who preached from the heart, without notes and in the vernacular. Both stressed the role of the laity, acting in common, to sustain each other's morality and to act as a force for sobriety, charity, and order in their community.

The Methodist itinerant revivalist Peter Cartwright may be taken as typical of the camp-meeting prophets who revitalized the South after 1800. Born in Virginia in 1785, he moved to Logan County, Kentucky, with his parents in a wagon train at the age of two or three. The country was still filled with marauding Indians, struggling to keep back the white man's invasion; five persons in this wagon train were killed by Indians when they fell behind. However, the country filled up rapidly. Kentucky became a state in 1792. The Indians made peace in 1794. By 1800, when the famous Cane Ridge camp meeting took place near Cartwright's home, the state had 230,000 inhabitants scattered across it. Converted at the age of seventeen, Cartwright was licensed to preach as a Methodist circuit rider soon after. From that time until his death, he took part in countless camp meetings, from Kentucky to Illinois. His autobiography, written when he was 71, is an endless series of dramatic confrontations between himself and the scoffers, deists, infidels, and rival preachers he encountered. His ability to outshout and outfight the riffraff who challenged him and to outwit the Baptists, Shakers, Stoneites, Campbellites, and Universalists who competed with him for converts is the central feature of his account. Unlike the Yankees, who wanted at least a semblance of learning and doctrine from their preachers, the southern Methodists spurned learning:

> Our pocket Bible, Hymn Book, and [Methodist] Discipline constituted
> our library. It is true we could not, many of us, conjugate a verb or
> parse a sentence and murdered the king's English almost every lick. But
> there was a Divine unction attended the word preached, and thousands
> fell under the might power of God.

Many of Cartwright's stories go, as he said, "to show the ignorance the early Methodist preachers had to contend with" in the West. But it was an ignorance shared by preacher and flock.

Describing the early camp meetings, Cartwright notes that five to ten thousand persons "would collect from forty to fifty miles around" and stay together from four days to four weeks. During the meetings,

> Ten, twenty and sometimes thirty ministers of different denominations
> would come together and preach night and day . . . and great good
> resulted from them. I have seen more than a hundred sinners fall like
> dead men under one powerful sermon, and I have seen and heard more
> than five hundred Christians all shouting aloud the high praises of God
> at once.

As in the North, the prevailing cultural world view of southerners had been Calvinistic, but Calvinism faded fast after 1800. At first, Cartwright said, the Presbyterians and Baptists tried to uphold the old doctrines, but soon "they almost to a man gave up these points of high Calvinism and preached a free salvation to all mankind." The Methodists, who had always believed in free will and a general atonement, came into their own at last. Many southern Presbyterians claimed to be more orthodox Calvinists than the New School Presbyterians and Congregationalists to the North; but, like Whitefield (and Beecher), they preached as though salvation was open to "whosoever will," as Cartwright notes.

Cartwright claims that the Methodists preached against the more extravagant emotional hysteria of the camp meetings, "called the running, jumping, barking exercise" and the "trances and visions." But his accounts indicate that many revivalists encouraged this form of stress release because these exercises "made such an appeal to the ignorance, superstition, and credulity of the people." Much of Cartwright's effort went into reclaiming souls who had strayed from Methodism into the "delusions" of Shakerism, Universalism, or the erroneous Baptist position. He also notes how quickly and easily his converts were recruited into churches:

> I addressed the multitude about three hours and when I closed my arguments I opened the door of the Church and invited all that would renounce Shakerism to come and give me their hand. Forty-seven came forward and then and there openly renounced the dreadful delusion. The next day I followed those that fled . . . from cabin to cabin, taking the names of those that returned to the solid foundation of truth and my number rose to eighty-seven. I then organized them into a regular [Methodist] society and the next fall had a preacher sent to them.

Cartwright's preoccupation with the numbers he had converted, with getting them committed by a handshake, and with obtaining ministers to keep the group together was remarkably similar to the work of Beecher, Finney, and other revivalists in the North.

The reason why southern revivalism failed to produce the same kind of political reform and institutional restructuring that occurred among "romantic perfectionists" in the North lies in the problem of slavery. Even a major prophet like Peter Cartwright dared not touch on the issue of slavery in his sermons after 1830, and when he tried in other ways to oppose that institution, he was finally forced to give up preaching in the South. He was not afraid to say that slavery was "a domestic, political, and moral evil," but southern folk were unwilling to hear it. This mixing of social reform and spiritual affairs cut too deeply into the traditional fabric of the southern way of life. It threatened rather than consolidated communities; it promised violence when the function of religion was to curtail violence. The kind of perfectionism the Methodists and other evangelical denominations sought was inward and personal holiness, and southern preachers could find nothing in the Bible that told them to declare that the institution of slavery was a sin. In fact, taken literally, the Bible seemed much more clearly to accept slavery as a sad but necessary condition for some people.

Commenting on the intense concern with personal morality in
southern religion, John Boles has written, "If anything, pietistic
revivalism on the individual level decreased concern with politics."
Christianizing the social order in the South, as among the more
intense holiness groups in the North, meant converting every
individual to the basic moral pattern or rural middle-class virtue.
The awakening challenged southern culture—or was allowed to—
only in terms of private self-control. In a land with little real
poverty, no urban slums or factory towns, minimal cultural conflict
with Roman Catholic immigrants, with the Indians removed to the
West and the blacks considered childlike beneficiaries of civilization, the white southerner felt that his region of the nation was
already closer to millennial perfection than any other part of the
country. Was not the South a region of farmers, and had not
Jefferson said that the farmer was "nature's nobleman" and that
the republic was safe in his hands? As the camp meetings and new
churches Christianized the southern frontiersmen and stabilized
their rough habits, the South's celestial railroad seemed further
along its track to the kingdom of God than any of the celestial
railroads in the North.

In the North, the Second Great Awakening challenged the older
way of life at every turn, producing endless schisms and theological
debates. In the South, after some initial denominational turmoil in
the first decade of the century, this awakening confirmed the
prevalent life-style, increased religious homogeneity, and made the
Methodists and Baptists so dominant that other sects were an
almost invisible minority. Southern white Christians were not
averse to benevolent reform if that meant encouraging personal
temperance and helping the orphan or widow, the deaf, the dumb,
the blind, the insane. But if it meant rearranging the social order,
tampering with slavery, interfering with state sovereignty, defending the Indians' right to remain on good farm and cotton land,
then benevolent reform was totally misguided. It was in fact
un-Christian, since it created political tests for spiritual organizations. Whether a man held slaves or not was irrelevant to his right
to join a church.

For the southern white Evangelical, one of the great virtues of
leaving social reform outside the realm of revivalism and the
churches was that it bound the nation together. Conservative

northern Evangelicals agreed and strove desperately after 1830 to prevent the radical perfectionists from dividing the national denominations into northern and southern wings over the issue of slavery. The southern white Christians also found political quietism advantageous because it permitted white and black Evangelicals to believe that, whatever their social differences, they worshiped the same God. Blacks who took Christian teaching seriously would expect Christian masters to be more benevolent toward them; whites expected Christian teaching would make the blacks more docile. A façade of Christian evangelism was thus pasted over the great chasm separating black and white (as well as white and red) Americans.

The blacks, however, had their own evangelical hope, which they furtively expressed in folktales and gospel songs (and, not so furtively, in escapes to freedom). But the millennial goal of black Evangelicals was not the same as that of the white southern Evangelical; their Kingdom of God on earth did not include the continuation of slavery. Masking their desire for freedom behind a symbolic identification of slavery with that of the Jewish bondage in Egypt, black preachers and revivalists called metaphorically for a Moses to lead their people out of bondage. But their Canaan did not correspond with that of northern Evangelicals, who hoped for total assimilation of blacks, or of those who hoped that all blacks would find their Canaan in Africa. The black millennial dream of freedom and equality ran counter to the narrowing definition of what it meant to be an American that emerged from this awakening. Black Evangelical prophets saw more realistically than the white prophets of revitalization that a long hard road lay ahead.

## Democratized Theology and Romantic Nationalism

As long as the white southern churches could keep Evangelicalism (the generic term for the Arminianized Calvinism that constituted the new ideological consensus after 1830) apolitical, the Second Great Awakening was a source of national unity and hope. But pietistic perfectionism carried within it the seeds of a cataclysm that no compromises could postpone forever. The concept of manifest destiny and Christian union had carried Americans through the

troublesome years of their adolescence and into national maturity.
Out of it came the new democratic faith in the common man that
made Jacksonian democracy possible. Out of its more mystical side
of communion with God in nature came a new cultural milieu from
which a truly national literature, art, and architecture could
develop, as well as the literary flowering of New England in the
Transcendental movement. The Second Great Awakening was
America's coming-of-age as a subculture; if it was not yet the equal,
it was no longer the child of Europe. The dominant white,
Protestant majority had committed the nation to developing its
own human and natural resources in its own unique way.

In politics, the awakening resulted in what historians call
"Jacksonian democracy," with its perfectionist preference for the
heart over the head and its postmillennial optimism. "I believe,"
said Andrew Jackson in his First Inaugural in 1828,

> that man can be elevated; man can become more and more endowed
> with divinity; and as he does he becomes more God-like in his character
> and capable of governing himself. Let us go on elevating our people,
> perfecting our institutions, until democracy shall reach such a point of
> perfection that we can acclaim with truth that the voice of the people is
> the voice of God.

As John William Ward puts it, in *Andrew Jackson, Symbol for an
Age* (1953), "Where Jeffersonians rested their case [for democracy]
on the power of the mind, the Jacksonians rested theirs on the
power of man's heart."

The secular expression of the new ideological consensus can be
found in the writings of Walt Whitman, George Bancroft, Orestes
Brownson, and John L. O'Sullivan. O'Sullivan said that the cause
of Jacksonian democracy "is the cause of Christianity." Bancroft
argued that intuition, inspiration, and innate ideas (what he called
"Reason" with a capital "R") were more important than "Understanding" (rationalism, intellectual, academic logic) in deciding
the important questions of the day. And,

> If Reason is a universal faculty, the universal decision [of the masses] is
> the nearest criterion of truth. The common mind winnows opinions; it
> is the sieve which separates error from certainty. . . . A government of
> equal rights must, therefore, rest upon mind, not wealth and brute
> force; the sum of the moral intelligence of the community should rule
> the State.

We may contrast this with Jefferson's claim that "The people are the most honest and safe, though not the most wise, repository of the public interest." The eighteenth-century Enlightened man of "Understanding" was replaced after 1830 by the Romantic man of "Reason"—that is, of the heart, the spirit. The age of Kant, Coleridge, Wordsworth, and Emerson had replaced that of Locke, Voltaire, Pope, and Paine. The transformation was well summarized by Orestes Brownson's description of a democrat (i.e., an American):

> A democrat is not he who only believes in the people's capacity of being taught and therefore graciously condescends to be their instructor, but he who believes that Reason, the light which shines out from God's throne, shines into the heart of every man and that truth lights her torch in the inner temple of every man's soul, whether patrician or plebeian, a shepherd or a philosopher, a Croesus or a beggar. It is only on the reality of this inner light, and on the fact that it is universal in all men, and in every man, that you can found a democracy.

It is not surprising that Bancroft's history of the American people, started in the 1830, stressed the great contribution of the Quakers to the development of democracy (not the contribution of the Puritan Calvinists). The Quakers were the originators of the religious concept of the inner light in all men that lights their way to truth. The American people did not read much theology, history, or philosophy, but they understood precisely what these Jacksonian political leaders were saying. They had experienced the truth of these statements in their revivals, and the dynamic thrust of that revitalization movement succeeded in carrying the nation through its most serious national crisis. The Union was preserved because God willed it. The quintessence of the Evangelical consensus that dominated nineteenth-century American culture can be found in the most symbolic song of that era (and one that still lies close to the nation's ideological core), *The Battle Hymn of the Republic* (written by a daughter of Lyman Beecher):

> In the beauty of the lilies
>     Christ was born across the sea
> With a glory in his bosom
>     That transfigures you and me;
> As He died to make men holy,
>     Let us die to make men free,
> His Truth is marching on.

# 5

# *The Third Great Awakening, 1890–1920*

## *Revivalism between Awakenings*

Some historians have seen the "Great Prayer Meeting Revival of 1857–58" as America's Third Great Awakening. Others have portrayed the great urban revival campaigns of Dwight L. Moody and Ira Sankey, from 1875 to 1885, in these terms. But measured against the definition we have utilized in this essay, neither of these movements qualifies as an awakening or revitalization movement. It is true that there were grave social tensions in the United States in both periods: tensions over the slavery issue and the financial panic in 1857; tensions over an economic depression and widespread labor agitation in 1875–85. Yet in neither of these brief spans of time was there any major shift in the prevailing ideological consensus or any major reorientation in the belief-value system that had emerged after the Second Great Awakening. In fact, both movements confirmed and sustained that consensus. They were extensions or reaffirmations of it. One might point to some "new measures" or techniques for saving souls in these movements, but new evangelistic methods did not change the terms of salvation or Americans' understanding of their relationship to God's will and laws.

The Prayer Meeting Revival of 1857–58 is best explained as the acceptance of mass revivalism by urban businessmen seeking God's help in time of trouble. Contemporary accounts call it the "Businessman's Revival" or evidence of "God in commerce." It was closely associated with important changes taking place in technology and mass communications, which included, among other things, the installation of the Atlantic cable, the national telegraphy system, and the circulation battles of the cheap penny newspapers (particularly James Gordon Bennett's New York *Herald* and Horace Greeley's New York *Tribune*, both of which gave detailed coverage to the revival). "What hath God wrought?" was the first long-distance message ticked over the telegraph in Morse code. In 1857-58 God wrought an urban revival by establishing the means whereby worried ("panic"-stricken) businessmen, holding noon prayer meetings in the downtown business section of one city during the lunch hour, could send telegraphic accounts of their piety to businessmen at similar noon prayer meetings in other cities. Not that these businessmen were insincere, but their prayers were essentially a ritual plea for God's assistance during a temporary business crisis.

D. L. Moody's revival meetings, on the other hand, might be characterized as the result of superabundant confidence among evangelical businessmen in the 1870s. These captains of industry believed that an effective lay preacher (as Moody was), together with a sentimental "gospel singer" (like Sankey), given thousands of dollars to spend on highly organized six-to-eight-week revival campaigns in the nation's largest cities, could reach the unemployed clerks, salesgirls, and working people with a Christian message that would calm their anxieties over unemployment and turn their attention to higher thoughts than labor agitation. It is no coincidence that Moody was the first revivalist singled out by socialists as an enemy of the working class, a man who made religion "the opiate of the masses." George Bernard Shaw said this of Moody's revival in Dublin, and Friedrich Engels called "Moody and Sankey and the like" the tools of the capitalist class.

Timothy L. Smith has argued that the Great Prayer Meeting Revival, at least insofar as it was associated with the holiness movement of Phoebe Palmer, was a prelude to the Social Gospel movement. If this were so, it might be possible to link it with the Third Great Awakening, of which the Social Gospel movement was certainly a key part. But Smith's own evidence indicates that Palmer was essentially concerned with personal perfection, not social reform. Perfectionists were "otherworldly," he says; "denouncing social and political injustice remained for them a prerogative of divinity." The Social Gospel movement after 1890 took precisely the opposite tack; denouncing social and political injustice was, said its spokesmen, preeminently the task of the ministers and churches.

Similarly, James Findlay has claimed that Moody's religious concern lay deeper than saving the souls of the urban poor. Moody realized after 1885 the failure of his mass revivals to reach the unchurched and tried to devise other means to help the lower classes improve their condition. But Findlay admits that Moody was no Social Gospel reformer. When Moody concluded, after 1885, that his "simple message" of salvation did not cope with "the problems connected with industrialization," Findlay writes, he "began yet another career outside the ambit of revivalism." That new ambit was, however, "Christian education," not social reform.

The best case that might be made for the cultural significance of the Prayer Meeting Revival would be to prove that it was a concerted effort by Americans, North and South, to relieve the social tensions of the slavery and secession crisis and to assert some new sense of national identity that could create the climate for yet another sectional compromise by Whigs and Democrats. It is true that some revivalists and ministers, then and later, made much of the fact that, by concentrating public atteniton on salvation, the leaders of the revivals of 1857–58 consciously avoided controversial topics like slavery or doctrinal difference. But most historians now agree that, far from increasing national harmony, the prayer-meeting revivals exacerbated sectional animosity. As an urban revival, it solidified the North. Such piety as it aroused helped tip the secular businessman toward the importance of maintaining the Union at any cost. In order to sustain the nation's covenant with God and its manifest destiny as a people, the people elected Lincoln and thereby induced the very sectional division that the revival is credited with overcoming, or seeking to overcome.

The best case that can be made for the significance of Moody's revivals of 1875–85 is that they represented a nativistic response to the rising cultural distortion that was building up to the "new light" of the Social Gospel and Liberal Protestantism. If we could label Moody "the first Fundamentalist," he could then be described as the spokesman for the "old lights" (the traditionalist phase of the Third Great Awakening). There is some truth in this. Moody did reject Darwinism and the higher criticism of the Bible. He did cling to ''the old-time religion'' (Evangelicalism) and reject ''Modernism.'' Most important, he sometimes adopted the pessimistic, premillennial tone that came to characterize the Fundamentalist reaction to the cultural crisis at the end of the century. In one sermon in 1877 Moody said he simply could not find in the Bible those justifications for a postmillennial interpretation of history that had seemed so obvious to Finney, Beecher, and Cartwright (and remained true for the Modernists): ''I look upon this world as a wrecked vessel,'' he said; ''God has given me a lifeboat and said to me, 'Moody, save all you can.' ''

But, by and large, this was not typical of Moody or of the vast majority of ministers and laymen who supported his revival campaigns. He was brought to the cities in times of unemployment by middle-class churchgoers and businessmen precisely to tell the workers that the American dream was true, that the system was fundamentally sound. People should not grumble or complain in hard times, because, sooner or later, the laws of supply and demand would bring a readjustment in the market, business would pick up, the factories would hum, good times would return. Meanwhile, they should tighten their belts, take any work that was available, and have faith in God's laws of economics. Moody even suggested that there was still plenty of land in the West and that farming was always a ready outlet for surplus urban labor. ''We live in a land flowing with milk and honey,'' he said to a revival audience in New York City in 1875 (where 50,000 were out of work): ''God has blessed this nation; yet men complain of hard times.'' To Evangelical believers in the Protestant ethic, the poor were poor because they had some flaw of character that conversion would quickly remove: ''It is a wonderful fact,'' Moody preached, ''that men and women saved by the blood of Jesus rarely remain the subjects of charity, but rise at once to comfort and respectability.''

In the end, however, Moody had to admit that his revivals did not reach the poor in the cities. His audiences were essentially middle-class, rural-born native Americans who had come to the city to make their fortunes; they believed that he spoke God's truth in extolling hard work and free enterprise. But he was not a spokes-

man for those who were becoming discouraged or disillusioned with
the success myth; nor did he reach the foreign-born or Catholic
poor who made up so large a proportion of the labor class. His
revivals represented an effort to reassure the middle class (or those
rising into it) that urban and industrial problems were minimal and
temporary. Professional revivalism of this sort was an effective
stress-relief mechanism for the majority in these years. Until the
1890s evangelists (and their audiences) continued to believe
complacently that this was the best of all possible worlds; God was
in his heaven, and all was right with America.

Nevertheless, tensions continued to grow. The old answers
became less and less convincing. Men did not easily rise to the top
or avoid poverty simply by hard work, thrift, and sobriety.
Increasing unrest and violence raised doubts that all was well.
American (and British) evangelical churchgoers (Moody was as
popular in Britain as in America) began to show signs of confusion
and doubt. Only then were they ready for a third great awakening.
By then Moody's career was over.

## Billy Sunday as a National Prophet

Moody died in 1899, just three years after Billy Sunday started his
career as a major urban revivalist. Since the height of Sunday's fame
fell in the years when the Third Great Awakening took place, his
role in it deserves attention. For all the criticism of him that arose
after 1920, with the ridicule heaped upon Fundamentalism and the
Scopes trial by H. L. Mencken and "the smart set" of the Jazz Age,
Sunday is too important a figure to be lightly dismissed by
historians. He was fully as important to his era as Billy Graham is to
the Fourth Great Awakening (and he filled virtually the same role).
He was the champion of "the old-time religion" and the old
evangelical beliefs and values of the nineteenth century. He spoke
more clearly than Moody for the old lights (because the cultural
reorientation offered by the new lights was much more clearly
defined after 1890). He used his revival platform to denounce
Darwinism, to support Prohibition, to deplore the new naturalism
and the concessions to it by "Liberal Protestants," whom he
scathingly called "Modernists." In addition, he appealed to the

fears of many evangelicals of the more rigid sort, who found horrific dangers of subversion (or destruction) of ''the American way of life'' in the immense influx of ''new'' immigrants (from eastern and southern Europe) after 1890.

Billy Sunday stands at the heart of the cultural confusion of the years 1890 to 1920. At the root of this confusion lay the fear that science (formerly considered the expositor of God's laws of creation) had become the enemy of God's revealed law. Evolution and the naturalistic, pragmatic philosophy of the ''new social science''— particularly the behaviorist and Freudian psychological theories— seemed to undermine the whole basis of Christian faith as the romantic evangelicals understood it (and as it had been incorporated into the Scottish Common Sense Philosophy so central to American ideology in the nineteenth century). When Billy Sunday attacked the new scientific theories, he was defending the old light of the Second Great Awakening; in so doing, he represented the fears and confusions of millions of pious Americans in the cities as well as in the rural ''Bible Belt.'' Oddly enough, the central issue once again was determinism versus freedom of the will.

Born in Ames, Iowa, in 1862, Sunday was a baseball player until he was converted in front of a saloon by an urban slum-mission worker in Chicago in 1886. He gave up baseball and became a lay preacher for the YMCA. His oratorical gifts led him into professional revivalism, first as the assistant of the Reverend Jay Wilbur Chapman and then, in 1896, as a revival preacher. Ordained in 1908, primarily on the basis of his successful soul-winning (he had no schooling beyond eighth grade), Sunday rose to immense fame and popularity between 1905 and 1920. His massive urban crusades utilized all aspects of professional public relations (John D. Rockefeller, Jr., asked Ivy Lee, one of the founders of modern advertising, to assist Sunday during the New York City revival of 1917). He developed an elaborate team of ''experts'' and utilized ''revival machinery'' far more sophisticated and expensive than Finney or Moody ever dreamed of. Sunday's success, measured in conversion statistics (those who ''hit the sawdust trail''), surpassed that of any previous revivalist. He had no difficulty in requiring the vast majority of the Protestant churches to close down their services while he was in a city and send their congregations to his specially built ''tabernacles'' (holding 15,000 to 20,000) to be ''revived.''

To those clergy who sided with the new lights (i.e., the Liberal Protestants) Sunday was often a source of embarrassment. They did not want to repudiate him entirely, for many of their church members devoutly believed Sunday was a messanger from God in the midst of a national crisis of faith. But by the same token many of their church members, especially among the young and better educated, found Sunday's theology and social theory reactionary, bigoted, or "old-fashioned." Moreover, his style was slangy and flamboyant; he leaped around his revival platform like an acrobat, shouting and telling funny stories and waving the American flag as he stood on top of the pulpit. His theology was blatantly Fundamentalist, and, at a time when many religious liberals were concerned about the exploitation of the working class by the "robber barons" of industry, Sunday's campaigns (like Moody's) were being financed by some of the leading industrial exploiters. Furthermore, although Sunday was paid only by "free-will offerings" collected at his meetings, the sums of these offerings were often staggering. He seemed to be making millions out of the revival business.

Sunday, however, was not unaware of the changing social and intellectual climate. He devoted a great deal of effort to what he considered the leading social issue of the day, Prohibition. It was a reform that many liberals in the churches and progressives in politics also considered important. He further capitalized on the furor over corruption in politics and argued that his revivals galvanized respectable citizens to join reform movements, overthrow "the bosses," and elect reform mayors and governors. Newspapers often headlined this aspect of his work: *"W. A. Sunday Ushers in Big Clean-Up. Fiery Evangelist in Opening Sermon Tells of Good He Will Accomplish in Ridding Ottumwa of Crime."* After his revival in Burlington, Iowa, the headline read, "BURLINGTON IS DRY: BILLY SUNDAY HAS MADE GRAVEYARD OF ONCE FAST TOWN." The muckraker, Ray Stannard Baker, in a book entitled *The Spiritual Unrest*, in 1910 noted that many church leaders in midwestern cities were enthusiastically supporting Sunday's revival campaigns because they felt he would help reform their city in one way or another. After his revival in Pittsburgh in 1914 a newspaper headline said, "What Years of Reform Work Could Not Do, He Has Wrought in a Few Short Weeks." In

Philadelphia in 1915, a front-page line drawing depicted him leading the fight "For Decent Citizenship."

Though most of his sermons dealt with repentance and salvation, Sunday sometimes tried to wrestle with the problems raised by naturalism and science over free will and the moral responsibility of the individual:

> I believe if society permits any considerable proportion of people to live in foul, unlighted rooms where from eight to ten people live, cook, eat, and sleep, working year in and year out from fourteen to fifteen hours every day, I believe if society allows deserving men to stagger along with less than a living wage, if society permits the shoulders of widowed motherhood to be forced down under industrial burdens and throws the unripe strength of children into the hopper of corporate greed to be ground into dividends, then society must share the responsibility if these people become criminals, thieves, cut-throats, drunkards, and prostitutes.

Yet later in the same sermon he complained, "A man is not supposed to be the victim of his environment. . . . I don't like to see you trying to put it all on environment and take away responsibility from the individual who's got a rotten heart." The phrase "is not supposed to be" lay at the heart of Sunday's popularity and of the confusions of the rural-born Evangelicals to whom he essentially appealed. They did not want to believe what the new-light philosophers and social scientists were telling them about how the universe operated.

Typical also of the social and ethical confusion that Sunday's old-light message represented was his attitude toward the new efforts of "social engineering" to uplift the poor in the slums. While he never attacked humanitarian reformers like Jane Addams or pragmatic philosophers like John Dewey, he could see no reason why the churches should urge people to devote more and more of their time to "social service" and less and less time to saving souls. "The trouble with the church, the YMCA, and the Young People's Societies," Sunday said, "is that they have taken up sociology and settlement work but are not winning souls to Christ." He thought "The Social Creed of the Churches," issued by the Federal Council of Churches in 1912 to persuade Protestant ministers to encourage social action, was a mistake. "We've had enough of this godless social service nonsense,'' he told a reporter in 1915. The way to end poverty and crime was to convert men to the principles of the Protestant ethic; then they would not need welfare aid (which, after all, only taxed the hard-working middle class to support the shiftless).

It is significant that Sunday at first opposed American involvement in the great war that broke out in Europe in 1914. He thought it was none of our business: ''A lot of fools over there are murdering each other to satisfy the damnable ambitions of a few mutts who sit on thrones.'' Like William Jennings Bryan (then secretary of state), Sunday feared foreign entanglements with decadent European nations, but after the sinking of the *Lusitania* and continued German submarine attacks on American shipping, he finally joined Theodore Roosevelt in urging military preparedness. And once Wilson had persuaded the country to enter the ''war to end war,'' Sunday became one of the most ardent patriots, helping to raise thousands of dollars in war bonds to aid the crusade against ''the Hun.'' After the war he joined other ''100% Americans'' in praise of the Palmer Raids and the shipping of ''dangerous aliens'' back to Europe. In some of his southern campaigns in the 1920s he allowed hooded members of the new Ku Klux Klan to march into his tabernacles to participate in the services. He warned his congregations throughout his career that ''hordes'' of ''foreigners'' were endangering American institutions, and he welcomed the immigration-restriction laws of the 1920s. The Russian Revolution aroused his concern as a ''Bolshevik'' plot to undermine American freedom; he supported General Leonard Wood for the Republican nomination in 1920, on the ground that strong military might was the defense of freedom. Above all he blamed ''the foreign vote'' for trying to block passage of Prohibition and, later, its enforcement: ''It will take a great Anglo-Saxon majority to overcome this foreign influence'' in America, he warned.

Sunday was obviously out of touch with the prevailing shift in American culture. But his views, during the generation from 1890 to 1920, represented those of millions of American churchgoers who shared his fears that the changes that were taking place would alter for the worse the nation's beliefs, values, and institutions. His popularity, however, steadily diminished. The social issues that confronted Americans in this Third Great Awakening were no longer answerable in the old terms he offered. Ironically, the greatest professional revivalist of his day was an old light in this awakening. Sunday was not a prophet offering new visions and guidelines for a people whose mazeways were blocked. The way out of the cultural distortion of these years was pointed by other men with new light from God or from the God of science.

## Theistic Evolution and Progressive Orthodoxy

By 1890 the world seemed to be closing in on many groups in America; freedom and equal opportunity seemed to be dying out. For many Evangelicals, postmillennial hope and optimism died with the coming of Darwinism, urbanism, and the fading role of the self-subsistent farmer. The census of 1890 announced the closing of the frontier. But farmers had felt the iron grip of industrial change much earlier. The rise of agribusiness meant a loss in status for the small independent farmer who could no longer make a go of it. After 1890 the small farmer ceased to be an honored symbol of the culture, "the backbone of the nation." The population of the nation now centered in the urban areas; industrial growth was idealized. The populist movement made the average farmer seem cranky, fanatical, naive. His lack of success in his vocation marked him as a failure. As early as the 1870s rebellious young writers began to disparage the small-town way of life, formerly hallowed for its moral integrity and closeness to nature. In the 1890s the farmer found himself portrayed as "a hick" and a "hayseed"—the laughingstock of city people, not even respected by his own children, who, at the first opportunity, left the farm to go to the city and grow up with the Industrial Revolution.

Yet when these hopeful young people went to the city to follow the socially structured avenues of aspiration, many found their way blocked by immense problems. The city seemed anything but the road to opportunity and success. Even its environment seemed dark and foreboding. Tenements and "skyscrapers" blotted out the sky; smoke cut out the light; crowded streets made it difficult to walk; criminals threatened safety. City politics seemed closed to the middle-class native American as ward bosses and immigrants took over the polls and stuffed the ballot boxes. Evidence of fraud appeared even in state and federal legislatures as "vested interests" manipulated the lawmakers for the ends of "big business." Big business and its millionaire captains, hitherto a source of national pride and emulation, were now revealed by muckraking journalists to have feet of clay. Through bribery, cut-throat competition, and monopolistic practices they were curtailing freedom of opportunity for the small businessman and were charging the consumer "all the traffic will bear."

Simultaneously, the rise of labor unions and violent unrest among the workers in industrial centers threatened freedom and good order from the bottom of society. After the Haymarket Riot of 1886, many Americans again became paranoid about foreign conspiracies led by anarchists, communists, socialists, or Roman Catholics with guns in the cellars of their churches. Caught between the rich plutocrats and the turbulent proletariat, the young, who hoped to make their way to the top, as well as the middle class, who feared they might be pushed downward, became fearful. A stratified social system with restricted mobility seemed about to replace the classless open society upon which the American dream rested.

The loss of confidence in divine support of old beliefs and values mounted from year to year. Just when the social order seemed to be closing in on all sides, God (as Americans knew and understood him) began to disappear. He could not be found in revival meetings, in churches, on college campuses, or in the winds of doctrine whistling through the cracks in the decaying edifice of Evangelicalism. Darwinism, which had seemed a remote and abstract theory when *The Origin of Species* appeared in 1859, now loomed up in every book, sermon, periodical, and tract to challenge the most fundamental tenets of the old faith. It challenged the Bible by denying its account of creation. It challenged the concept of an absolute moral law by its doctrine of survival of the fittest. It challenged the millennial goal by describing nature as amoral and purposeless. Species, like civilizations, rose and fell. Mankind was no more certain of survival than the dinosaur or the pterodactyl. By 1890 God was described, even in some evangelical pulpits, as the

First Cause, Prime Mover, or Vital Energy rather than as a Father, Shepherd, Guide, or Personal Savior. Herbert Spencer, the chief spokesman for science, reduced God to "the Great Unknown." Renowned biblical scholars challenged not only the infallibility of the Bible but the divine birth and historical existence of Jesus of Nazareth. Christmas, just coming into popularity as a symbol of domestic affluence and a ritual of the father-mother gods of hearth and home, was described by sociologists as pagan in origin and commercial in function. Santa Claus was a giver of material, not spiritual, gifts.

New ideas and a new vocabulary were being used to explain man's place in the universe. Man was redefined as the descendant of a "hairy quadruped" that, over eons of time, had evolved from an amoeba-like cell in "the primordial slime." While Christianity had learned to cope with the Copernican astronomy and the geological challenge to biblical chronology, the crisis that arose in orthodoxy after 1890 was unlike anything Western culture had ever faced. If the evolutionists were right, man seemed an alien in an empty universe, a mere animal, of doubtful future, struggling to adapt to a hostile, or at best neutral, natural environment. The sacred mythology was a fabrication of prescientific man. Human beings, like birds and beasts, were pawns driven by forces beyond their control. Or so the positivists, psychologists, and naturalists of the more skeptical sort maintained. The prophets of the Third Great Awakening had to undertake an enormous rescue operation to sustain the culture. They had to redefine and relocate God, provide means of access to him, and sacralize a new world view.

The new answers were formulated as theistic evolution, Progressive Orthodoxy, and Christian sociology. The prophets of the cultural reorientation included theologians like Washington Gladden and Harry Emerson Fosdick; philosophers like John Dewey and William James; scientists like Asa Gray and Alfred North Whitehead; political scientists like Herbert Croly and Walter Lippmann; humanitarians like Jane Addams and Lillian Wald; sociologists like Thorstein Veblen and Lester Frank Ward; economists like Richard T. Ely and John Bates Clark; college presidents like Woodrow Wilson and John Bascom. Morton White describes this revitalization process as "the revolt against formalism," an effort to open up the "block universe" of an older era. Its key concepts were relativism, pragmatism, historicism, cultural organicism, and creative intelligence. Robert Wiebe described it as "the search for order," in which the new values became efficiency, integration, systematization, regularization, and professionalization. Like all awakenings, it was an organizing or reorganizing process. The divided denominations reorganized into a federation of Christians; overlapping voluntary charity societies reorganized into city, state, and national "welfare" bureaucracies; schools reorganized into carefully graded classes and interlocking grammar, junior high, and high schools; college reorganized to give specialized professional degrees to supplement "classical" or liberal-arts degrees; competing regional businesses reorganized into national corporations to minimize competition; city governments reorganized, and the federal government abandoned its role as mere umpire of private enterprise and assumed a positive responsibility to regulate and control business and labor.

The middle-class urban, educated citizens who accepted this new outlook became the bureaucratic managers of technocracy. Progressive orthodoxy in religion and Progressive politics in society combined their new guidelines into a new vision of manifest destiny under new prophets. But many in the lower middle class and among the rural folk—the less well-off and less well-educated —rejected the new light and clung to the old. Fundamentalists, Pentecostals, and Holiness people organized "prophetic conferences" to discuss the imminent end of the world and the Second Coming; they held revivals where the power of the Holy Spirit gave them "baptisms by fire," inner perfection, faith to heal illness which "faith-less" doctors could not heal, and the ecstasy of communing "in tongues" with the Spirit of God. Where Fundamentalists and Pentecostals "bore witness" to their faith in oral testimonies of their conversion or other encounters with God, the new-light "Liberals" bore witness to their faith by social action. The former thought of religion in terms of subjective relationships to God, the latter in terms of social relations with God's children or "the brotherhood of man." This division in Christian orthodoxy weakened both sides, leaving a vacuum into which agnostic humanitarianism, professional altruism, and behaviorist social engineering slipped as a surrogate religion.

At first sight Darwin's theory of evolution had seemed an

insurmountable roadblock to Christian faith and postmillennial meliorism. Evangelical leaders, like Charles Hodge of Princeton Seminary, dismissed it in 1874 as "atheism." But when scientists of undeniable Christian faith, like the Harvard biologist Asa Gray, accepted its validity, more imaginative ministers and philosophers found ways to give it a theistic interpretation. Gray led the way by saying that Darwin, though an agnostic, had postulated "a first cause" in nature. Many simply tucked God into that niche and left him there, as "Prime Mover of the universe." But that was cold comfort to pietistic Americans. Gray therefore went further, by making the negative aspects of Darwin's work seem positive. "I do not understand him to deny purpose, intention, or the cooperation of God in nature," he wrote in an early review. And, what Darwin did not deny, broad-minded Christians were quick to assume.

The Reverend Henry Ward Beecher, son of the New England revivalist and a national spokesman for "Romantic Evangelicalism," declared in 1882 that he was "a Christian evolutionist." Beecher stressed the cooperative roles of religion and science. He called biologists, archeologists, and paleontologists "that noble body of investigators who are deciphering the hieroglyphics of God inscribed upon this temple of the earth." They were "to be honored and encouraged," not denounced as atheists. But when Beecher tried to be more explicit about how evolutionism was related to theism, he took refuge behind romantic rhetoric. Evolution was "the divine method," and "Science is but the deciphering of God's thought as revealed in the structure of this world." Beecher saw God as the warm Sun germinating the seeds of human development: "I hold that Divine Nature broods over the human family everywhere and tenderly stirs men to rise from a lower to a higher state of action."

Beecher's pantheistic or transcendentalist reconciliation of Darwinism and Christianity was supplanted by a more empirical reconciliation in Lyman Abbott's *The Theology of an Evolutionist* (1891). Abbott coined the phrase "evolution is God's way of doing things." But he frankly said, "Evolution is not to be identified with Darwinism." He meant that it was not to be identified with the amoral theory of "the struggle for existence" and "survival of the fittest." "Evolution is, broadly speaking, the doctrine of growth applied to life . . . the doctrine that all life proceeds by natural and normal processes from lower to higher stages." When Abbott spoke of God as "the Infinite and Eternal Energy from which all things proceed," he seemed to place God in nature. Yet he also insisted that evolution was "a vital force or forces operating from without." Trying to straddle this fence between an immanent and a dualistic view of the universe, Abbott had to reject the older imagery of Evangelicalism: "The theistic evolutionist does not believe in an embodied King sitting on a great white throne." That view made him "remote, inaccessible, a God afar off." The modern theologian, he said, "believes that God is truly in the universe and manifests himself through all the multifarious forces of nature; that what we call the laws of nature are the laws of God's own being." Laws of nature are, of course, subject to proof and measurement, and Abbott was therefore hard put to deny that scientists are theologians of a sort. When they pointed out contradictions between Scripture and scientific laws, they had to be taken seriously. The wise minister, Abbott concluded, will say to the scientist on controversial biblical questions, "Since you have studied this subject and this is your verdict, I accept it, and I will see what light it throws upon the problems of moral life." New light thus came to religion from science in this awakening, whereas in previous awakenings the reverse had been true.

Scientific theology was carried even further by secular writers like John Fiske and John Bascom. In *Through Nature to God* (1899), Fiske coined yet other names for God: "Absolute Power" and "Omnipresent Power." Fiske had no objection to equating these with God as long as it was clear that this was not the personal God of Evangelicalism. He denied Spencer's view that God is "unknowable," because Omnipresent Power is "knowable in the order of its phenomenal manifestations, knowable in a symbolic way as the Power which is disclosed in every throb of the mighty rhythmic life of the universe." In learning to act in harmony with this rhythmic power—through psychology, sociology, political economy—God is "knowable as the eternal Source of moral law which is implicated with each action of our lives and in obedience to which lies our only guaranty of the happiness which is incorruptible."

#### Chapter 5

Under closer analysis, this harmony with Omnipresent Power seems
to boil down to adjustment to the environment, adjustment to the
world as it is.

For all its optimism about the inevitability of progress through
science, there was a fundamentally conservative cultural shift in the
new light of this awakening. The old perfectionism and free will of
Romantic Evangelicalism portrayed man as unconditioned by
nature, unbound by contingencies of heredity and environment,
and capable of miraculous power over all obstacles in personal or
social reformation. But the new light of this Third Awakening
described God's power as locked into nature's laws. Even with
God's help men could not leap over nature or culture to challenge
the "realities" of life as it is. Religion under Liberal Protestantism
or Modernism was bereft of its miraculous and transcendent
quality. Only the Pentecostals and Holiness people held to this
faith, and for them it was purely personal; it saved them from a real
world that was doomed by its materialism. In 1917, when John
Dewey, one of the chief spokesmen for the new philosophy,
justified America's entry into World War I, Randolph Bourne
voiced a criticism of it that many Pentecostals might have echoed;
in this philosophy, Bourne said, "You never transcend anything.
You grow, but your spirit never jumps out of your skin to go on
wild adventures."

John Bascom, minister and president of the University of
Wisconsin, provided the most sophisticated statement of the new
relationship between religion and science in *Evolution and Religion,
or Faith as a Part of a Complete System* (1897). Christianity as he
saw it was a spiritual process of adjustment to environment;
salvation was the slow, evolutionary progress of the race in conformity with the laws of nature:

> Christ bids us lose our lives, the immediate joy and comfort of them, in
> a universal struggle for the true conditions of life, and to win back a
> masterful life, carrying its own conquering impulses into our hourly
> experience. We are to plant, cultivate, and ripen our virtues in the sterile
> soil and under the harsh climate which enclose it, till there comes to be
> a spiritual fertility begotten of the corrected process of culture itself.
> We conquer by submission, but we conquer.

In Bascom's reinterpretation of the Protestant ethic and the doctrine of the free and morally responsible individual, men grow spiritually by asserting self-control over their crude, undeveloped, animal natures. Social science tells us what God's moral laws are so that we can discipline ourselves by submitting to them. "Growth is a spiritual direction," not an aimless conflict.

At the same time that theistic evolutionists were harmonizing science and religion, progressive theologians were reconciling revealed truth with "the higher criticism" of the Bible. The older (or lower) form of biblical criticism was the study of church doctrine and biblical texts; the new critical method utilized history, comparative linguistics, anthropology, and archeology to test the accuracy and consistency of Scripture by objective, nonbiblical evidence. Those willing to accept this form of critical analysis came to be called Liberal Protestants (or Modernists) as opposed to the Fundamentalists, who held to the literal inerrancy of Scripture. Kenneth Cauthen defines Liberal Protestantism as "the attempt of men who were convinced of the truth of historic Christianity to adjust this ancient faith to the demands of the modern era." Bernard Reardon defines the Liberals as those influenced by the neo-Kantian interpretation of Christianity led by Friedrich Schleiermacher and Albrecht Ritschl in Germany between 1830 and 1890. Many Liberal Protestants went to Germany to study theology under these men and their disciples. Most of the Liberals were "Christocentric," retaining the significance of an emotional and personal relationship between the believer and God, though not through the stereotyped conversion experience of revival meetings. Some placed a more mystical emphasis on it (following Schleiermacher), while others stressed its ethical importance (following Ritschl). Theologically, however, the Liberal came perilously close to Pelagianism, the belief that man, through his own efforts and good works, can achieve his own salvation. They justified their faith not in terms of the miraculous birth and resurrection of Jesus but by the role of Jesus in human history. As Reardon puts it, they believed that "the historical Jesus had been for man the source of a new life of spiritual communion with God." Jesus was "the perfect realization of the human ideal," and, through faith in that,

Christians developed a profound concern to improve the human condition, in imitation of Jesus, and to fulfill his purpose.

The new light of Liberal Protestantism turned the attention of the converted Christian not toward saving souls or perfecting his own inner holiness but toward efforts to raise the whole human race. The true Christian, as they understood it, attains fulfillment in the service of others. Ritschl taught that "moral goodness can be achieved only in society; the godly life is a social life, in which the individual fulfills his responsibilities to his fellow men. . . . Any attempt to separate faith in God from public spirit and recognition of one's duty to community is, from the Christian's standpoint, a profound error." Hence, Liberal Christianity's role lay "in promoting *this*-worldly activity and enabling man to exercise his God-given dominion" over nature and culture. An admirer of Kant's system of ethical imperatives, Ritschl inspired Liberals to attach the same importance to social morality as to personal morality. The central feature of Christ's message, Ritschl said, is the duty of man to bring about the Kingdom of God on earth in social action: "In Christianity the religious motive of ethical action lies here, that the Kingdom of God, which it is our task to realize, also represents the highest good which God destines for us as our supramundane goal."

In their studies of Liberal Protestantism Reardon and Cauthen note that its advocates faced a complex task. First, they tried to sustain the Christian belief that man has freedom and free will (i.e., that he is not a product of naturalistic determinism); second, they tried to direct Christian idealism toward social reform without implying that salvation lies in good works and without becoming too pragmatic or relativistic in their accommodation of Christian strategy to cultural values and ends. They tried to tell Christians, in Ritschl's words, that free will lies in the ability (through faith in Christ) to rise above cultural values: "Religion springs up as faith in super-human spiritual powers by whose help the power which man possesses of himself is in some way supplemented and elevated into a unity of its own kind which is a match for the pressures of the natural world." But in reality the ability of man to have dominion over nature (and his own fate) depended so heavily on his knowledge of God's scientific laws that Liberal Protestants became the captives of science—particularly in the areas of psychology, sociology, and economics.

At the turn of the century, churchgoing Americans of any sophistication were unable to accept the old light of Evangelicalism (fast hardening into Fundamentalist dogma) and consequently found in Liberal Protestantism a more helpful understanding of God's covenant with them and the path to the millennium. By putting Christians to work in social service, the Liberals also sustained the belief in the free and morally responsible individual. And by urging the achievement of the Kingdom of God on earth they transformed the perfectionist impulse into social engineering. How close this new theology came at times to pragmatism can be seen in its claim that "the verification of faith," as Reardon puts it in *Liberal Protestantism* (1968), "is experience, not abstract logic," and that "the nature and function of religion are inherently pragmatic." Christian and secular reformers, ministers and social scientists, could and did work harmoniously together in this cultural transformation, adjusting idealism to the practical contingencies of prevailing conditions; reform, like politics, was the art of the possible. If the Christians thereby compromised their "transcendence," the naturalistic scientists also compromised their intrinsic determinism. The former were more practical than they should have been, the latter more idealistic.

Kenneth Cauthen points out, in *The Impact of American Religious Liberalism* (1962), that while some Liberals remained "metaphysical" in their theology and others devoted themselves almost exclusively to social ethics, a third group (for whom he uses the term "Modernists") emerged after 1915 with a more empirical, less evangelical, leaning than the great majority of Liberals. For our purpose, since this is not a study of theology per se, the important distinction lies between those Liberals (Cauthen calls them "evangelical Liberals") who continued to stress the moral and personal aspects of good works and those who advocated more far-reaching social and institutional restructuring. It is clear, for example, that many Liberals held such a personal view of ethics that they had little quarrel with the old laissez-faire theory of progress. But the more prophetic Liberals spoke of ethics in terms of social justice, which required severe limitations on free enterprise through government regulation of the economy. This latter group, the social and political activists, have generally been known as the Social Gospelers, and it was they who had most in common with the secular humanitarians of the Progressive political movement.

The efforts of Liberal Protestants to utilize "the historical Jesus" as a basis for Christian social service were often less shocking to Fundamentalists than their efforts to reconcile historical or scientific evidence with biblical literalism. For without a literally inerrant Scripture, nothing seemed fixed; the world would be awash in relativism. Yet the Liberals pressed on. Durant Drake was one of the most blunt spokesmen for the view that "higher criticism" of the Bible had conclusively disproved its infallibility.

> It has been definitely proved that the traditional ascriptions of the authorship of many of the Bible books are mistaken. . . . Many inconsistencies exist [in Scripture] between different traditions that have been incorporated . . . ; [and] not merely inconsistent . . . but obviously untrue are many of the Biblical statements. . . . The whole account of creation . . . reflects a very primitive conception of nature . . . ; not a few statements in the historical books have been proved untrue by extant monuments and the records of surrounding nations; it is plain to the historical student that the Jewish chronicles are biased and to a considerable extent untrustworthy. It is clear that the evangelists [Matthew, Mark, Luke, John] were in many points mistaken in their views of the events of Jesus' life.

To many ordinary churchgoers these criticisms of the Bible were frightening and blasphemous. Billy Sunday roundly denounced such views, and, when more and more seminary-trained pastors adopted them, the major denominations lost thousands of members to the Fundamentalists.

For those willing to hear them out, however, the Modernists went on to say that biblical errors did not undermine biblical truth. "These bits of dross amid the gold do not destroy the worth of the Bible." Twentieth-century men must be willing to accept the fact that the Bible was written by men of a primitive era of human development. It "is a very human book." The writers of the Bible, though perhaps inspired by God, were creatures of their own limited time and culture, totally unacquainted with our recent discoveries in astronomy, geology, biology. Hence God could not adequately express his most complex truths to such untutored

minds. Only an obscurantist would insist on literal interpretations
of the myths, symbols, and metaphors through which God's
ancient scribes tried to convey his laws and moral principles.
Concerning the miracles that the superstitious people of Jesus'
time wrote down as fact, "The Modernist has come to the clear
realization," wrote one of them, "that these are not in any sense
religious but purely scientific questions, and should be set aside for
scientific investigators to pass upon." Harry Emerson Fosdick, the
most popular of the Modernists, said of the Virgin Birth that the
writers of the Gospel "phrased it in terms of a biological miracle
that our modern minds cannot accept." However, this did not
invalidate the moral and spiritual truths of Jesus' preaching. To
many better-educated churchgoers this seemed a viable compromise.

When Liberals came to apply the moral laws of Jesus to the
problems of the day, they divided among themselves. The more
conservative, though willing to abandon the literal infallibility of
the Bible and to accept evolution, were not willing to abandon the
individualistic aspects of the Protestant ethic. They accepted the
fact that man was evolving toward higher spiritual goals, but they
believed that this process required, essentially, self-discipline and
self-control. The problems of urban poverty, political corruption,
and labor agitation they saw in much the same terms as Billy
Sunday and the old lights had seen them: those at the bottom of
the social ladder lacked the will power to practice delayed gratifica-
tion; they lapsed into their animal nature; they were lazy. Such
people were sinners against Christian evolution, backsliders from
progress, misfits or degenerates. Conversely, those who were successful had developed the traits of character that enabled them to
adapt to the complexities of modern industrial society. Of course,
the very rich, the millionaires or robber barons, were themselves
sinners because they had probably broken the ethical rules of
society and the Bible. They were inhuman in their predatory,
cutthroat behavior toward their fellow man; they broke the Golden
Rule and broke the law. Success achieved by these sinful and
inhumane means was not to be admired or emulated. Better to
have a modest income and live in a modest suburban home than to
risk jail, exposure, or loss of spiritual growth.

Liberal Protestants of this ethical persuasion were happy to see robber barons prosecuted for corruption, but they did not believe that there was anything basically wrong with the system of free-enterprise capitalism. As successful members of the middle class, they could argue that the system worked. The ministers of their congregations tended to sanctify the economic laws of Adam Smith, Malthus, and Ricardo as scientific and not to be tampered with. As Christians they believed in charity toward "the deserving poor," but they saw no need to encourage labor unions or the government to regulate and control the nation's economy or to interfere with the ways in which honest businessmen managed their workforce. Reform as they understood it meant voting for honest men.

## Social Gospelers, Reform Darwinists, and Progressives

The more progressive, or Social Gospel, wing of Liberal Protestantism took a very different view of the moral laws of Scripture and the teachings of the historical Jesus. In their view, Jesus taught a social ethic, not an individualistic one. If America was to revitalize its culture, it would have to severely modify the Protestant ethic and its political corollary, laissez-faire. The starting point of the Social Gospel was its claim that Jesus taught a doctrine of community and fraternity, "the Fatherhood of God, the brotherhood of man, the coming of the Kingdom." Richard Hofstadter has identified this group as "Reform Darwinists." Inspired in part by the sociologist Lester Frank Ward and in part by the work of German economists and social scientists, these reformers fell into two groups: those who were avowedly Christians and those who were avowedly humanists (agnostics, atheists, behaviorists, positivists, naturalists). The leading figure in the Christ-centered group was the economist Richard T. Ely; the leader of the humanists was John Dewey (educator, psychologist, philosopher).

The leading Social Gospel ministers (Washington Gladden, George Herron, Walter Rauschenbusch) had no qualms about working with both groups. Some were even willing to support the democratic socialism of Eugene V. Debs, for though Debs claimed to get his inspiration from Marx and Engels, he always praised the social teachings of Jesus. The Third Great Awakening as a revitalization movement includes all of these disparate groups, for each in its own way hoped to use religion and science together to "uplift the masses" rather than to leave them to the mercy of laissez-faire individualism.

Lester Ward, a self-trained scientist who spent most of his early career in government but ended it as the first professor of sociology at Brown University (from 1906 to 1913) made four major contributions to the reorientation of American beliefs and values in the Third Awakening: he provided empirical, scientific evidence to refute Herbert Spencer's view that evolution worked best by laissez-faire. Second, pointing out that the human brain is also a product of evolution, Ward argued that "the psychic factor in civilization" enables man to control, as well as adapt to, his environment. Third, he insisted that Darwin found "the social instinct" in biological determinism more important than the individualistic and hence that "fraternalism" is the basis for political order and progress, not competition. Finally, he declared that education is the key to man's mastery of his environment and therefore that the highly trained social scientist must assume an active role in the government to assist elected officials in setting the wisest policies for national growth, prosperity, and progress.

In the early stages of human evolution, Ward said, when the caveman was but little removed from the brute, he operated on the simple principles that animals follow in their daily routine. He hunted, mated, slept, and fought as pleasure or pain dictated. But because of his innate "social instinct," which led him to join with his fellows for protection, friendship, and sustenance, man gradually developed a more complex brain structure, which became the basis of his learning to cope with nature:

> With man in a social state, however primitive, foresight was exercised, which is itself a form of intuitive faculty [or psychic factor], and the habit of making provision for the future arose. . . . Both the passion [for acquisition] and the means of satisfying it were conditions of the development of society itself, and, rightly viewed, they have also been the leading factors in civilization.

Man ceased to rely on brute force and low cunning and began to use his brains, his memory, his capacity for "more refined and subtle manifestations of the same psychic principle." He evolved social

institutions and "codes of conduct requisite to life in collectivity."
Applying Darwin's fundamental principle of natural selection,
Ward concluded that man gradually found that his "rude animal
methods were intolerable and, by natural selection, . . . society
discarded them." That is, men organized in groups, chose as their
leaders those who were more intelligent, refined, and thoughtful,
and came to regard as the least fit those rough, aggressive, and
undisciplined types who cared only to satisfy their own needs.
Employing the methods of cultural historicism in this way, Ward
accepted the views of the new science of anthropology, which traced
the evolution of religion from primitive superstition to magic,
polytheism, monotheism, and finally science. As a scientist, Ward
was a militant atheist, considering all religious concepts hangovers
from man's less civilized period of social organization and primitive
comprehension of nature.

Logically, when man developed foresight, he learned to plan for
the future; planning in and for groups led to cooperation. "The
psychic element" thus came to supplant "nature by art," to move
from laissez-faire to social control:

> If we call biological processes natural, we must call social processes
> artificial. The fundamental principle of biology is natural selection, that
> of sociology [the science of society] is artificial selection. The survival of
> the fittest is simply the survival of the strong, which implies, and would
> better be called, the destruction of the weak. If nature progresses
> through the destruction of the weak, man progresses through the protec-
> tion of the weak. . . . The terms are all reversed.

This was the key to humanitarian reform in the Progressive and
New Deal eras, and it led to a rejection of laissez-faire politics. It
also led to an intense interest in education (which Ward called "the
Great Panacea") as a means of training the social-science experts
who would be needed to direct a planned society. The trouble with
an unplanned society was not simply that it regressed to oppression
of the weak by the strong; it also led to "inefficiency"—perhaps
the most negative value in the whole Progressive ethic. Monopolistic capitalism had developed out of laissez-faire in government;
while useful in its day, it was now hypertrophied. Giant trusts and
cartels produced artificial shortages and increased costs to benefit
the few at the expense of the many. Under Ward's program.

experts in sociology would become "efficiency experts" able to regulate supply and demand, maximize production, decrease costs, and provide more goods and a higher standard of living for everyone.

Well aware that he would be accused of socialism as soon as he discussed planning and of paternalism when he discussed efficiency experts, Ward spelled out a political theory called "Sociocracy," which, he claimed, was neither. "Modern society is suffering from the very opposite of paternalism—from under-government, from the failure of government to keep pace with the change which civilization has wrought." Without planning, society suffered from an excess of brute cunning and selfishness, and the dysfunctional "acquisitive faculty" dominated social ethics. "The true function of government is not to better but to liberate the forces of society . . . ; unbridled competition destroys itself. The only competition which endures is that which goes under judicious regulation." Here was the keynote of Progressive political legislation: do not use government paternalistically to lift society, but regulate the evils of monopolistic self-aggrandizement and thereby "liberate" the natural energies and imagination of those whose intelligence (psychic factor) will innovate new and more productive means for meeting society's needs. Excessive individualism "creates artificial inequalities"; socialism (excessive planning or control) "creates artificial equalities." But Sociocracy "recognizes natural inequalities and aims to abolish artificial inequalities."

The workingman need not resort to radical schemes (anarchy, communism) to improve his lot, Ward said. "The working people should realize that the government is their own and will be just what they make it." The ballot box would suffice for reform if men would throw off all slavish party allegiance and vote for policies provided by the scientific experts. Sociocracy, moreover, was an open society—open to the talent, brains, skill, and imagination that the public schools would develop in the citizenry: "Intelligence, hitherto a [natural] growth, is destined to become a manufacture." It was from this point that John Dewey took off with his concept of "progressive education." The Progressive reformers started with efforts to return the government to the people, to take it away from the bosses and vested interests by the initiative, referendum, recall, secret ballot, and direct election of senators. They ended by suggesting a partnership of government and business under the wise regulation of social scientists—social planners and policy-makers. Their ultimate aim was to free the system from constrictions produced by misguided laissez-faire.

There was nothing socially or politically radical in Ward's theory. It posed no threat to private property or capitalist enterprise. It was liberal because it liberated individual initiative from unplanned monopoly; it moved forward cautiously, a step at a time, pragmatically. "This ideal solution [Sociocracy] will be realized [only] through a long series of slight advances which constitutes true social progress." Nevertheless, Ward sounded the postmillennial note so dear to liberal hearts: "Higher and higher types of statesmanship will follow the advancing intelligence of mankind, until one by one the difficult social problems will be solved."

The link between Ward's theory and Progressive reform was John Dewey. Ward was such a militant atheist, wrote in such a crabbed style, and was generally so cantankerous that he founded no school and, when he died in 1913, left no followers. But Dewey became the leading liberal intellectual of the first half of the twentieth century. Born before the Civil War in Vermont, raised in an Evangelical rural family, and at first, as a student, enamored of Hegelian idealism, Dewey always managed to convey a warm humanitarianism in his writings and personal relationships. He not only had a large following of friends and students in the colleges where he taught but until his death in 1952 was constantly active in public affairs, becoming an active socialist in the 1930s. His humanistic (or post-Christian) pietism provided the basic world view for many secular reformers in the first half of the twentieth century who had grown up as Evangelicals but had drifted away from the church after 1890. Progressive humanists like Jane Addams, Frederic C. Howe, and Lincoln Steffens were almost indistinguishable in their political and social philosophies from the Social Gospelers and Christian sociologists with whom they often worked closely. To them Dewey was the prophet who provided the most convincing answers to the questions raised by the cultural crisis at the turn of the century.

The highest value in Dewey's pragmatic philosophy was "the

creative intelligence'' of man, a term that resembled Ward's
''psychic factor'' and, like it, indicated the importance of continued growth. ''The process and method of constructing *goods* is
the only thing that can be called *the* good,'' Dewey said. It was
creative intelligence that allowed man to think through possibilities, raise options, make plans, and experiment with constructing
''goods.'' ''The process of growth which produces whole clusters of
values, personal and social, from phase to phase, and which at the
same time creates the condition for further growth, is the only thing
that can be called the end of growth.'' Though he lost whatever
Christian faith he had had as a youth and never talked of a
millennium, Dewey wrote, worked, and taught as though mankind
could improve or advance intelligence and planning to the point
where harmonious cooperation among men and pragmatic solu-
tions to problems in a peaceful, democratic manner would in effect
approach the millennial ideal. Like the religious reformers, Dewey
believed that ''We must work on the environment, not merely on
the heart of men.''

The phrase, ''the heart of men,'' was typical of Dewey's
willingness to speak in the accents of Liberal Protestantism. Furthermore, he seems to have resented, as many lapsed Protestants
did, those who spoke of humanists and nonchurchgoers as non-
religious. ''It is widely supposed,'' he wrote, ''that a person who
does not accept any religion is thereby shown to be a non-religious
person.'' This misconception had arisen only because creeds and
churches ''now prevented, because of their weight of historic
encumbrances, the religious quality of experience from coming to
consciousness and finding the expression that is appropriate to
present conditions.'' It was ''the religious quality of experience''
(he later called it ''the common faith'') that sustained him and
most post-Christian pietists in their humanitarian efforts for
reform. Though he stated it with his usual inversion, he appeared
to find the democratic process moral for this reason: ''Democracy
has many meanings, but if it has a moral meaning, it is found in
resolving that the supreme test of all political institutions and
industrial arrangements shall be the contribution they make to the
all around growth of every member of society.'' Or, more directly,
''Any activity pursued in behalf of an ideal and against obstacles

and in spite of threats of personal loss because of conviction of its general and enduring value is religious in quality." Dewey and his followers felt a religious quality in committing themselves on faith to building a better world. "It is this *active* relation between ideal and actual to which I would give the name 'God,'" Dewey concluded in 1934.

The Christian reformers who still attended church and who claimed the social teachings of Jesus as the inspiration for their reformism differed little in practical values from the secular Progressive humanists. As one Modernist wrote in 1919, "The mind of today is intensely practical, if not pragmatic. It insists that for it, at least, a valid Christianity is to be known not by its roots but by its fruits." However, Christian faith placed important limits on pragmatism, and belief in the coming Kingdom of God provided a transcendent hope that humanists lacked. The leading figure among the avowedly Christian social scientists of the day were Richard T. Ely, John Bates Clark, Graham Taylor, E. A. Ross, Simon N. Patten, Henry Carter Adams, and Edmund James. Most of them got their training in German graduate schools and returned to the United States to teach in the new graduate programs in the larger American universities. In an era when scientists became the chief messengers of God because of their superior and direct insight into his "Omnipresent Power" and "divine method," these economists, sociologists, and political scientists inspired the rising generation with the hope of combining Christian faith and professional expertise in the advancement of the millennium. They built their careers around efforts to redress the balance between individualism and fraternalism, self-interest and community, free will and determinism—the key issues of the ideological crisis of 1890–1920. Rebelling against the closed intellectual systems of Evangelicalism, the Scottish Philosophy, and Positivism, they found a new social perspective in the work of German social scientists who, at the end of the century, worked with and for the government to overcome the problems of urban industrialism. And from their German professors they learned that there was nothing absolute, eternal, or universal about the so-called economic laws elaborated by Adam Smith, Malthus, and Ricardo. Economic and political systems were not designed by God in heaven but were

developed by men on earth to meet the needs of their particular
environment, technological skills, resources, markets, and commercial facilities and the political and scientific sophistication of
their people. Through empirical studies and inductive analysis the
Germans were learning how to regulate, manage, and systematize
their own economic order for both greater efficiency and greater
social justice.

In 1885 Richard T. Ely and a group of young economists and
Social Gospelers formed the American Economic Association to
spread their new vision for revitalizing the nation. Most of them
were pietistic Protestants who believed that the church as well as the
state has a role to play in creating a better social order. Christian
humanitarianism inspired these economists and sociologists as
much as the new social science and "the new economics." Their
efforts contained elements of a religious crusade. Like itinerant
evangelists, these new economists and Social Gospelers traveled
back and forth across the nation, speaking in churches and
auditoriums, organizing conferences, publishing tracts and peri-
odicals, and spreading by every available means the new gospel of
reform. Their goal was the spiritual rebirth of society, not of
individual souls.

Richard T. Ely's draft for the statement of purpose of the A.E.A.
in 1885 read: "We regard the state as an educational and ethical
agency whose positive aid is an indispensable condition of human
progress. While we recognize the necessity of individual initiative
in industrial life, we hold that the doctrine of laissez-faire is unsafe
in politics and unsound in morals and that it suggests an inadequate explanation of the relations between the state and its
citizens." An adequate explanation of these relations would describe the state as the agent of the people acting to regulate the
total economic order for the common good, yet leaving the
enterprising individual free enough to display economic initiative.
One of the planks of the A.E.A. program stated, "We hold that
the conflict of labor and capital has brought into prominence a vast
number of social problems whose solution requires the united
efforts, each in its own sphere, of the church, the state, and of
science." Another plank spelled out the evolutionary nature of
their approach: "We believe that political economy is still in an

early stage of development . . . and we look not so much to speculation as to historical and statistical study of actual conditions of economic life for the satisfactory accomplishment of that study.''

In the awakening that followed, this organization provided much of the leadership. Members of the A.E.A. worked closely with Theodore Roosevelt for the ''Square Deal,'' for the ''New Nationalism,'' and for Woodrow Wilson's ''New Freedom.'' Roosevelt praised Ely's books, and Wilson studied under him as a graduate student at Johns Hopkins. Young lawyers joined the association and brought its new statistical methodology into their briefs. The new theory of law that Louis Brandeis, Oliver Wendell Holmes, and Roscoe Pound championed as ''sociological jurisprudence'' owed much to the ideas and methods of this new economics. When Holmes said in the *Lochner* case that ''the Fourteenth Amendment does not enact Mr. Herbert Spencer's *Social Statics*,'' he was attempting to persuade the Supreme Court to loosen up its old-light assumption that the higher laws of economics were made in heaven and embedded in the Constitution. It could be argued that the Third Great Awakening was not completed until the majority of the Court, late in the 1930s, accepted Holmes's position and proceeded to endorse the kinds of New Deal legislation that previous decisions had declared unconstitutional.

Ely, like his colleagues in the A.E.A., took care to distinguish his views from those of socialists, though some historians have described him as a ''Christian socialist.'' ''I condemn alike,'' he said, ''that individualism which would allow the state no room for industrial action and that socialism which would absorb in the state the functions of the individual.'' Ely called his middle way ''fraternalism,'' which was the new version of the old covenant ideal. He helped to found the American Institute of Christian Sociology and, as an Episcopal layman, worked closely with its various Social Gospel organizations. The ethical theory of Christian sociology held that men act as frequently from altruistic motives as selfish ones—love of family, love of country, love of honor, love of humanity—and that true virtue is self-sacrifice in social service to God and man. Contemporary journals described the religious spirit of the era as ''a social Awakening.''

''Private self-interest,'' said Ely's friend Henry Carter Adams, "is too powerful or too ignorant to promote the common good without compulsion." Hence, regulatory laws and commissions were not restraints on economic freedom but compulsions to social altruism. Labor unions were not restrictions upon "freedom of contract" for the individual workers but fraternal organizations to compel men to see that the good of all requires the solidarity of all. At a time when the Supreme Court was declaring unions to be "conspiracies in restraint of trade," Ely was arguing that they were "the natural and inevitable outcome of existing industrial conditions" and deserved full legal rights to bargain collectively with employers' associations. "The labor movement in its broadest terms is the effort of men to live the life of men," to reject the notion that labor is a mere commodity in the industrial process. The union movement "is a force pushing toward the attainment of the purpose of humanity . . . namely, the full and harmonious development in each individual of all human faculties." The Christian economist or sociologist must therefore throw his weight in with the Social Gospel minister to alleviate the oppression of the workers; they must seek workmen's-compensation laws, better sanitary conditions in the factories, abolition of child labor, the eight-hour day, boards of arbitration, and help for women in industry. Outside the industrial area they must work for parks and playgrounds, forest conservation, slum renovation, organized poor relief, public health clinics, mutual savings banks, old-age insurance, health insurance, public employment offices, public works programs. This was the institutional restructuring for which these new lights (Christian and secular) preached, wrote, and lobbied. "Government," as Ely put it, "should interfere in all instances where its interference will tell for better health, better education, better morals [including Prohibition], greater comfort of the community."

## The Social Gospel Movement

The Social Gospel movement got its name because it rejected individual salvation as the beginning and end of Christ's message and because it argued that men must come to God not as discrete, atomistic individuals, pure only in and of themselves, but as parts of the brotherhood of man, in which each is spiritually and ethically united to his neighbor. Numerically the Social Gospel ministers were few at the turn of the century. According to one estimate, no more than 662 of the more than 100,000 ministers in the nation in 1892 were "deeply interested in the labor problem" (considered the key issue by the movement). But they grew in numbers during the course of the awakening, and, after the Great Depression began in 1929, many conservative Liberal Protestants were ready to abandon laissez-faire and accept the need for state interference in economic affairs. While statistics indicate that the bulk of the Protestant clergy voted against Franklin Roosevelt, nevertheless, in 1934, 95 percent of 21,000 ministers responding to a questionnaire said that they favored "a cooperative commonwealth" over a capitalist system, and 51 percent favored a "drastically reformed capitalism." This was obviously a great shift in clerical opinion from its almost unanimous support of laissez-faire in the years 1865–90.

The foremost leader of the Social Gospel movement was a Baptist, Walter Rauschenbusch. He summed it up by saying that the problems facing America "have their evils in the wrongful abandonment or the perversion of the great aim of Christ," the Kingdom of God. The Social Gospelers sought to restore that aim to the center of Christian thought and action. "As the idea of the Kingdom is the key to the teachings and work of Christ," Rauschenbusch said, "so its abandonment or misconstruction is the key to the false or one-sided conceptions of Christianity." The source of evil lay in the intense preoccupation of Protestant evangelicalism with soul-winning and revivalism:

> Because the Kingdom has been dropped as the primary and complete aim of Christianity and personal salvation has been substituted for it, therefore men seek to save their own souls and . . . the individualistic conception of personal salvation has pushed out of sight the collective idea of a Kingdom of God on earth, and Christian men . . . are comparatively indifferent to the spread of the spirit of Christ in the political, industrial, social, scientific and artistic life of humanity.

Evangelicals had of course claimed to be advancing the Kingdom by saving souls, but in effect "The Kingdom of God has been understood as a state to be realized in the future rather than . . . here and now."

Politically Rauschenbusch was more radical than most Social Gospelers. The conservative program for the Kingdom did not favor government action beyond "busting" monopolistic trusts and mediating labor disputes. They mixed concern for social injustice with attacks on intemperance, gambling, prostitution, crime, and shiftlessness. The poor had their responsibilities as well as the rich. Occasionally these conservatives would join a crusade against civic corruption (like the Reverend Charles H. Parkhurst's effort to clean up New York City in 1892) or to elect honest Christian men to office (like "Golden Rule" Jones in Toledo and Tom Johnson in Cleveland). Some of them urged their churches to start settlement work in the slums, mixing soul-winning with the distribution of food and clothing or street preaching with efforts to find jobs for the unemployed. They were most sympathetic to reforms that would improve the general quality of life (from which the middle class would benefit as much as the poor): providing more parks and playgrounds, organizing orphanages and health clinics, improving police protection and juvenile courts. Lowering taxes and increasing administrative efficiency were important to this group, especially efficiency in the dispensing of charity. There was more interest in putting church members into useful social-service activities than in lobbying for major legislative reforms.

The more liberal Social Gospelers took a much greater interest in social legislation. Washington Gladden, the widely read author of a dozen Social Gospel books and pastor of a Congregational church in Columbus, Ohio, spelled out the importance of redressing the balance between individual salvation and social reform in 1909:

> The gospel has been very imperfectly heard by anyone to whom it has brought no other tidings than that of personal salvation. For in truth the individual is saved only when he is put into right relations to the community in which he lives, and the establishment of these right relations among men is the very work that Christ came to do. The individual gospel and the social gospel are therefore vitally related, inseparably bound together, and salvation can no more come to the man apart from the community than life can come to the branch when it is separated from the vine. And the social gospel can be adequately presented only in the terms of the common life.

For that reason, when Billy Sunday came to Columbus in 1912 to conduct one of his mass campaigns for personal salvation, Gladden refused to lend his support. The old-time religion was an un-balanced gospel.

Gladden generally spoke for those who took a middle road between the radical and conservative Social Gospel positions. This group was more eager to obtain government intervention to reform the worst abuses of urban industrialism and laissez-faire. They urged legislative action to provide better hours and wages and were willing to have public tax money spent for social welfare. Some of them supported profit-sharing, cooperative manufacturing and merchandising, workmen's compensation, and unemployment and health insurance. Most important, they were more ready than the conservatives to champion the cause of labor unions (if they were not socialistic or anarchistic). On the whole, however, they felt that compulsory arbitration was superior to strikes and boycotts in obtaining social justice. Many favored women's suffrage on the grounds that women citizens would be sympathetic to welfare legislation, Prohibition, and improving the tone of community life. Probably the best-known Social Gospelers were among these moderates. In addition to Gladden, they included Bishop Henry Codman Potter, Frederick D. Huntington, Charles Stelzle, and Samuel Z. Batten. A few of them sometimes spoke in favor of government ownership of natural resources and national monop-olies (railroads, telephone, telegraph, public utilities). Washington Gladden wrote, as early as 1895, "Government ownership and control of the machinery of transportation is the only logical solution to the [railroad] problem." But he added, with typical caution, "it may be sufficient for the people to own the tracks and to lease them for limited terms to operating syndicates, the government prescribing the rates and supervising the business but leaving the conduct of it to private enterprise." Gladden's general position was for a regulated capitalism, with some positive govern-ment intervention for social service. "We may yet go far beyond Mr. Spencer's limits and yet stop a great way this side of socialism," he wrote.

The radical wing of the Social Gospel movement, represented by Rauschenbusch, Jesse H. Jones, George D. Herron, and William D. P. Bliss, sometimes moved close to Christian Democratic Socialism. It held that Jesus and his apostles were the first socialists, citing Acts

4:32-35: "Neither said any of them that aught of the things which
he possessed was his own; but they had all things in common . . .
and distribution was made unto every man according as he had
need." Bliss founded a magazing called *Dawn* in 1890, designed

> To show that the aim of socialism is embraced in the aims of
> Christianity and to awaken members of Christian churches to the fact
> that the teachings of Jesus Christ lead directly to some specific form or
> forms of socialism; that therefore the church has a definite duty upon
> this matter and must, in simple obedience to Christ, apply itself to the
> realization of the social principles of Christianity.

Bliss had no use for those moderate Social Gospelers who thought
capitalism could be reformed and regulated: "Business itself today
is wrong. . . . It is based on competitive strife for profits. But this is
the exact opposite of Christianity. . . . We must change the
system."

Rauschenbusch, the most articulate of the radicals, had spent the
first ten years of his career (1886-96) as pastor of a slum church in
New York City. Later he became a professor at the Baptist seminary
in Rochester, New York. Having seen the oppression caused by the
capitalist system, he became convinced that the spirit of capitalism
was anti-Christian, at least as Jesus preached Christianity:

> I hold that the church and the money power are not friends, but
> enemies, opposed to each other in the same sense in which God and the
> world are opposed to each other. . . . The church is both a partial
> realization of the new society in which God's will is done and also the
> appointed instrument for the further realization of that new society in
> the world about it.

Having repudiated mass revivalism, the Social Gospelers advanced
its new light by writing more than by preaching, and in the first of
three important works, *Christianity and the Social Crisis* (1907),
Rauschenbusch argued that Jesus should be seen as the last of the
Hebrew prophets (a claim that the Reform Jewish rabbi Stephen S.
Wise of New York, a moderate Social Gospeler, endorsed). The
Jewish ethic of social justice was applied by Jesus to all mankind and
was the heart of his social teaching. "Jesus has been called the first
socialist," Rauschenbusch wrote. "He was more, he was the
inauguration of a new humanity . . . ; he bore within him the

germs of a new social and political order." The organic imagery of
the evolving germ was typical of the evolutionary concept underlying the Social Gospel movement. Social Gospelers, who were all
Modernists in theology and believers in the higher criticism,
believed that the Christian church itself had evolved and was still
evolving. Their great objection to Fundamentalism was that it was
trying to "fossilize" the church. As Harry Emerson Fosdick put it,
Christianity "is a life in fellowship with the living God, it will think
new thoughts, build new organizations, expand into new symbolic
expressions. . . . Stagnation, not change, is Christianity's deadly
enemy, for this is a progressive world."

Rauschenbusch conceived of Jesus as the first Christian sociologist: "Jesus had the scientific insight which comes to most men only
by training but to the elect few by divine gift. He grasped the
substance of that law of organic development in nature and history
which our day at last has begun to elaborate systematically." Jesus
was not a premillennial catastrophist but a postmillennialist. "He
was seeking to displace the crude and misleading catastrophic
conceptions by a saner theory about the coming of the Kingdom."
And "the concept of growth" that Jesus preached was one of social
cooperation, not individual competition: "Competition tends to
make good men selfish; cooperation would compel selfish men to
develop public spirit." Just as Lester Ward reversed the whole
Spencerian concept of evolution through laissez-faire, so Rauschenbusch reversed the whole Evangelical conception of individual
salvation and the Protestant ethic.

In *Christianizing the Social Order*, written the year Eugene Debs
and the Socialist Party of America won 6 percent of the popular
vote, Rauschenbusch spoke of the "tragic dilemma" of religious
men like himself who disliked the anticlericalism of Marxian
socialism yet recognized that socialism was "the most thorough and
consistent economic elaboration of the Christian ideal." Whether
the socialists (and the Christian churches) knew it or not, they were
"tools in the hands of the Almighty." "God had to raise up
Socialism because the organized church was too blind or too slow to
realize God's ends." But socialism was in the end only a halfway
step toward the Kingdom. Eventually, when socialism had purged
American economic life of the greed and selfishness of capitalism, it

would have to return to the Christianity it had mistakenly repudiated. "Progress is more than natural. It is divine."

In his last book, *A Theology for the Social Gospel* (1917), Rauschenbusch tried to refashion orthodox Christianity to fit the Social Gospel interpretation. Original sin, which all men have inherited, was not the result of Adam's Fall but symbolized the inability of humanity to overcome the cultural prejudices of race, nation, class, creed, and sex without divine help. "Sin is lodged in social customs and institutions and is absorbed by the individual from his social group" and transmitted from generation to generation by the inertia, tradition, and conventionalism embedded in institutions. To be converted meant to turn from selfish motives, profit motives, cultural prejudices, and toward brotherhood, sharing, cooperation. The atonement was Jesus' suffering for man's corrupt social vision; he was killed by the mob that preferred Barabbas. Faith is the "faith to see God at work in the world and to claim a share in his job"; it is an "energetic act of the will in affirming our fellowship with God and men, declaring our solidarity with the Kingdom of God and repudiating selfish isolation."

Because he was of German ancestry and, like so many Social Gospelers, admired German theological scholarship and philosophy, Rauschenbusch viewed World War I as a tragedy. Like Randolph Bourne (but unlike John Dewey), Rauschenbusch could not see how good could come out of violence and bloodshed. Like Eugene Debs and Jane Addams and other pacifists, Rauschenbusch had come to believe that modern man, with his insight into the laws of sociology and psychology, politics and economics, should have been able to solve even the most complex modern problems without reverting to the barbaric savagery of war. For him the war was a defeat for most of the ideals he believed important. Jesus was "the Prince of Peace," and the sword he brought was a sword against social injustice.

But most Social Gospelers, most Liberal Protestants or Modernists, most Fundamentalists and revivalists came (by 1917) to see the war in the terms Woodrow Wilson proposed—as the last great crusade, the war to end war, the war to make the world safe for democracy. There had always been within the Social Gospel movement a confidence in the moral superiority of America and its people. This can be seen in the endorsement by most Social Gospelers of the need to convert, assimilate, and "Americanize" the newly arrived foreign-born. It can be seen in their continued interest in the foreign-mission movement, in their general support for the Spanish-American War, and in their subsequent support of Theodore Roosevelt's imperialism. It can be seen also in the patronizing manner in which Social Gospelers condescended to indulge in comparative religion, allowing that the Buddhists, Muslims, Confucians, and Hindus had some important ethical and spiritual insights that Christians could respect. Washington Gladden, though he frequently criticized the survival-of-the-fittest ethic among Social Darwinists, inconsistently applied it to comparative religion and foreign missions:

> If we want the nations of the earth to understand Christianity, we have got to have a Christianized nation to show them. Small samples will not serve. The real question is, after all, what Christianity is able to do for the civilization of a people. The keen-witted Orientals, to whom we are making our appeal, the Japanese, the Chinaman, the Hindus, the Turks, understand this perfectly, and we must be ready for a rigid application of this test. It is perfectly fair. We are judging them in the same way. The religions of the world are forced by the contacts and collisions of world politics into a struggle for existence; the evolutionary processes are sifting them; and we shall see the survival of the fittest— that religion which best meets the deepest needs of human nature.

Gladden had no question about which would survive: "Doubtless each will make some contribution to that synthesis of faith which the ages are working out, but none of us doubts which one of them will stamp its character most strongly upon the final result."

In 1917 most Americans convinced themselves, largely because of the new self-confidence that the Third Great Awakening had instilled, that it was part of their mission to stamp their character on the decadent civilizations of Europe. Once the last of those autocratic empires was defeated, the millennium would be close at hand. Then America, now grown to full adulthood in the family of nations, would take its rightful place at the peace table in Europe to sustain a just peace and institute a League of Nations and a World Court, which would, forever after, solve international problems according to a higher law. A revitalized America was convinced it could Americanize the world.

# 6

# *The Fourth Great Awakening, 1960–90(?)*

## *The Failure of Liberalism*

Once again American culture is suffering from a crisis of legitimacy. The old consensus has broken down. Our norms do not match our daily experience. Our system is under pressure "to adjust its institutions to its central value system in order to alleviate strains created by changing social relations." We have been in this crisis since 1960, and it will be with us for a generation. Some might push the initial phase of this awakening, its nativist phase, back to the 1950s, when we Americans desperately sought to reaffirm our old values, to get "back to God," to rid ourselves of subversives who were conspiring to destroy our way of life. But in fact the consensus that had united religion and science in the Third Awakening continued into the early sixties. John F. Kennedy's administration was seen as liberal, continuing most aspects of the old New Deal or even extending them into "New Frontiers" (like the "War on Poverty"). It is only by looking back that we can see how the Kennedy years marked a major watershed in our history.

The ferment of the sixties has begun to produce a new shift in our belief-value system, a transformation of our world view that may be the most drastic in our history as a nation. Today the end of the world seems closer than the millennium. Scientific progress more often seems a threat than a help in adjusting to our environment. The Vietnam War has brought serious doubt about our mission and manifest destiny. The welfare state has bogged down in inertia and bureaucracy. There is more crime and cynicism than faith and optimism. We do not seem to know how or where to find God or how to define his power. Protestant, Catholic, and Jewish institutions are riven with confusion and schism, and many humanists are searching for a different order of reality than pragmatic behaviorism offers. There is a striking new interest in the wisdom of the East as that of the West loses its power to give order and meaning to life.

Of course the faith in science was never total. The old lights never disappear; no new-light consensus is ever complete. Millions of Fundamentalists were never willing to locate God in the laws of evolutionary growth; in fact, they had used their votes where they could to bar the teaching of evolutionary heresy (no matter how glossed over with theism) in the public schools. At the other pole, many intellectuals doubted that psychologists and sociologists, however well-intentioned their concepts of uplift, adjustment, or fraternalism, could really fashion a millennial Kingdom on earth. In 1929, Joseph Wood Krutch, in *The Modern Temper*, expressed their doubts in terms that seem pertinent today: "There is no reason to suppose that [human] life has any more meaning than the life of the humblest insect that crawls from one annihilation to another." In 1931 Aldous Huxley wrote the classic satire on human engineering and behavior modification, *Brave New World*. Physicists, after studying Einstein's theory of relativity and Werner Heisenberg's "uncertainty principle," concluded that there is no certainty in the operations of matter and energy, no clear relationships of cause and effect. The Harvard physicist Percy W. Bridgman, writing in *Harper's* in 1929, voiced the anxieties of this avant-garde long before the public became aware of them:

> The physicist finds himself in a world from which the bottom has dropped clean out; as he penetrates deeper and deeper it eludes him and fades away by the highly unsportsmanlike device of becoming meaningless. . . . The world is not a world of reason, understandable by the intellect of men, but as we penetrate ever deeper the very laws of cause and effect, which we had thought to be a formula to which we could force God to subscribe, cease to have any meaning. The world is not intrinsically reasonable and understandable.

Despite the confidence of religious and humanist Liberalism after 1920, the work of Freud and Jung added to the doubts about the

rationality of human existence. Postulating a series of powerful
hidden drives in man that were beyond his skill to control and that,
when suppressed, produced compulsions that forced him into the
most heinous crimes and crippling illnesses, Freud virtually eliminated free will and the moral responsibility of the individual. He
also eliminated the formerly self-evident borderline between sanity
and insanity. What was worse, if taken seriously, Freud undermined the basic democratic principles of John Locke and Thomas
Jefferson: if men could neither discern right from wrong nor
rationally act on logical choices, then how were they capable of
governing society? They could not even govern themselves.
Roderick Nash, in *The Nervous Generation* (1970), points out that,
"After the psychologists had spoken, man could no longer be
confidently regarded as master of his fate. . . . And the mounting
evidence that opinion could be molded to any purpose by propa-
ganda and advertising made it difficult to sustain the notion of
free, responsible political action."

Among the first shocks to Liberalism were the popular elections
of Benito Mussolini and Adolf Hitler by the democratic process.
Then the Soviet Union, considered the world's best hope for a
rationally planned society, utilized Pavlovian brain-washing techniques to extract "confessions" at the Moscow purge trials in 1935.
The potential threat of behavior modification did not strike the
great mass of Americans until the Korean War, when our captured
soldiers were "persuaded" to denounce publicly the nation for
which they had formerly been willing to sacrifice their lives.

The first signs of a religious reaction against pragmatic Liberalism
began among a group of Protestants who urged a return to more
orthodox views of Christian faith. The "neo-orthodox movement,"
originating with Karl Barth's pessimistic reaction to World War I in
Europe, insisted that it was foolish of Liberalism to neglect the
ultimate facts of the human condition—the innate depravity of
human nature and the mystery of God's will. Led by Reinhold and
Richard Niebuhr and (after his flight from Nazi Germany) Paul
Tillich, the neo-orthodox school in America spoke of their view as
"Christian realism" in order to distinguish it from the unrealistic,
fuzzy-minded idealism of Liberal Protestantism, with its naive faith
in reason, progressive education, and human rationality. Reinhold

Niebuhr launched the attack on "the illusion of liberalism" in his book *Moral Man and Immoral Society* in 1932. In it he argued that Christianity did not teach the sentimental idealism claimed by the Modernists and Social Gospelers: "we are dealing with a possible and prudential ethic in the gospel," not the perfectionist utopianism of the Kingdom of God on earth.

Niebuhr found the gospel a dialectical or paradoxical book of personal and social ethics. It spoke in parables of "impossible possibilities" that only soft-headed theistic evolutionists took literally. At best a few saintly individuals might "approximate" the Christian ethic in their private lives, but no nation, no culture, no group (labor, capital, or farmer; Anglo-Saxon, Latin, or Slav; intellectual, bourgeois, or populist) could ever live by it. Nations cannot turn the other cheek. Social groups of all kinds are fundamentally self-interested and immoral. They cannot be brought into harmony by appeals to reason or love or brotherhood but only by hardheaded power politics. Social organisms have to work together by compromising (often a dirty word to Liberal idealists) because it is in the very nature of political groups to press for the self-interested claims of their own members against the claims of other groups. Labor and capital, democracy and fascism, cannot live by the Golden Rule. They must achieve a balance of power.

Niebuhr pointed to the bitter labor struggles of the 1930s to prove his point and urged that only an equally hardheaded sense of power politics could effect a balance of power among nations. His hardheaded realism struck many Liberals (who in the 1930s were often pacifists) as heretically anti-Christian. "If a season of violence," Niebuhr said in justification of labor's battles, "can establish a just social system and can create the possibilities of its preservation, there is no purely ethical ground upon which violence and revolution can be ruled out." He heaped scorn on progressive reformers like Richard T. Ely, Washington Gladden, John Dewey —"the moralists, both religious and secular, who imagine that the egoism of individuals is being progressively checked by the development of rationality or the growth of religiously inspired goodwill, and that nothing but the continuance of this process is necessary to establish social harmony between all the societies and collectives."

In short, "social justice cannot be resolved by moral and rational suasion alone. . . . Conflict is inevitable, and, in this conflict, power must be challenged by power."

This *Realpolitik*, praised by labor reformers and antifascists in the 1930s, was to come back to haunt Niebuhr's admirers in the days of Vietnam, when his neo-Liberal followers applied it to public policy, especially foreign policy, in the Kennedy and Johnson administrations only to have this same "tough" approach dealt out to them in spades by neoconservatives in the Nixon administration. But in the 1930s Niebuhr's following was small precisely because it ran counter to the beliefs and values of the liberal consensus that had emerged in the Third Awakening. Rational idealists "do not see," Niebuhr said, "that the limitations of the human imagination, the easy subservience of reason to prejudice and passion, and the consequent persistence of irrational egoism, particularly in group behavior, make social conflict an inevitability in human history to its very end." In this theology there was no hope for a postmillennial theory of progress. Although Niebuhr's own private commitment to many of the reforms of his day brought him the grudging admiration of those who disliked his new orthodoxy, his theology seemed alien and abstruse to the vast majority of Americans until the 1950s, when a wave of public crises in domestic and foreign affairs suddenly challenged the whole basis of liberal faith and optimism.

It is difficult to say just when the majority of Americans lost faith in Liberalism. Some date it from the conviction of Alger Hiss in 1950; others from the defeat of Adlai Stevenson in 1952; still others find its origin in the rising fears of the Cold War after 1947 or the stalemated war in Korea. Clearly the traumatic growth of communist power at the very time America took its place as the leading nation of the Western world had a lot to do with it. When the Soviet Union became the first to launch a rocket into space orbit in 1957, Americans faced the possibility that their scientific skills were no longer the most advanced in the world. The rise of the Third World nations in the same decade, most of whom tried to remain neutral rather than accept the leadership of the United States, cast a major shadow over the concept of manifest destiny. Difficulties in foreign affairs were matched by crises at home. The fear of communist subversion led to the rise of McCarthyism and the Rosenberg executions. The Supreme Court's abandonment of the policy of "separate but equal" status for Afro-Americans and the wave of public confrontations over their integration or separate status in the South (and later in the North) raised questions whether white Americans could face the fact of true equality (many wanted to impeach Earl Warren for his use of "sociological jurisprudence" and reverse the court's decision). Perhaps the most frightening factor in the 1950s, cutting across all class, political, and racial lines, was the possibility of World War III and a nuclear holocaust. Even atomic testing in preparation for such a war (not only by the United States but by an increasing number of other nations) posed threats of genetic damage to millions of innocent people. Science seemed to have unleashed powers it could not control. God, if he were a God of love, was not revealing himself through history and evolution. Salvation no longer seemed securely locked into the advance of science and modernism.

In 1963 Michael Harrington's *The Other America* further undermined faith in Liberalism by pointing out that, despite all the humanitarian legislation of the New Deal and Fair Deal, the welfare state had not solved the problem of poverty. Millions of Americans were still living below the poverty level, and some families were entering their third generation "on welfare." The mixed economy, which was supposed to amalgamate the best aspects of humanitarianism, social engineering, and free-enterprise capitalism, appeared to be a colossal failure. As government became more bureaucratic, as labor unions were given equal bargaining power with big business, and as the farm bloc made agribusiness a major political force, the consumer—the average citizen—began to feel more harassed and hemmed in than he had ever been. In the freeest nation in the world, freedom seemed to be diminishing rather than increasing. Americans became uncertain of their future and frightened over their inability to cope with a world so complex and unpredictable. As Joseph Wood Krutch had put it much earlier, "The Universe is one in which the human spirit cannot find a comfortable home."

This self-doubt and pessimism were new in American culture. And while some still spoke in the 1950s of Americans as a people of plenty or of their "affluent society," others began to speak of "the crack in the picture window" and of the Age of Anxiety. When men become self-conscious and analytical about their most cherished cultural myths, they have ceased to believe in them. When the individual members of a society feel that they have lost control over their lives, it indicates that the society itself is out of control. Since the heart of America's culture core had been faith in the self-reliant, morally free, and responsible individual (acting in a special covenant with God), "the end of ideology," as Daniel Bell's popular book of 1960 was entitled, signaled that Americans were unsure of themselves. Another era of cultural distortion had begun.

## The Nativist Phase of the Awakening

The first response to the crisis was an effort to reaffirm the beliefs and values of an older era. Some textbooks now refer to the 1950s as an age of neoconservatism. Fundamentalists asserted the virtues of the cross and the flag, while intellectuals called for a return to eternal verities. Economists who disliked the welfare state rallied behind prophets like Friedrich Hayek, who insisted that the country was on "the road to serfdom" and that, to be free, it must return to the fundamental laws of laissez-faire capitalism. Political scientists like Walter Lippmann urged a new elitism in the management of diplomacy, since the public was too ill-informed to understand world affairs. William F. Buckley attacked the godless educational principles of higher education, while Max Rafferty urged a rejection of "progressive" education in the public schools and a return to the "basics" of *McGuffey's Readers*, as taught in the little red schoolhouse of bygone days. Conservative philosophers like Russell Kirk and writers like Peter Viereck expounded on the virtues of the humanities, of social hierarchy, tradition, and religious faith. "The churches," said Viereck in *Conservatism Revisited* (1949)

draw the fangs of the Noble Savage and clip his ignoble claws. . . .
Marx gave the ablest summary of the issue when he dreaded religion as "the opiate of the people"—that is, the tamer, pacifier, civilizer of the people. . . . Despite eloquent advocates of progressive education, the function of education is conservative: not to deify the child's "glorious self-expression" [as John Dewey was accused of advocating] but to limit

his instincts and behavior by unbreakable ethical habits. . . . What prevents a [modern] baby from remaining a caveman is the conservative force of law and tradition.

Russell Kirk, in *The Conservative Mind* (1953), echoed these sentiments, lauding the principles of Edmund Burke in politics and Irving Babbitt in philosophy. The true conservative, he argued, holds to the belief that "a divine intent rules society as well as conscience, forging an eternal chain of right and duty. . . . Political problems, at bottom, are religious and moral problems. A narrow rationality . . . cannot itself satisfy human needs." A truly civilized society "requires orders and classes. The only true equality is moral equality . . . ; economic levelling is not economic progress. Separate property from private possession and liberty is erased. . . . Tradition and sound prejudice provide checks upon man's anarchic impulse . . . ; change and reform are not identical. . . . Providence is the proper instrument for change," not economic planning or bureaucratic welfare programs.

While political prophets like Nixon, Mundt, McCarthy, and Velde sought to get the government back on its old patriotic course by rooting out subversive communist agents and dupes in the State Department, the bureaucracy, and the Army, new religious prophets like Norman Vincent Peale, Monsignor (later Bishop) Fulton J. Sheen, and Billy Graham aroused the public to its need to return to the cultural values that had preceded the advent of atheistic Liberalism. Peale wrote a famous article for *Reader's Digest* in 1953 entitled "Let the Churches Stand Up for Capitalism," and in his extremely popular books he preached the old doctrines of self-reliance and the Protestant ethic. Sheen aroused conservative Roman Catholics to the danger of communist advances around the world and the destruction of Christian mission activities in the Third World by communist-inspired nationalists. Billy Graham, the most popular of the three, utilized radio, television, and movies, as well as mass urban revival "crusades," to demonstrate that Fundamentalism was not dead but in fact held the key to the return of law, order, decency, and national progress. In the 1950s and again in the late 1960s he became the unofficial White House chaplain, frequently visiting Eisenhower and Nixon to help them guide their decisions by the power of prayer.

Because of his national and international reputation as a preacher
and his continuous activity from 1950 to the present, some
commentators have identified Graham's revivalism as the center of
the Fourth Great Awakening. But Graham's message has always
been traditionalist and backward-looking, and, by his seeming
endorsement of the reactionary politics of the 1960s and his close
personal ties with Nixon, it became too partisan for many who had
formerly considered him a messenger from God. Nevertheless, if we
are to follow the development of this revitalization movement, it is
necessary to understand Graham's popularity. Born in 1918 in
Charlotte, North Carolina, converted by a Fundamentalist itinerant
revivalist in a tent meeting at the age of sixteen, Graham was raised
in the subculture of those who rejected the new consensus produced
by the Third Awakening. His family, and the community in which
he lived, carefully insulated itself from the heresies of the Modernists, Social Gospelers, and pragmatic Liberals. They thrived by
attacking these views and clinging to their older evangelical
position (as that position had hardened into the premillennial creed
of Fundamentalism). In their view, Darwin, Dewey, and Freud
were tools of Satan, trying to undermine the faith in the inerrancy
of Scripture. By establishing their own schools, summer camps, and
radio stations, these "Bible-believing Christians" nurtured the
older faith in their homes and came to think of themselves as the
saving remnant.

Graham's family was delighted when he chose professional
Christian work as his vocation and dedicated himself to battling the
evil forces undermining God's covenant with America. Graham
began his career as a minister in 1947 with an organization called
Youth for Christ, designed to combat juvenile delinquency in the
post–World War II years. The young are generally the first victims
of a crisis in cultural legitimacy, for they most desperately need the
sense of order and meaning that cultural institutions provide.
Graham entered into the very heart of the growing social breakdown when he addressed himself to the difficulties parents and
children faced as the old consensus began to wane. But Graham's
response ignored changing social conditions and urged simply a
reassertion of older child-rearing norms, i.e., those preserved
among the saving remnant in his own subculture. His Youth for

Christ sermons on this topic were incorporated into his sermons as a professional mass revivalist after 1950.

These sermons, which Graham printed and distributed free to millions of radio listeners in the 1950s, were entitled "Our Teen-Age Problem," "The Answer to Teen-Age Delinquency," "Juvenile Delinquency and Its Cure," "The Answer to Broken Homes," "The Responsibilities of Parents," and "The Home God Honors." (The campaign sponsored by the American Council on Advertising in the 1950s struck the same theme with billboards around the country carrying the slogan "The Family that Prays Together, Stays Together." Hollywood took a different tack and glorified the delinquents and their problems in movies like James Dean's *Rebel Without a Cause*.) The answers to these problems began with a call for the assertion of parental authority and the subservience of wives to their husbands. The validity of this norm for family life was demonstrated by quotations from the Bible, God's Word, the highest of all authorities: "Wives, submit yourselves unto your own husbands, as it is fit in the Lord." From this followed the obedience of children: "Children, obey your parents in all things." From his own experience as a child in a "God-centered home," Graham demonstrated that the old-fashioned home, with old-fashioned parents, was the home God honored (by keeping it free of discord and delinquency): "I'll never forget my father and mother. They raised their children in the fear of the Lord. I never heard my parents argue. I do not even remember their having used a slang word, much less a word of profanity." In too many modern homes the wives were trying to "wear the trousers." But, "Because of sin in the Garden of Eden, one of the curses God sent upon the woman was that the man shall rule over her."

> We in America are dealing with a holy, righteous and pure God. He will not long tolerate our evils and sins. How long is this pure God going to endure our divorce rate, our [lax] teen-age morals, our immorality in government circles, our truce-breaking, our drunkenness, our swearing? How long is God going to tolerate our pride, gossiping, malice, slandering, love of money, ease, and pleasure?

The problems in the home were caused by Satan: there was no doubt, he said, "of what Satan is doing to destroy the morals of America and break down our homes." But Satan was aided by

many agents, among them the communists: "One of the great
goals of Communism is to destroy the American home. If the
Communists can destroy the American home and cause moral
deterioration in this country, that group will have done to us what
they did to France when the German armies invaded the Maginot
Line." The home was the last bulwark of national defense. Among
the group who were working "like a fifth column" to subvert the
home were the followers of Darwinism, of Dewey's progressive
education, of Freud's unspeakable theories of human psychology.
These were all "alien philosophies"—alien, that is, to the old and
true ways of our fathers. Like Senators Joseph McCarthy and
Richard Nixon, Graham found these alien philosophies not only in
the pragmatic liberalism of the State Department but in the
schools, the churches, and the legal system. How else could one
explain decisions of the United States Supreme Court permitting
students to refuse to salute the flag and taking prayer out of the
public schools?

Graham was introduced to his radio audience each week as "a
man with God's message for these crisis times"; and while he
devoted most of his sermon message to the need for each man and
woman to make an "immediate decision for Christ," he usually
started his talks with references to current social and political issues.
Indirectly (and often directly) Graham attacked the United Nations, the United Council of Churches, and the welfare state (or
New Deal). The United Nations had undermined American sovereignty; the Council of Churches had undermined biblical orthodoxy and substituted social service for religious conversion as the
test of a true Christian; and the New Deal had betrayed the
God-ordained principles of laissez-faire economics, the Protestant
ethic, and individual self-reliance. He referred to the bureaucratic
regulation of business and the welfare programs as having undermined "the rugged individualism that Christ brought." He portrayed the rise of communism and the decline of foreign missions as
"the dangers that face capitalistic America." Capitalizing on
current disillusion with the labor movement in the 1950s, he
described the Garden of Eden as a place where there were "no
union dues, no labor unions, no snakes, no disease."

Not unlike the preaching of Peale and Sheen, Graham's sermons
stressed that Christianity's survival depended on the power of

American capitalism and military strength and that these in turn required the personal commitment to biblical Christianity by all Americans. Otherwise God would punish America for deserting his ways. "American is truly the last bulwark of Christian civilization," Graham told his immense audiences in cities across the nation. "If America falls, Western culture will disintegrate." "If you would be a true patriot, then become a Christian. If you would be a loyal American, then become a loyal Christian." He portrayed the crisis in world affairs as America's last chance to be true to its divine mission. "America cannot survive, she cannot fulfill her divine purpose, she cannot carry out her God-appointed mission without the spiritual emphasis which was hers from the outset." If Americans did not heed the message he brought, the nation would be destroyed, probably in an atomic war with Russia. "Do you know," he asked his revival audience in Los Angeles, soon after the Russians had exploded their first atomic bomb, "the area that is marked out for the enemy's first atomic bomb? New York! Secondly, Chicago; and thirdly, the city of Los Angeles." "My own theory about Communism," he said in 1957, "is that it is master-minded by Satan." Like most nativist prophets, Graham predicted the imminent end of the world: "I sincerely believe that the Lord draweth nigh." "We may have another year, maybe two years," he said in 1950, "to work for Jesus Christ, and [then], ladies and gentlemen, I believe it is all going to be over. . . . Two years, and it's all going to be over." Two years later he said, "Unless this nation turns to Christ within the next few months, I despair of its future."

Despair of the future was the essence of this first phase of cultural distortion, and Graham was only one of many spokesmen for traditionalism. The fact that Fulton Sheen, a Roman Catholic, rose to fame as a writer and television star in the same years, with a similar effort to provide authority and certainty to people lost in doubt, indicated that this was not simply a Protestant awakening. Like Senator Joseph McCarthy, the political spokesman for nativist fears, Sheen and Graham had a wide audience among Protestants, Catholics, Jews, and humanists. Will Herberg pointed out, in his book *Protestant, Catholic, Jew* (1955), that the three major faiths held more in common than they realized. All three had come to identify their supposedly transcendent beliefs and values with the cultural norms of the United States: "To be a Protestant, a Catholic, or a Jew," said Herberg, "are today the alternative ways of being an American." The "underlying culture-religion" of most of those who went to church and synagogue was essentially "the American way of life."

The election of a Roman Catholic to the presidency in 1960 was a symbol of the end of Protestant hegemony and the beginning of what some historians have called "the post-Protestant era" or "the second disestablishment." The choice of Kennedy was possible largely because the fear of communist expansion enabled conservative Protestants, Catholics, and Jews to bury their mutual animosities in defense of the American way of life. Insofar as John F. Kennedy was elected out of this fear (many Liberals found him at fault for his failure to take a strong stand against McCarthyism), the election of 1960 was less a return to Liberalism than a culmination of the nativist phase of the awakening. The sixties, with three assassinations of major political leaders, produced the most severe social crisis in the United States since secession. And having at last entered into the cultural mainstream, Catholics and Jews suffered from the same institutional stresses as Protestants.

While the conservative Catholics admired Fulton Sheen and Cardinal Spellman, the liberal Catholics turned to Pope John XXIII. Through the Vatican Council of 1963–65 Pope John tried to throw open the church's windows to the winds of social and doctrinal change. But his successor, Pope Paul VI, found the result so tempestuous that he hastily tried to close them. The result was increased confusion and loss of confidence in ecclesiastical authority. Pope Paul's encyclical prohibiting the use of artificial birth-control methods, just at the time when the birth-control pill was at last placing in women's hands the ability to protect their bodies against unwanted pregnancies, caused a disastrous rift, not only among the laity but among the clergy and religious orders. The revolution in sexual mores entered the church in the form of a widening debate over clerical celibacy, which led over 600 priests to leave their office in 1968 alone. Nor could Catholics, any more than Protestants or Jews, find unity on such pressing aspects of political concern as the civil-rights movement and opposition to the war in Vietnam. Jews had the additional problem of trying to explain the meaning of the Holocaust, the Israeli position in the Middle East, and the significance of the internal division among Reform, Conservative, and Orthodox factions within the faith.

The awakening entered all three faiths in a new concern over direct personal encounters with God's Spirit. Jews experienced it in the revival of orthodoxy and in a rising interest in Hasidism. Catholics experienced it in the charismatic movement, Protestants in the rising interest in Pentecostalism. Underlying these pietistic movements in all three faiths was a loss of faith in the old forms, doctrines, and rituals and a feeling that those whose duty it was to explain God's will in their daily lives were incapable of doing so. The old priests, pastors, and rabbis simply could not provide answers to the most pressing of personal problems, let alone to national and world problems; the young priests, pastors, and rabbis seemed as rebellious and divided as their flocks. Authorities within the church pitted the faithful against each other; and, if anyone turned outside the church, to the scientists, the answers were equally contradictory. Birth control and population control constituted only one such unanswerable question. Women's liberation and the use of abortion were even more controversial. There seemed to be no clear religious or scientific guidelines for old or young. The churches did not know whether homosexuals (let alone transsexuals) could be "orthodox" or have congregations to meet their needs. Neither scientists nor ministers could agree on whether a fetus was human (or *when* it was), whether Karen Quinlan was a vegetable, whether euthanasia was more merciful than prolonged cancer. Ordinary people were left without guidance or consolation on the most pressing of all questions—on love, life, and death.

Clerical efforts to respond to the demands of their people merely fractured theological unity. The most serious crisis had to do with how God manifests himself in this world. Liberalism, though it had placed God's power within history and evolution, had made it impossible for God to make himself manifest in person or through miracles. Yet Katheryn Kuhlman, a Presbyterian minister from Pittsburgh, traveled around the nation in the 1950s and 1960s holding enormous revival meetings whose central feature was faith healing: "I believe in miracles," Kuhlman told her audiences; and many who had turned in vain to medical science for help claimed to find healing under her ministry. At Pentecostal meetings men and women who had found no spiritual communion in regular church services experienced direct communion with the Holy Spirit, who entered their hearts, causing them to speak and prophesy "in tongues." The works of Dietrich Bonhoeffer became popular because he told Christians to act as though God did not exist, for then they would rely less upon rituals and institutions in searching for him. Thomas Altizer and Gabriel Vahanian, though associated with the phrase "God is dead," really said that God's spirit is more important than his institutions: "Christ is the God who remains in the world. The death of God was the passage from transcendence to immanence." But this was not the immanence of the theistic evolutionist; it was the immanence of the Antinomian or the Quakers. God's power is available, they said, not through the intellect of the advanced scientist, but through the heart of the true believer.

## The Death of God and the Secular City

The Fourth Great Awakening began in the 1960s, but its birth was obscured by the belief that Kennedy's program marked a revival of Liberalism in politics, even though many of his advisors shared Reinhold Niebuhr's neo-orthodox view of human nature and destiny. Niebuhr's pessimistic view of rationalism and idealism was only a partial answer to the old consensus. Many Christian and humanist (or agnostic) Liberals simply adopted the hardheaded aspects of Niebuhr's *Realpolitik* to achieve Liberal ends. "Interest-group politics" at home and "negotiating from power" abroad were the new means to old Liberal ends. The neo-Liberals who supported Kennedy felt "chastened" of their old idealism, which had allowed them to be such easy dupes of the Left in the 1930s. They too had wanted America purged of communist subversion in the 1950s. But they remained pragmatists, willing to pit one group's power against another in struggles where each made the ends justify the means. Soon after Lyndon Johnson transformed the New Frontier into the Great Society, many who had high hopes for neo-Liberalism became utterly disillusioned. The awakening then

produced a great wave of civil disobedience, violence, and moralistic third-party politics that marked the final breakup of the old
consensus.

What seemed new about the War on Poverty, the civil-rights
movement, and the other Liberal causes during the Kennedy and
Johnson administrations was that they abandoned Social Gospel
idealism and frankly avowed the use of power and compromise in
the fight for social justice. Both the war on poverty and the civil-
rights effort used federal power and money to outflank local
political machines intent on maintaining the status quo. They did
not seek to educate prejudice out of existence or solve it by appeals
to love and brotherhood. Martin Luther King, Jr., was closer to
Niebuhr than to Gladden in his use of "coercive nonviolence"; his
model was Mahatma Gandhi, whose fight against British colonial-
ism won the admiration of Niebuhr for its cunning manipulation of
mass power. With Gandhi in mind, Niebuhr had said, in 1932,
"nonviolent methods of coercion and resistance" offer the largest
opportunities "for an oppressed group which is hopelessly in the
minority and has no possibility of developing sufficient power to set
against its oppressors. The emancipation of the Negro race in
America probably waits upon the adequate development of this
kind of social and political strategy." King acknowledged his debt
to Niebuhr in the application of this strategy to his boycotts and
marches against the oppressive majority in the Deep South. In this
struggle, King was aided by a group of neo-Social Gospelers from
the North who were willing to "lay their bodies on the line" in
support of "coercive nonviolence."

The same technique was applied by civil-rights groups and
welfare organizers in the North. Saul Alinsky developed this
strategy against oppressive slum landlords, George Wiley used it for
the National Welfare Rights Organization, and it was endorsed by
Harvey Cox for a wide range of social reforms in *The Secular City*
(1965). Cox argued that the best way to help the poor in the urban
slums is to teach them how to apply political pressure to those who
hold economic power: "The Negro revolt is not aimed at winning
friends but at winning freedom, not inter-personal warmth [as old
Social Gospel idealists might urge] but institutional justice."
Increasing the relative power of the inner city," Cox maintained,

"means decreasing the relative power of the suburbs." Not reason, love, and education but tough-minded confrontation of power by power is the feature of neo-Social Gospel reform: "Inner-city people represent the oppressed to whom Jesus said he had come to bring not warm words but liberty. The inmates of the urban concentration camps do not long for fraternization with the guards; what they want is the abolition of the prison." Cox seemed to be arguing that the time was ripe for the massing of power on behalf of social justice in God's name, even if that meant pitting large groups of people against each other. The result was a decade of head-on collisions over civil rights and the war in Vietnam.

First the North rallied to support the civil rights of Southern blacks, braving the mobs and police there. But violent action by southerners against nonresistant demonstrators led some to assert the right of self-defense. First came Robert Williams' "Deacons for Defense" in Georgia; then S.N.C.C. (Student Nonviolent Coordinating Committee) moved from nonviolence to Black Power under Stokely Carmichael and H. Rap Brown; then the militant Black Panthers, Malcolm X, and Angela Davis seemed prepared to go even farther. Malcolm X frankly raised the question whether the ballot or the bullet was more adequate to minority needs in the power situation.

Southern intransigence had to be met by increased federal power, and this brought Lester Maddox and George C. Wallace to national prominence. At the same time, blacks in the North, noting that de facto segregation was being ignored, called attention to it by waves of riots in Watts, Detroit, Newark, and a dozen northern cities. Coercive nonviolence appeared to be a far more dangerous weapon than anyone had realized. Further proof of this came when "politics in the street" moved against the undeclared war in Vietnam.

The peace movement, starting with massive sit-ins on college campuses, boiled over into the burning of draft cards (led by the Reverend William Sloane Coffin, Jr.), the destruction of draft-board records (by the Berrigan brothers), and finally the organized violence of the Weathermen after the S.D.S. (Students for a Democratic Society) had split on the issue of tactics. Claiming "national security," the government struck back. In the process of asserting protective power, local, state, and federal law-enforcement agencies broke the laws they were sworn to uphold: Mayor Daley's police brutally smashed Senator Eugene McCarthy's supporters; the National Guard shot unarmed students at Kent State; and Attorney General John Mitchell illegally arrested 10,000 citizens in Washington, D.C.

Theologians struggled to keep up with the rapidly shifting currents. They developed new and more radical rationales for social action: first a special "black theology" and then a "revolutionary theology" to replace the old nonviolent theologies. "The church is the avant-garde of the new regime," said Harvey Cox. "God is ever at work making freedom and personhood possible. There is no neutral ground. Man either masters and manages his environment or he is mastered by it." But in the escalating frenzy, many began to doubt those who called for social revolution in God's name. The disillusioned concluded that Judeo-Christian theology had no answers, that God was literally dead. One popular religious joke of the mid-sixties combined the feeling that space travel had destroyed the symbolic location of heaven "out there" with the cynicism of those who called upon God to support political reform "down here": "I have seen God," said the returning astronaut, "and she is black." At this point Liberalism and neo-Liberalism, Social Gospel and neo-Social Gospel, conservatism and neoconservatism, Fundamentalism and Liberalism, seemed to have reached dead ends. They did not disappear, but their thrust was too fragmented to provide coherence. New visions and alternatives were needed. Some of them had, in fact, begun to develop before the end of the 1950s.

## The Beat Generation

The first of the alternative philosophies and life-styles adopted by the more flexible and younger members of the culture was associated with the "Beat" poets and writers of California. In the late 1950s this group achieved national notoriety for their antinomianism, their rejection of bourgeois values, and their experiments with marijuana and Zen Buddhism. Associated with Allen Ginsberg, Lawrence Ferlinghetti, Alan Watts, Gary Snyder, and

Jack Kerouac, the Beats were noted for their casual life-style, their experimental writings, and their interest in the Orient. To conservative adherents of the Protestant ethic they seemed little different from juvenile delinquents, except that their writing was taken seriously by the more tolerant critics and scholars. The Beats refused to take seriously the cultural goals of hard work, vocational training, and material success within accepted institutions. Welcomed on college campuses for their exciting new aesthetic and emotional insights into the possibilities of human feeling, they later cooperated with the rebels against academic censorship and with those seeking more student participation in the governance of the universities.

The Beat movement began as protest poetry in the broadest sense—protest against the deadening hand of technology and bureaucracy upon the human spirit. Its early poems and novels celebrated life, spontaneity, and religious energy. Aesthetically the Beats adopted a loose, flowing, romantic style, reminiscent of Walt Whitman's in its subjectivity. Like Whitman, the Beats waxed lyrical about the possibilities of ordinary men and women in everyday life. They proclaimed (often with four-letter words) the earthy joys of the body, the ecstasies of the heart, the endless variety and possibilities of life, and in their own lives tried to live up to their fullest human potential, regardless of convention. Kerouac's *On the Road* (1955) and Ginsberg's *Howl* (1956) were testimonies of religious rebellion and experience, telling Americans that there was another side to life besides the mechanical escalator of success, the stultifying treadmill of white-collar life. They urged the young to stop worrying about their future and learn to live for the present —to enjoy their feelings, to accept sensuality, to free the essence of their common humanity from lifeless ritual and routine.

Beat poetry testified to the personal conversion experiences of these "new lights." Their works said, in effect, "I used to feel all tied up in knots, angry, confused, despairing; then suddenly I realized that I was a human being and not a cog in the social machinery; I experienced an ecstatic rebirth, an enlightenment about the human condition; I awoke to new possibilities and potentials within me; and since then I have been free from my burdens, a new man; I see the world in a new way and I come to offer this gift of freedom to you." Theodore Roszak in *The Making of a Counter-Culture* (1969) quotes Ginsberg's early poem of frustration as an example of what in his experience appealed so directly to that of many others:

> I feel as if I am a dead
> end and so I am finished
> All spiritual facts I realize
> are true but I never escape
> the feeling of being closed in
> and the sordidness of self,
> the futility of all that I
> have seen and done and said.

This, in secular form, is like the testimony of older Christian converts who said, "I knew what religion was; I went to church, I lived according to the accepted moral code of my neighbors, but nevertheless I felt numb and burdened and guilty." But then, after the experience of enlightenment, Ginsberg wrote (again like a religious convert):

> This is the one and only
> firmament. . .
> I am living in Eternity.
> The ways of this world
> are the ways of Heaven.

This is the transcendentalism that, like Emerson's and Whitman's, saw heaven in a blade of grass and eternity in an hour. It is pantheistic and this-worldly in its perspective, abandoning the dualism of the Judeo-Christian world view. All that is eternal and spiritual lies in man and in nature, not in some life after death, some paradise in space, some future millennium. Reality is here and now. Heaven is in you.

From protest against the stultification of the human spirit in bourgeois society and celebration of the sensibilities of man, the Beats went on to prove the innate potential, the unexplored inner being, of the spirit by smoking marijuana and by the mystical experience of Zen *satori*. In works like Ginsberg's *Sunflower Satori* and Kerouac's *The Dharma Bums* (1958) the Beats reversed the canons of neoconservatism by insisting that men and women must not hold back their inner instincts but let them loose. Like Walt Whitman, the Beats "let it all hang out," all the feelings that tense, inhibited, "up-tight" Americans tried to suppress or hide. They became prophets questioning the prevailing cultural norms and saying, like Emerson, "Whoso would be a man, let him be a nonconformist." In the Beat movement the Fourth Great Awakening first developed a countercultural alternative. But it seemed so extreme, so "far out" or "spaced out," that only a few of the young dared try it. However, by calling attention to the alternative philosophies of the East (as Emerson, too, had done), the Beats offered a way around the blocked mazeways that many others found very helpful.

## Zen and Other Oriental Alternatives

The counterculture, as it has developed since 1960, has been un-American in five profound ways. It has rejected the dualistic view of man and nature, man and God, this world and the next, that is so ingrained in Western thought. It espouses a new sense of time, or timelessness—a preference for measuring life in terms of eternity rather than in terms of the near future or millennial future. It admires the East instead of considering its wisdom backward, quaint, or incomplete. It prefers to think of humanity in terms of "the family of man" instead of in terms of particular ethnic groups, races, classes, or "chosen" people; it tends also to think of man as merely one form of life among all the others, not necessarily superior to them or empowered to have dominion over them. Finally, it would rather be passive than activist in the current crisis because, by the old-light version of progress (via technical manipulation of man and the environment), any change is bound to be more destructive than constructive; we must wait, the counterculture argues—get our heads together, get reoriented in time and space, spirit and life—before we continue on the path that has already brought us to the brink of total disaster.

In all these respects the philosophies of the Orient have an appeal that Judeo-Christianity lacks. To the average Westerner, however, those who practice Oriental religions seem to have lost touch with reality—to be withdrawn, narcissistic, escapist. Alan Watts, one of the first in this awakening to study Buddhism seriously, wrote *The Way of Zen* in 1957 to explain the importance of breaking the ethnocentric cultural outlook that viewed the Far East as either missionary territory or a source of markets. Watts, like Emerson, believed that the East has much to teach the West about the human condition. Although the world is much smaller now in terms of travel—or bombing strikes—its problems of communication are larger. Americans speak few foreign languages. To remain incapable of comprehending the culture and language of the Far East, Watts said, is scandalous and dangerous, especially when our own culture seems in such desperate straits. At a time when many Americans were becoming disenchanted with "the success myth," "the organization man," "the man in the grey-flannel suit," "the status-seekers," "the other-directed man," and "the power elite" (to name some of the more popular symbols of the 1950s) the possibility of finding new values in Oriental religion was attractive to many people outside Beat circles. They were attracted because of their own aversion to the aggressive, hard-driving Calvinist ethic, which placed so much emphasis on personal aggrandizement and materialism. America's philosophy seemed to mold men to become cogs in the great industrial machine (knowing more and more about less and less); Eastern philosophy tried to make man feel at home in the universe. Where American life seemed hectic and disordered, Eastern culture offered calm and order. Where the Judeo-Christian theology portrayed the world as sinful, man as separated from God, and assumed the basic depravity of human nature, the Zen Buddhist held that "the natural man is to be trusted." Man's duty is not to get from this world into the next; life is not a perpetual battle against internal sin and external evil but a search for the unity between man and nature. From the viewpoint of Eastern philosophy, Watts said,

> it appears that the Western mistrust of human nature—whether theological or technical—is a kind of schizophrenia. It would be impossible in their [Eastern] view to believe oneself innately evil without discrediting the very belief, since all the notions of a perverted mind would be perverted notions. However religiously "emancipated," the technological mind shows that it has inherited the same division against itself when it tries to subject the whole human order to the control of conscious reason.

This "division against itself" is inherent not only in Western religion but in Western man's concept of nature. The Book of

Genesis says that God created man to "have dominion over" nature and to live "by the sweat of his brow" in accumulating goods. It is a myth that has less appeal today than it did in the time of our Calvinistic forefathers, facing virgin forests. Zen Buddhism suggests that the West reconsider its concept of postmillennial progress (the dream of bringing heaven to earth) and consider that the earth may be all man has to live with. In place of linear, step-at-a-time Western engineering and linguistics, the Oriental world view offered "total consciousness" and "intuitive awareness"— seeing the whole universe or, rather, the wholeness of the universe. It questioned the Western definitions of time and space, energy and matter. Wholism was, for many who tried Zen, a more meaningful kind of holiness than "the divided self" and the dualistic universe. To lose one's self in a sense of oneness with nature or harmony with the universe is truly to find one's innermost being.

Wholism of this sort appealed particularly to those Americans who left the city in the 1960s to find harmony with nature by living in rural communes and placing themselves in closer touch with the seasonal rhythms of land, earth, and sky. The subscribers to *The Whole Earth Catalogue* subscribed to its view of planet Earth: "We can't put it together; it is together." Unspoken in this was the knowledge that madmen could at any moment blow it apart. The Judeo-Christian theology made man feel anxious and guilty, urging him always to scrutinize his conscience for sins. Eighteenth-century Enlightenment philosophy urged men always to seek the cause for every effect. But Buddhism taught, Watts said, that it is not necessary always to "seek the wherefore" and the "why" of every act or feeling. It is often better to "let it be." The fear of the imminent end of the earth has made many Americans feel that this planet is more precious—turning them back in time when before they had always looked to the future.

Gary Snyder, writing in *Turtle Island* in 1975, tried to give Americans a better sense of their own time-span by stressing their relationship to the past of America's Indians (who were once Orientals):

> Our own heads: Is where it starts. Knowing that we are the first human
> beings in history to have so much of man's culture and previous
> experience available to our study, and being free enough of the weight

of traditional cultures to seek out a larger identity; the first members of a civilized society since the Neolithic to wish to look clearly into the eyes of the wild and see our self-hood, our family, there. We have these advantages to set off the obvious disadvantages of being as screwed up as we are—which gives us a fair chance to penetrate some of the riddles of ourselves and the universe, and to go beyond the idea of "man's survival" or "survival of the biosphere" and to draw our strength from the realization that at the heart of things is some kind of serene and ecstatic process which is beyond qualitites and beyond birth-and-death.

The interest in Zen Buddhism, Taoism, Hinduism, the I Ching, and other Oriental philosophies is not likely, in this awakening, to produce a fusion of East and West, but it offers valuable alternative stances or new perspectives from which to view our place in the universe and a new perception of its meaning. For many, of course, Eastern religion may simply be a temporary effort to find self-oblivion. For others its appeals are utilitarian: Yoga offers new ways to exercise and relax; Kung Fu offers new techniques for self-defense; acupuncture offers medical cures without surgery; Transcendental Meditation offers peace of mind and relief from tension; Zen centers offer new kinds of friendly human relationships. Most people lack the commitment and self-discipline to come to a full appreciation of these ways of life. The widespread interest, however, reflects a recognition that the Eastern religions may serve as correctives against imbalances in Western culture and help it return to a more fruitful and harmonious relationship between man and nature, between technology and contemplation.

## LSD, Flower Power, the Occult, and Rock Concerts

Closely related to the Beat movement and the interest in Oriental religions were the experimental life-styles associated with drugs, the hippies, the practice of occultism, and rock concerts. To many hippies the answer to the world's problems was for everyone simply to be "nice" to everyone else: "Make love, not war." In smoking pot they developed a ritual of sharing experiences of tranquillity and good fellowship. Passing the reefer from hand to hand had many of the elements of passing the communion cup among church brethren. As they sat casually about in silent harmony, relaxed, happy, and "mellow," they seemed to come in closer touch with

each other and with a power of benevolence beyond themselves yet
linking them to everyone else. Reversing the acquisitive, com-
petitive-comparative values of the Protestant ethic, the hippie
counterculture stressed sharing, giving, loving. Lysergic acid di-
ethylamide provided the emotional excitement for the hippie
religious experience. Dropping acid "blew the mind," cleared it of
the "bad vibrations" of bourgeois society, producing psychedelic
trips out of this world, demonstrating astonishing powers of
awareness and sensibility within men and women that had been
locked up by the repressive routines of bureaucratic life in school,
business, and surburbia. The mass production of LSD after 1963
opened up a whole new realm of experience for millions of
Americans. What "baptism by fire" did for the Pentecostalist and
Zen *satori* did for the disciplined practitioner of Zen became
immediately available at any time to anyone who could afford a
couple of dollars for a "hit" or a "tab" of acid. To get "high" on
LSD was to transcend this grey world and enter a many-splendored
paradise ("bad trips" excepted). Timothy Leary and Ken Kesey
became the high priests or gurus of this new form of spiritual
ecstasy, and in spontaneous groups all around the country people
found an alternative to Judeo-Christian worship and church brotherhood. For many it was a miraculous revelation; and though they
never established formal organizations, they constituted a phenomenal new-light movement.

There were others whose rebellion against suburban, bourgeois
values took more aggressive and destructive (often self-destructive)
forms. The darker side of the counterculture, these people were as
violent as the hippies were pacific. One form this took was the
motorcycle gangs—the Hell's Angels or the East Coast Mother
Fuckers. Another form was the practice of "Satanism," an inversion of Christian doctrine and rituals. The most extreme form,
represented by the Manson Family, accepted a charismatic leader as
the voice of god and yielded themselves totally to his power. Such
total transvaluations of values are not uncommon in periods of
social crisis, as Norman Cohn pointed out in *The Pursuit of the
Millennium*. While some seek possession by the Holy Spirit in their
despair, others seek possession by the devil. Witchcraft has been
practiced in this as in other awakenings, sometimes in the form of
white magic (which utilizes occult power to heal sickness, find lost

valuables, bring lovers together, predict the future) and sometimes as black magic (which puts a curse or hex on enemies in the hope of causing them injury or death). Some occultists claimed the power to leave their bodies (astral projection) and move about as spirits. In whatever form it took, occultism, like the drug subculture, was a search for power beyond one's self.

For many, this search for a different order of reality was best understood through reading the works of Carlos Castaneda. Castaneda, a doctoral candidate in anthropology at U.C.L.A., set out in 1960 to study the religious rituals connected with peyote and the *Datura* root among the Yaqui Indians of Mexico. He was converted from skepticism to discipleship through the charismatic power of the Yaqui medicine man or sorcerer, Don Juan, who taught him how to perform the elaborate rituals in gathering peyote and then guided him through the hallucinogenic experience that resulted from eating it. Castaneda's accounts assure the reader that there is as much validity to the Yaqui way of knowledge through peyote as there is to European or American empiricism.

In all these (and other) alternate life-styles and ritual performances there were conversion experiences comparable in power and effect to those in the Christian tradition. Hippie communities, Hare Krishna groups, and drug experiences did change lives and often made them more healthy, functional, and creative, though by the standards of outsiders they seemed abnormal, strange, "weird," or "freaky." Richard Alpert, who performed with Timothy Leary some of the first experiments with lysergic acid while he was a professor of psychology at Harvard in 1961, described his conversion in his book *Be Here Now*. With only slight changes it could pass for the conversion of a Christian who had lived in sin, caught up in material pleasures, but had then found new light:

> I had an apartment in Cambridge that was filled with antiques and I gave charming dinner parties. I had a Mercedes-Benz sedan and a Triumph and a Cessna 172 airplane and an MG sportscar. [But I felt that] something was wrong with my world [and] that all the stuff I was teaching was just like little molecular bits of stuff, but they didn't add up to a feeling of wisdom. [I feared that I] was going to spend the next forty years not knowing [truth] and that this was par for the course. [Trying LSD]. . . was a terribly frustrating experience, as if you came into the kingdom of heaven and you saw how it all was and you felt

these new states of awareness, and then you got cast out again. . . and
again, and I began to feel an extraordinary kind of depression set in.

Alpert concluded that LSD was only a partial and inadequate
means of finding truth, so he went to India to study Oriental
philosophy. Here he found that he could experience a more deep,
pure, and lasting sense of spiritual awareness without drugs. He
studied under a guru, changed his name to Ram Dass, and became
"a new man."

As in previous awakenings, changing child-rearing patterns had a
great deal to do with the emergence of this one. The "generation
gap" may be a perennial problem, but in times of severe cultural
strain that gap becomes a prime symptom of the breakdown of an
old consensus and the start of cultural disjunction. The young need
the sense of order, predictability, identity, and confidence that the
family (as a social institution) is supposed to provide. When there is
a disjunction between norms and experience, it shows up very
quickly in the family. In the 1950s and '60s a large proportion of
the young were torn between the feeling that they were hopelessly
trapped, on the one hand, and hopelessly adrift, on the other. They
were adrift because the behavior patterns inculcated by their
parents made no sense to them; they were trapped because the
educational patterns forced them into vocational choices they found
unbearable.

Conservatives (traditionalists) blamed the rebelliousness of children on scapegoats like Dr. Benjamin Spock (for his permissive
child-guidance manuals) or John Dewey (for his equally permissive
educational theories). Humanistic Liberals like Paul Goodman,
author of *Growing Up Absurd* (1956), blamed the soul-killing
technocratic educational system, with its boring goal of "the good
life" in suburbia. David Potter, the historian, suggested in *People
of Plenty* (1954) that too much affluence, leisure, and freedom
were the causes of the alienation of the young. Others suggested
that parents had lost interest in raising children because they had
nothing to teach them and because often both parents were
working. Parents made very little emotional investment in their
children. Children and parents commonly complained that they
could not talk to, or relate to, each other in any meaningful way.
Much of the child-rearing task was foisted off on the school system

or a psychologist. The young reacted by taking their direction from their peers rather than their parents or parent surrogates.

Alienation from parents, schools, and vocational goals produced an emotional deadness or affectlessness in the young. In order to "feel alive," they looked for excitement. In order to find security, they formed groups. In order to find guidelines, they looked for authority figures. For self-discipline they tried religion—often Oriental religion because of their reaction against Judaism or Christianity. In order to find excitement, they tried pills or drugs. Having seen their parents take pills to "calm their nerves" or "give them a lift," and having often had pills prescribed for them by doctors and psychologists, it seemed natural to try marijuana or LSD (and exciting because it was illegal to do so). In previous generations juvenile delinquency had been associated with the poor in the slums (those who "had no advantages"); by 1960, it had become a major problem in the suburbs, where kids "had everything."

Encouraging this revolt of the young against the absurd enculturation process of the 1950s, Paul Goodman hoped to see it produce significant political and institutional restructuring. For a time in the early 1960s this appeared to be happening as the young confronted "the establishment" at every level (but especially in the schools and colleges), demanding drastic changes. But as time passed, Goodman found that the path from rebellion to political restructuring was a much longer and more tortuous one than he had thought. Cultural distortion had gone too far. The young could not understand his humanistic appeals for "right proportion," "social balance," and "humane learning." Goodman (and many others "over thirty" who had sympathized with the alienation of the young) were unprepared for the emotional upsurge and spiritual hunger that welled up as the old order collapsed. The movement of the counterculture was not rational but impulsive. It did not care for self-discipline or intellect but for inspiration and intuition. By 1969 Goodman recognized that "Alienation is a powerful motivation of unrest, fantasy, and reckless action. It leads . . . to religious innovation, new sacraments to give life meaning. But it is a poor basis for politics, including revolutionary politics." Goodman proved as perceptive in recognizing the quality of the awakening as he had been in exposing its sources:

> I have imagined [in 1962] that the world-wide student protest had to
> do with changing political and moral institutions, to which I was
> sympathetic, but I now saw [1969] that we had to do with a religious
> crisis of the magnitude of the Reformation in the fifteen hundreds,
> when not only all institutions but all learning had been corrupted by
> the Whore of Babylon.

The whore in this case appeared to be "scientism" in the abstract
and the military-industrial complex in particular. Goodman's hope
for rational, orderly, and rapid reform was shortsighted. The crisis
was too deep. "In the end," he said of the younger generation, "it
is religion that constitutes the strength of this generation, and not,
as I used to think, their morality, political will, and common
sense." To a nonreligious humanist, this was a power with which he
could not cope. In every awakening the liberal rationalist is the
most poignant figure. He sympathizes with the revolt against
corruption, but he cannot get into the "Spirit" that pervades it.

Although technocracy and scientism were the enemies of the
counterculture, not all Americans lost faith in the ability of science
to solve man's problems and fathom the secrets of the universe. The
keen interest in Rhine's experiments with ESP (parapsychology), in
Scientology, and in B. F. Skinner's *Walden II* indicate that many
still expect from science the miracles they will not accept from
religion. Psychiatry and behavior modification seemed to offer
scientific stress release for those who lacked religious faith. "En-
counter sessions," Esalen Institutes, and est courses provided relief
from guilt and self-doubt for those with faith in them. These tend
to be people of an older generation, many of whom tried to get
answers from their ministers or solace from their church rituals and
could not.

In this Fourth Great Awakening, as in all awakenings, the line
between science and magic, the real and the unreal, has temporarily
disappeared. People are ready to believe almost anything. Did
psychokinetic research reveal the existence of psychic powers that
science would someday direct, or were they, on the contrary, powers
that science would never control? Was astrology a science or a
religion? Did Rosicrucians know secrets of the universe that scientists did not know? Is Uri Geller a mountebank, or does he have
extraordinary powers? Were "space probes" any more scientific
than the search for Noah's Ark? Americans read avidly about the

magic regions of Tolkien's Hobbits and just as avidly read reports of
the Army's interest in UFOs. Interest in spiritualism, astrology,
and Ouija boards flourished in the 1960s. So did science fiction. It
was difficult to distinguish between real voyages to Mars and those
seen on "Star Trek" or in *2001*. The search for King Kong seemed
no less real than the search for the Loch Ness monster or Big Foot or
the Abominable Snowman. The search for another order of reality
in these "outlandish" activities marked the failure of the ordinary
religious institutions to provide satisfactory answers about the
mysterious, the unknown, the unexplainable, and of course it also
marked the failure of science to do so.

The counterculture in its more extreme forms—among the Beats
or hippies, on rural communes or at Electric Kool-Aid Acid Tests—
did not attract the vast majority of the young, except in very diluted
forms. What did seem to attract and unite them all was the new
rock-and-roll music. In many respects the rock concerts and festivals
deserve comparison to the old camp meetings, where people
entered into a special arena of religious enthusiasm with like-
minded souls seeking release from confusion and ready to "let
loose" in orgies of emotional enthusiasm. Sometimes in large
urban coliseums but more often in the open air under the trees and
the stars, amidst deafening noise and constant motion, young
people found a way to deliver themselves up from the problems of
this world. In between these mass celebrations they carried the aura
back into daily life by listening to transistor radios, car radios, or
stereo sets or by playing their own guitars. They sang the new songs
of liberation like gospel hymns.

The emotional release of rock concerts often frightened the older
generation, for it frequently got out of hand. As in frontier camp
meetings, violence frequently erupted when people let loose what
was burning them up. The harmony of Woodstock was matched by
the horror at Altamont. Forces of love and hate easily got out of
control. The rituals of smoking pot or drinking apple wine were like
a communion, but bad trips on LSD or barbiturates could produce
a Black Mass. The high priests of these revivalistic ceremonies
alternately mixed songs of love and songs of protest, which kept the
emotions in constant tension. It was a new form of folk art; the
words and music brought the varied feelings of unrest into
articulate configurations that to outsiders (those not "with it")

appeared to be little more than senseless clamor and cacophony. Rock music and folk songs expressed the various moods of the new-light movement but could give it no direction. Like a Pentecostal meeting, the Spirit gripped different people in different ways, and each was left to express it in the form in which it spoke to him or her.

In the early '60s the predominant note was that of social protest. Closely associated with marches and rallies in support of civil rights, many concerts included gospel songs and songs from the labor-union movement of the 1930s. Pete Seeger often led these as singalongs, combining familiar tunes with new words. Later, Bob Dylan, Joan Baez, Buffy St. Marie, Arlo Guthrie, and Peter, Paul, and Mary wrote new protest songs. When the civil-rights protest began to merge into the antiwar rallies, the songs took on a more openly political tone. At the same time, other singers, ignoring the politics of protest, expressed private anguish, frenzy, or pain. Janis Joplin, Jimi Hendrix, and the Rolling Stones led the more frenzied forms of this anguish, while Simon and Garfunkel, Judy Collins, and Joni Mitchell expressed the quieter pain and longing. The Beatles, most popular of all, managed to include the whole gamut of emotions in music and lyrics that attracted not only the young but many of their parents.

The inability of the young to stop the war or effect rapid change in the system, plus the government's savage reprisals against protesters, brought a new phase to the music of the '60s as the decade drew to a close. Many singers became harshly critical of the patriotic myths used to support the war and became sardonic about a society that justified its cruelties in the name of God and democracy. Dylan's "With God on Our Side" and "The John Birch Society Blues" expressed this disillusionment and cynicism, while the Rolling Stones rose to fame by transvaluing old ideals into "Sympathy for the Devil." In addition to wearing flower symbols, the hippie protesters now wore the American flag upside down on the seats of their pants. John Lennon of the Beatles expressed the revolt against "official goodness" when he said, in 1966, "Christianity will go. It will vanish and shrink. We're more popular than Jesus now." He meant that the protest songs and love songs were more popular than the Jesus of Billy Graham and the Christianity of those who upheld established piety and order; the established forms of Judeo-Christianity, as Herberg had said, were captives of the culture.

The young were far from irreligious, but they sang and marched to a different beat and saw the world in a different light. The pietistic element in the counterculture found its symbol in the Woodstock Nation after a particularly idyllic concert festival in 1969. Joni Mitchell's song "Woodstock" captures the revivalistic mood of the 100,000 young people who gathered from all over the country at Yasgur's farm to sing and commune with each other under the trees:

> I came upon a child of God,
> He was walking along the road,
> And I asked him, "Tell me,
> Where are you going?"

> "I am going down to Yasgur's farm,
> I'm going to join a Rock an' Roll band,
> I'm going to get back to the land,
> And try to get my soul free."

> We are stardust,
> We are golden,
> We are caught in the Devil's barter
> And we've got to get ourselves
> Back to the garden.

> Then can I walk beside you?
> I have come here to lose the smog,
> And I feel just like a cog
> In something turning.

> Well, maybe it's the time of year,
> Or maybe it's the time of man,
> I don't know who I am,
> But life is for learning.

> By the time we got to Woodstock
> We were half a million strong
> And everywhere there was a song
> And celebration.
> And I dreamed I saw the bomber deathplanes
> Riding shotgun in the sky
> And they were turning into butterflies
> Above our nation.

There were many similarities between the spirit of pantheistic piety expressed in this song and in the spirit of the Jesus Movement among those who had "come out" from the regular churches. Like the Woodstock Nation, the Jesus People were seeking alternative ways of transforming the belief-value system. They too wanted a new way to express the transcendent spirit of the culture core, to find the universal fraternalism of the primitive Christian church before it became bogged down with doctrines, dogmas, rituals, and institutional restrictions upon the Spirit that moves the world. In the Second Great Awakening, Emerson had spoken of Jesus as "the first transcendentalist," and Theodore Parker had noted the difference between "the transient and the permanent in Christianity." In the Third Great Awakening, Social Gospel reformers had spoken of Jesus as "the first Social Gospeler," while humanists spoke of him as "the first socialist." In this Fourth Awakening, many have called Jesus "the first hippie" ("Jesus wore long hair," the preeminent symbol of a reforming or counterculture hero).

This search for symbols that can give new meaning and order to life is the essence of this and all awakenings. It lies even within the openly atheistic New Left movement. C. Wright Mills, Herbert Marcuse, Theodor Adorno, and Angela Davis have abandoned the economic determinism of "vulgar Marxism." They look for the creation of a "new consciousness" that will free the bourgeoisie as well as the working class from the "false consciousness" of a dehumanized social order, at war with itself. Under true Marxism, they believe, oppression and war and government will wither away, human nature will alter, and the world will leap into a new utopian harmony. Minorities now denied the opportunity to fulfill their human potential (Blacks, Chicanos, Indians, women, Third-World people), as well as alienated, suppressed, and exploited members of the bourgeoisie, will find liberation, and a new spirit will flow through all mankind.

## The Future of the Awakening

As we approach the end of the 1970s, it is clear that the nation is still far from reaching a new consensus in its belief-value system. Many products and many groups offer new ideological options, but the process of transforming our world view is still very much in process. While the nativist phase in the 1950s failed to return the culture to its traditional ways, it has made certain aspects of evangelicalism a live option again (as President Carter's election demonstrates). The various experiments in countercultural life-styles begun in the 1960s have already modified older life-styles in many respects (Gary Snyder won the Pulitzer prize in 1975; long hair, blue jeans, unisex, four-letter words, and changing sexual mores have entered the mainstream). Transcendental Meditation is practiced by suburban housewives. But institutional reform has made far less progress. The civil-rights movement passed its legal hurdles only to find social intransigence blocking implementation; the welfare programs are still hopelessly snarled in bureaucratic red tape; the war in Vietnam is over, but the voluntary army is hardly a viable alternative to the draft. Colleges and universities have made some important administrative reforms, but their curriculums and educational goals are still ambiguous. Public schools and public prisons seem to be worse off than ever; the cities have more problems than before; the courts are unable to provide consistent guidelines for social problems. And two of the most basic insti-tutions—the churches and the family—are in almost total con-fusion.

With the culture in metamorphosis and major problems like atomic war, the population explosion, ecological deterioration, and energy supplies still unsolved, it is not surprising that voices of doom still prevail. One of the more remarkable features of this awakening has been the shift from postmillennial optimism to premillennial pessimism among major segments of the population, including most of the intelligentsia.

Some commentators have suggested that the most promising movement toward ideological reorientation is to be found among the neo-Evangelicals and that President Carter is the embodiment of this emerging consensus. Carter's view, it is argued, represents a chastened Fundamentalism, shorn of its old anti-intellectualism, no longer adamantly committed to rugged individualism and laissez-faire capitalism, ready to abandon the imperialistic aspects of manifest destiny, white, Anglo-Saxon supremacy, and Protestant hegemony. Carter is said to be both a liberal and a conservative, a born-again Christian and a nuclear scientist, a southerner and a champion of black equality, a businessman and a social reformer.

He is also a southern Baptist interested in ecumenism. In his religious philosophy and his political theory there are, it is claimed, hope for a new focusing of national consciousness, direction for institutional restructuring, and grounds for a new national unity and common faith.

Such an interpretation of Carter's role in this awakening is based more on hope than on history. Some elements of Carter's world view may indeed be part of the new consensus—his casual style, his recognition that America must restrain its power, his sense of common humanity, his concern for ecology, his recognition that "the American way of life" is culturally limited and needs to be judged by some transcendent values. But our political leaders have never been the prophets of new light; they may implement it, but they do not originate it. Carter, at midpoint in this awakening, is subject to too many countervailing pressures to undertake effective restructuring. Until a consensus is reached from the bottom up, it cannot be instituted from the top down. Presidential leadership follows, it does not create, consensus. Elected by a small majority of the minority who even bothered to vote in 1976, Carter has no mandate for change. At best he can only tinker with the current debilitated system. Though he is closer to a new light than Gerald Ford was (while Nixon was a nativist reactionary), few Americans in 1976 could distinguish his political program from that of Ford. They voted for Carter's good intentions and his faith.

The current popularity of neo-Evangelicalism has led to the claim that 50 million born-again Christians are the avant-garde of the Fourth Great Awakening. This is hard to sustain. The old Bible-centered faith in an omniscient, omnipotent, yet personal, loving, comforting God, who forgives sins, answers prayers, and helps us solve problems by his direct spiritual presence and guidance is, of course, the kind of religion many Americans want today. Its conception of God is the opposite of the current impersonal, uncaring, frustrating, bureaucratic authority that controls our lives through science, medicine, and government; this God is familiar and comfortable in a stressful world. However, the world view of neo-Evangelicalism, by concentrating on the individual, is essentially an escape from seemingly insoluble, tension-ridden social and political problems. Neo-Evangelicalism offers a moratorium on politics—a rejection of the turbulent sixties. Like Zen Buddhism or the Yaqui way of knowledge, it turns the attention of its adherents to transcendent realities. By giving total attention to whether one's own or one's neighbor's heart is right with God, neo-Evangelicalism justifies turning one's back on worldly affairs so complex that only God can cope with them. It argues that we can change the world only when God has changed the hearts of everyone in it.

The internalization of values is a crucial process in any awakening; a people in cultural stress must come to some understanding of their own identity and place in the universe. In this respect, neo-Evangelicalism is significant. But too much of the old political and economic conservatism of the Fundamentalist ideology is implicit in neo-Evangelicalism. Too much narrow-minded authoritarianism and obscurantism is heard from its leading church spokesmen to enable it in its current formulations to offer "new light" for the future. Somewhere within it, among those unattached to any denominational institutions and unwedded to ritualized behavior and escapism, may well lie the seeds of this awakening's new light. But this light has yet to become distinct and evocative. Soul-winning neo-Evangelicalism is a divisive, not a unifying, force in a pluralistic world.

At some point in the future, early in the 1990s at best, a consensus will emerge that will thrust into political leadership a president with a platform committed to the kinds of fundamental restructuring that have followed our previous awakenings—in 1776, in 1830, and in 1932. Prior to this institutional restructuring must come an ideological reorientation. Such a reorientation will most likely include a new sense of the mystical unity of all mankind and of the vital power of harmony between man and nature. The godhead will be defined in less dualistic terms, and its power will be understood less in terms of an absolutist, sin-hating, death-dealing "Almighty Father in Heaven" and more in terms of a life-supporting, nurturing, empathetic, easygoing parental (Motherly as well as Fatherly) image. The nourishing spirit of mother earth, not the wrath of an angry father above, will dominate religious thought (though different faiths and denominations will communicate this ideal in different ways). Sacrifice of self will replace self-aggrandizement as a definition of virtue; helping others will replace competitiveness as a value; institutions will be organized for the fulfillment of individual needs by means of cooperative communal efforts rather than through the isolated nuclear family.

I would agree with Robert Bellah in *The Broken Covenant* (1976) that some form of Judeo-Christian socialism will be the new political ideology. Our "new vision of man," our "new sense of human possibility" and new "ordering of liberty," will not come from Marxism or the Orient but from our own cultural past. Revitalization and revival are by definition syncretic; self-renewal does not begin de novo. There are many elements in our mythology that can be revitalized: our emphasis on the sanctity of the individual and the importance of the general welfare; our sense of the holiness of life and the need to find it by losing it; our view that man is in this world but not of this world in its materialistic sense. "One can deny the God of the Bible," writes the anthropologist David Buchdahl, "but in order to think about 'reality' completely, some sort of 'god-term' is still required for a coherent symbol system." And it must be a term that confirms the reality of experience and the continuity of culture. At rock bottom our present awakening consists in a basic revision in epistemology and ontology. How do we know what is real, and how do we comprehend or sustain harmony with it?

> A change in the conception of God is a cultural event of some magnitude, especially because the character of a culture is heavily influenced by the notion of God that predominates within it. American culture bears the imprint of a particular conception of God, the God of Abraham, Isaac, and Jacob mediated through Protestants like Calvin, Cotton Mather, and Billy Graham. The counterculture represents an elaboration of reality independent of this notion and draws its character from a quite different if not altogether new understanding of what God is.

Buchdahl found this new concept most clearly expressed by those he studied and worked with in rural communes. For them God is close to what Martin Buber described: "Of course, God is the 'wholly Other'; but He is also the wholly Same, the wholly present. Of course, He is the 'Mysterium Tremendum' that appears and overthrows; but He is also the mystery of the self-evident; nearer to me than my I.'' Godhead in this sense may be found in the birth of a child or the fruit of an apple tree.

The beginning of a new belief-value system springing from this new respect for life and its mysterious source and continuity is found not only in the current distaste for defoliation weapons, carbon monoxide, insecticides, preservatives, fluorocarbons, detergents, nuclear fission, and toxic dyes but in the concern to preserve whales, dolphins, and other endangered species. It is found in greater respect for the helpless aged and the battered wife, the oppressed races and the incarcerated prisoner, in respect for the materials of craftsmanship and the patient skill with which the craftsman works. Today's countercultural behavior strives for relationships that are tolerant, soft-spoken, respectful of the feelings and opinions of others; it frowns on the aggressive, defensive, hostile, and possessive attitudes of the cultural past; it likes what men and women have in common as individuals and as groups and finds no ''specially chosen people.'' It does not measure success in terms of money, status, or power but in terms of friendship, generosity, and the ability to empathize and give. It is concerned preeminently with the quality of life, not its quantity. In that direction the awakening is moving and changing American life.

The reason an awakening takes a generation or more to work itself out is that it must grow with the young; it must escape the enculturation of the old ways. It is not worthwhile to ask who the prophet of this awakening is or to search for new ideological blueprints in the works of the learned. Revitalization is growing up around us in our children, who are both more innocent and more knowing than their parents and grandparents. It is their world that has yet to be reborn.

# Suggestions for
# Further Reading

One purpose of this book is to suggest the importance of an interdisciplinary study of religion in America. Whether one takes the view that ideology shapes human action or that it is the interaction between ideology and the modes of production and distribution that shape a culture, it seems obvious that historians cannot understand the religious history of a people without understanding how their beliefs and values relate to the total pattern of their lives. Nor can one properly study religion and culture without a concept of what causes beliefs and values to change over time. We cannot hope to comprehend the success and subsequent decline of Calvinism, deism, Evangelicalism, Liberal Protestantism, the Social Gospel, Fundamentalism, or Neo-Orthodoxy without understanding what made these systems of belief satisfying to so many Americans in one era and so unsatisfying to their descendants in succeeding generations.

Sociologists and anthropologists offer helpful methods and tools for analyses of such questions even when their books do not deal specifically with the religions of Americans. Therefore, any list of suggested reading for students of religion in America should start with the classical writings of Max Weber, Emile Durkheim, Karl Mannheim, Bronislaw Malinowski, Ferdinand Tönnies, Ernst Troeltsch, and E. E. Evans-Pritchard. Although the historian will be more concerned with changing child-rearing patterns than with the internal workings of the human psyche, still he cannot help being enlightened by the works on religion and human behavior by Sigmund Freud, William James, Erik Erikson, and William

Sargant. Unfortunately, the study of changing concepts of child-rearing in America is still in its infancy, but useful works in this field include Edmund S. Morgan, *The Puritan Family* (Boston: Boston Public Library, 1956); Philip Greven, *Child-rearing Concepts* (Itasca, Ill.: Peacock, 1972); Anne L. Kuhn, *The Mother's Role in Childhood Education* (New Haven: Yale University Press, 1947); Bernard Wishy, *The Child and the Republic* (Philadelphia: University of Pennsylvania Press, 1968); and W. G. McLoughlin and Lewis P. Lipsitt, "Evangelical Child-rearing in the Age of Jackson," *Journal of Social History* 9 (1975): 20–43.

I wish to call attention here to four books in sociology and anthropology that have directly influenced this book: the essays of Clifford Geertz in *The Interpretation of Cultures* (New York: Basic Books, 1973) helped to clarify the relationship between religion, culture, and ideology. Victor Turner's *The Forest of Symbols* (Ithaca: Cornell University Press, 1967) is particularly useful for understanding the process of conversion and *rites de passage*. Mary Douglas's *Natural Symbols* (London: Barrie & Rockliff, 1970) provides valuable insights on the relationship between child-rearing and religious behavior. Kai T. Erikson's *The Wayward Puritans* (New York: John Wiley, 1966) offers an approach for studying how cultures define themselves in terms of social deviance.

Studying cultural change inevitably leads to the concepts of ghost-dance religions and cargo cults, and I have found very useful the following books on these subjects: Kenelm Burridge, *New Heaven, New Earth* (London: Blackwell, 1969); Peter Worsley, *The Trumpet Shall Sound* (London: MacGibbon & Kee, 1968); James Mooney, *The Ghost Dance Religion* (Washington, D.C.: U.S. Government Printing Office, 1896); and Weston LaBarre, *The Ghost Dance* (New York: Doubleday, 1970).

My primary debt in regard to the relationships between religion and social change comes from three works of Anthony F. C. Wallace regarding what he calls "revitalization movements": *The Death and Rebirth of the Seneca* (New York: Knopf, 1970); *Religion: An Anthropological View* (New York: Random House, 1966); and "Revitalization Movements," *American Anthropology* 58 (1956): 264–81.

Among the many general interpretations of religion in America,

I have found the following the most helpful: Sydney E. Ahlstrom, *A Religious History of the American People* (New Haven: Yale University Press, 1972); H. R. Niebuhr, *The Social Sources of Denominationalism* (New York: Henry Holt, 1929); H. R. Niebuhr, *The Kingdom of God in America* (New York: Harper, 1937). The best collection of documents tracing the history of American Christianity is H. S. Smith, Robert Handy, and L. A. Loetscher, *American Christianity*, 2 vols. (New York: Scribners, 1960).

Two of the central themes in American cultural history that are integral to the study of its religious revivals are the millennial hopes of Americans and their belief that this nation, under God, has a special role to play in human destiny. The millennial tradition in English and American thought is well delineated in Ernest Tuveson, *The Redeemer Nation* (Chicago: University of Chicago Press, 1968). Other important aspects of millennialism can be found in Norman Cohn, *The Pursuit of the Millennium* (Fairlawn, N.J.: Essential Books, 1957); Ernest Sandeen, *The Roots of Fundamentalism* (Chicago: University of Chicago Press, 1970); Christopher Hill, *The World Turned Upside Down* (New York: Viking, 1972); E. J. Hobsbawm, *Primitive Rebels* (New York: Norton, 1965). An excellent anthology of American statements on the millennial theme is Conrad Cherry's *God's New Israel* (Englewood Cliffs, N.J.: Prentice-Hall, 1971). Albert K. Weinberg's *Manifest Destiny* (Baltimore: Johns Hopkins University Press, 1935) is still the basic study of the changing definitions of this myth. It should be supplemented with Frederick Merk's *Manifest Destiny and Mission* (New York: Knopf, 1963) and Henry Nash Smith's *Virgin Land* (New York: Knopf, 1950).

The best studies I have found on the general belief-value system at the core of American culture are Ralph H. Gabriel, *The Course of American Democratic Thought* (New York: Ronald Press, 1956); Stow Persons, *American Minds* (New York: Henry Holt, 1959); Cushing Strout, *The New Heavens and New Earth* (New York: Harper & Row, 1974); A. N. Kaul, *The American Vision* (New Haven: Yale University Press, 1963); and Charles Sanford, *The Quest for Paradise* (Urbana: University of Illinois Press, 1961). I have myself made two previous stabs at defining central themes in the American culture-core, "Pietism and the American Charac-

ter,'' *American Quarterly* 13 (1961), and ''Revivalism,'' in E. S.
Gaustad, ed., *The Rise of Adventism* (New York: Harper & Row,
1974), pp. 119-53.

## The Puritan Awakening

The works of Perry Miller are of course central to the study of the
Puritans, and I have drawn heavily here upon his introduction to
the anthology he edited with Thomas H. Johnson entitled *The
Puritans* (New York: American Book, 1938). I have also found R.
H. Tawney's *Religion and the Rise of Capitalism* (New York:
Harcourt, Brace, 1926) still useful, despite its shortcomings.
Important for the more radical aspects of Puritanism is Michael
Walzer's *The Revolution of the Saints* (Cambridge, Mass.: Harvard
University Press, 1965). E. S. Morgan's *The Puritan Dilemma*
(Boston: Little, Brown, 1958) provides the best introduction to the
Massachusetts Puritans. The conception of their American identity
by the New England Puritans is ably traced in Sacvan Bercovitch,
*The Puritan Origins of the American Self* (New Haven: Yale
University Press, 1975). Several recent studies illuminate the social
aspects of the Puritan life-style in New England: John Demos, *A
Little Commonwealth* (New York: Oxford University Press, 1970);
Kenneth A Lockridge, *A New England Town: The First Hundred
Years* (New York: Norton, 1970); and Darrett B. Rutman, *Amer-
ican Puritanism* (Philadelphia: J. B. Lippincott, 1970).

## The First Great Awakening

The most important interpretations of the First Great Awakening in
New England are Alan Heimert, *Religion and the American Mind*
(Cambridge, Mass.: Harvard University Press, 1966); C. C. Goen,
*Revivalism and Separatism in New England* (New Haven: Yale
University Press, 1962); W. G. McLoughlin, *Isaac Backus and the
American Pietistic Tradition* (Boston: Little, Brown, 1970); Edwin
S. Gaustad, *The Great Awakening in New England* (New York:
Harper & Row, 1957); and Perry Miller, *Jonathan Edwards* (New
York: William Sloane, 1949). Key articles dealing with the New

England phase of this awakening include: Perry Miller, "Jonathan Edwards and the Sociology of the Great Awakening," *New England Quarterly* 21 (March 1948): 50–77; Perry Miller, "Solomon Stoddard," *Harvard Theological Review* 34 (1941): 277–320; John C. Miller, "Religion, Finance, and Democracy in Massachusetts," *New England Quarterly* 6 (March 1933): 29–58; W. G. McLoughlin, "The Great Awakening as the Key to the Revolution," *Proceedings of the American Antiquarian Society* 87, pt. 1 (1977): 69–96; C. C. Goen, "Jonathan Edwards: A New Departure in Eschatology," *Church History* 28 (March 1959): 25–40; John M. Bumsted, "Revivalism and Separatism in New England," *William and Mary Quarterly* 24 (1967): 588–612; Harry S. Stout, "Religion, Communications, and the Ideological Origins of the Revolution," *William and Mary Quarterly* 3d ser. 34 (October 1977): 519–41.

Three books treat important aspects of the First Great Awakening in the Middle Colonies: Charles H. Maxson, *The Great Awakening in the Middle Colonies* (Chicago: University of Chicago Press, 1920); James Tanis, *Dutch Calvinistic Pietism in the Middle Colonies* (The Hague: Nijhoff, 1968); and Leonard J. Trinterud, *The Forming of an American Tradition* (Philadelphia: Westminster, 1949). The standard sources on the awakening in the South are Wesley M. Gewehr, *The Great Awakening in Virginia* (Durham, N.C.: Duke University Press, 1930), and Robert B. Semple, *The Rise and Progress of the Baptists in Virginia* (Richmond, Va.: n.p., 1810). However, these works should be supplemented by the work of Rhys Isaac, particularly "Evangelical Revolt," *William and Mary Quarterly* 3d ser. 31 (July 1974): 345–68. A good study of the role played by George Whitefield is the biography by Stuart C. Henry, *George Whitefield* (Nashville, Tenn.: Abingdon Press, 1957).

There are four very useful anthologies of the First Great Awakening: Alan Heimert and Perry Miller, *The Great Awakening* (Indianapolis: Bobbs-Merrill, 1967); J. M. Bumsted and John Van de Wetering, *What Must I Do to Be Saved?* (Hinsdale, Ill.: Dryden Press, 1976); David S. Lovejoy, *Religious Enthusiasm and the Great Awakening* (Englewood Cliffs, N.J.: Prentice-Hall, 1969); and Richard L. Bushman, *The Great Awakening* (New York: Atheneum Press, 1970). In tracing the breakdown of the Puritan world view and life-style during the seventeenth century I have relied on

Philip Greven, *Four Generations* (Ithaca: Cornell University Press, 1970); Richard Bushman, *From Puritan to Yankee* (Cambridge, Mass.: Harvard University Press, 1967); and Perry Miller, *The New England Mind from Colony to Providence* (Cambridge, Mass.: Harvard University Press, 1953).

The important analyses of the breakdown of the Calvinistic consensus between 1750 and 1830 are: Conrad Wright, *The Beginnings of Unitarianism in America* (Boston: Starr King, 1955); Henry F. May, *The Enlightenment in America* (New York: Oxford University Press, 1976); Joseph Haroutunian, *Piety vs. Moralism* (New York: Holt, Rinehart, 1932); Frank H. Foster, *A Genetic History of the New England Theology* (Chicago: University of Chicago Press, 1907); Joseph F. Conforti, "Samuel Hopkins and the New Divinity Movement," Ph.D. dissertation, Brown University, 1975; and Sidney E. Mead, *The Lively Experiment* (New York: Harper & Row, 1963). In *The Creation of the American Republic* (Chapel Hill, N.C.: University of North Carolina Press, 1969), Gordon Wood skillfully demonstrates the religious dimension of the Revolution.

## The Second Great Awakening

While books on the First Great Awakening are overbalanced in their emphasis on the New England phase, books on the Second Great Awakening tend to overemphasize the southern phase. However, among the studies of this awakening in New England that deserve attention are: Charles R. Keller, *The Second Great Awakening in Connecticut* (New Haven: Yale University Press, 1942); Sidney E. Mead, *Nathaniel W. Taylor* (Chicago: University of Chicago Press, 1942); Vernon W. Stauffer, *New England and the Bavarian Illuminati* (New York: Russell & Russell, 1967); Daniel W. Howe, *The Unitarian Conscience* (Cambridge, Mass.: Harvard University Press, 1970); and, of course, Lyman Beecher, *Autobiography*, ed. Barbara Cross (Cambridge, Mass.: Harvard University Press, 1961).

The significant studies of this awakening in the South include: John B. Boles, *The Great Revival, 1787–1895* (Lexington: University of Kentucky Press, 1972); Dickson D. Bruce, *And They All Sang Hallelujah* (Knoxville: University of Tennessee Press, 1974); Donald G. Mathews, *Religion in the Old South* (Chicago: Univeristy of Chicago Press, 1977); Charles A. Johnson, *Frontier Camp Meeting* (Dallas: Southern Methodist University Press, 1955); and Catherine Cleveland, *The Great Revival in the West* (Chicago: University of Chicago Press, 1916). Important also for this awakening is the rapid growth of Methodism, for which see: Emory S. Bucke, ed., *History of American Methodism*, 3 vols. (Nashville: Abingdon Press, 1964); Elizabeth Nottingham, *Methodism and the Frontier* (New York: Columbia University Press, 1944); Francis Asbury, *Journal and Letters*, ed. Elmer T. Clark (Nashville: Abingdon Press, 1958); and Peter Cartwright, *Autobiography*, ed. Charles L. Wallis (Nashville: Abingdon Press, 1956).

The phase of the Second Awakening that is associated with Charles G. Finney and the area from New York to Ohio is analyzed in Whitney R. Cross, *The Burned-Over District* (Ithaca: Cornell University Press, 1950); Robert S. Fletcher, *A History of Oberlin College*, 2 vols. (Oberlin, Ohio: Oberlin College, 1943); Gilbert H. Barnes, *The Anti-Slavery Impulse*, ed. W. G. McLoughlin (New York: Harcourt, Brace, 1964); W. G. McLoughlin, *Modern Revivalism* (New York: Ronald Press, 1959); T. Scott Miyakawa, *Protestants and Pioneers* (Chicago: University of Chicago Press, 1964); and, of course, Charles G. Finney, *Autobiography* (New York: A. S. Barnes, 1876).

Two general studies of this awakening that deserve attention are Perry Miller, *The Life of the Mind in America* (New York: Harcourt, Brace, 1965), and Charles C. Cole, *The Social Ideals of the Northern Evangelists* (New York: Columbia University Press, 1954).

Important articles about this awakening include: Donald G. Mathews, "The Second Great Awakening as an Organizing Progress," *American Quarterly* 21 (1969): 23–43; John L. Thomas, "Romantic Reform in America," *American Quarterly* 17 (1965): 656–81; and David B. Davis, "The Emergence of Immediatism," *Mississippi Valley Historical Review* 49 (1962): 209–30.

The philosophy that emerged from the Second Awakening, to dominate American beliefs as the underpinning for Evangelical

Protestantism, was known as the Scottish Philosophy or Scottish Realism. The best summary of this outlook can be found in E. H. Meyer, *The Instructed Conscience* (Philadelphia: University of Pennsylvania Press, 1972). The importance of this philosophical outlook to American theology is traced in Theodore D. Bozeman, *Protestants in an Age of Science* (Chapel Hill: University of North Carolina Press, 1977), and Sydney E. Ahlstrom, "The Scottish Philosophy in America," *Church History* 24 (1955): 257-72.

The Great Prayer Meeting revival of 1857-58 is studied in Timothy L. Smith, *Revivalism and Social Reform* (New York: Harper, 1957).

## The Third Great Awakening

Important works about the Third Great Awakening deal with a wide range of subjects, from Fundamentalist revivalism to Liberal Protestantism to the Social Gospel and Progressive movements. In respect to Fundamentalism (or, really, the decline and breakup of the Evangelical consensus of the mid-nineteenth century) see Ernest Sandeen, *The Roots of Fundamentalism* (Chicago: University of Chicago Press, 1970); S. G. Cole, *The History of Fundamentalism* (New York: Richard Smith, 1931); Norman H. Furniss, *The Fundamentalist Controversy* (New Haven: Yale University Press, 1954); Liston Pope, *Millhands and Preachers* (New Haven: Yale University Press, 1942); James Findlay, *Dwight L. Moody* (Chicago: University of Chicago Press, 1969); W. G. McLoughlin, *Billy Sunday Was His Real Name* (Chicago: University of Chicago Press, 1955); John T. Nichol, *Pentecostalism* (New York: Harper & Row, 1966); Charles E. Jones *Perfectionist Persuasion* (Metuchen, N.J.: Scarecrow Press, 1974).

The leading works on the Social Gospel movement include Charles H. Hopkins, *The Rise of the Social Gospel* (New Haven: Yale University Press, 1940); Henry F. May, *Protestant Churches and Industrial America* (New York: Harper, 1949); James Dombrowski, *The Early Days of Christian Socialism in America* (New York: Columbia University Press, 1936); Paul A. Carter, *The Decline and Revival of the Social Gospel* (Ithaca: Cornell University Press, 1954); Washington Gladden, *Recollections* (Boston:

Houghton, Mifflin, 1909); Jacob C. Dorn, *Washington Gladden* (Columbus; Ohio State University Press, 1966); Dores R. Sharpe, *Walter Rauschenbusch* (New York: Macmillan, 1942); Aaron Abell, *The Urban Impact on American Protestantism* (Cambridge, Mass.: Harvard University Press, 1943); Richard T. Ely, *Ground under Our Feet* (New York: Macmillan, 1938); and Allen F. Davis, *Spearheads for Reform* (New York: Oxford University Press, 1967).

The rise of Liberal Protestantism out of the old Evangelical consensus is traced in Kenneth Cauthen, *The Impact of Religious Liberalism* (New York: Harper & Row, 1962); B. M. G. Reardon, *Liberal Protestantism* (Stanford, Calif.: Stanford University Press, 1968); E. C. Vanderlaan, *Fundamentalism vs. Modernism* (New York: H. W. Wilson, 1925); A. C. McGiffert, Sr., *The Rise of Modern Religious Ideas* (New York: Macmillan, 1915); E. E. Aubrey, *Present Theological Tendencies* (New York: Harper, 1936); William R. Hutchison, ed., *American Protestant Thought* (New York: Harper & Row, 1968); Arthur O. Lovejoy, *The Great Chain of Being* (Cambridge, Mass.: Harvard University Press, 1936); John Herman Randall, Jr., *The Making of the Modern Mind* (Boston: Houghton, Mifflin, 1926); Alfred North Whitehead, *Science and the Modern World* (New York: Macmillan, 1925); William Moats Miller, *American Protestantism and Social Issues* (Chapel Hill: University of North Carolina Press, 1958); Donald B. Meyer, *The Protestant Search for Political Realism* (Berkeley: University of California Press, 1961); Charles F. Potter, *Humanism: A New Religion* (New York: Simon & Schuster, 1930); John Dewey, *A Common Faith* (New Haven: Yale University Press, 1934).

## The Fourth Great Awakening

The Fourth Great Awakening began in the 1960s, but the dissent from the Liberal Protestant (Social Gospel, Progressive, Humanist, Naturalist) consensus produced by the Third Great Awakening began in the 1920s. The gradual breakdown of this consensus can be traced in the following studies: Roderick Nash, *The Nervous Generation* (Chicago: Rand McNally, 1970); Richard H. Pells, *Radical Visions and American Dreams* (New York: Harper & Row,

1973); David Potter, *People of Plenty* (Chicago: University of Chicago Press, 1954); John K. Galbraith, *The Affluent Society* (Boston: Houghton, Mifflin, 1958); Gilbert Chinoy, *The Automobile Workers and the American Dream* (New York: Random House, 1955); C. Wright Mills, *White Collar* (New York: Oxford University Press, 1951); William H. Whyte, Jr., *The Organization Man* (New York: Doubleday, 1956); Joseph Wood Krutch, *The Modern Temper* (New York: Harcourt, Brace, 1929); Aldous Huxley, *Brave New World* (New York: Doubleday, 1932); Rufus E. Miles, Jr., *Awakening from the American Dream* (New York: Universe, 1976); David Riesman, Nathan Glazer, and Reuel Denney, *The Lonely Crowd* (New York: Doubleday, 1955).

The breakdown of the old world view led to reexamination of the theological perspective and a crisis in the faith of those who had trusted the social sciences (particularly psychology) to explain man's place in the cosmos. The questions over "the death of God" and the new relevance of Oriental religions and other mystical approaches to "reality" were evident in: Gabriel Vahanian, *The Death of God* (New York: Braziller, 1961); Daisetz Suzuki, *An Introduction to Zen Buddhism* (New York: Macmillan, 1966); Alan W. Watts, *The Way of Zen* (New York: Pantheon, 1957); Ray Mungo, *Total Loss Farm* (New York: Dutton, 1970); Gary Snyder, *Turtle Island* (New York: New Directions, 1974); Carlos Castaneda, *The Teachings of Don Juan* (Berkeley: University of California Press, 1968); Charles W. Kegley and R. W. Bretall, eds., *Reinhold Niebuhr* (New York: Macmillan, 1956); Will Herberg, *Protestant, Catholic, Jew* (Garden City, N.Y.: Doubleday, 1960); Edward Wakin and Joseph F. Scheuer, *The De-Romanization of the American Catholic Church* (New York: Macmillan, 1966); Harvey Cox, *The Secular City* (New York: Macmillan, 1965); Harvey Cox, *The Feast of Fools* (Cambridge, Mass.: Harvard University Press, 1969); Norman O. Brown, *Life against Death* (Middletown, Conn.: Wesleyan University Press, 1959); Paul Goodman, *Growing Up Absurd* (New York: Knopf, 1956); Philip Slater, *The Pursuit of Loneliness* (Boston: Beacon, 1971); Philip Rieff, *The Triumph of the Therapeutic* (New York: Harper & Row, 1966); Edwin Schur, *The Awareness Trap* (New York: New York Times Co., 1976); Robert E. Ornstein, *The Psychology of Con-*

*sciousness* (New York: W. H. Freeman, 1972); Edward A. Tir-
yakian, ed., *On the Margin of the Visible* (New York: John Wiley,
1975); J. Stillson Judah, *Hare Krishna and the Counterculture*
(New York: John Wiley, 1974); F. D. Goodman, Jeanette H.
Henney, and Esther Pressel, *Trance, Healing, and Hallucination*
(New York: John Wiley, 1974).

These new quests for "reality" lead to a separatist movement
from "the establishment" and the creation of a counterculture,
which is described in: Tom Wolfe, *The Electric Kool-Aid Acid Test*
(New York: Farrar, 1968); William I. Thompson, *At the Edge of
History* (New York: Harper & Row, 1972); Theodore Roszak, *The
Making of a Counter-Culture* (New York: Doubleday, 1969);
Theodore Roszak, *Where the Wasteland Ends* (New York: Double-
day, 1972); Theodore Roszak, *Unfinished Animal* (New York:
Harper & Row, 1975); Charles Reich, *The Greening of America*
(New York: Random House, 1970); Robert N. Bellah, *The Broken
Covenant* (New York: Seabury, 1975); Herbert Marcuse, *One
Dimensional Man* (Boston: Beacon, 1964); Paul Robinson, *The
Freudian Left* (New York: Harper & Row, 1969); Kenneth Ken-
iston, *The Uncommitted* (New York: Harcourt, Brace, 1960);
Kenneth Keniston, *Youth and Dissent* (New York: Harcourt,
Brace, 1971); Jacob Neusner, *American Judaism* (Englewood Cliffs,
N.J.: Prentice-Hall, 1972); Irwin Unger, *The Movement* (New
York: Dodd, Mead, 1974); Howard Zinn, *S.N.C.C.: The New
Abolitionists* (Boston: Beacon, 1965); William O'Neill, *Coming
Apart* (New York: N.Y. Times Co., 1971); Richard Poirier, *The
Performing Self* (New York: Oxford University Press, 1971);
Lawrence Lipton, *The Holy Barbarians* (New York: Messner, 1959);
John Tytell, *Naked Angels* (New York: McGraw-Hill, 1976);
Robert L. Pirsig, *Zen and the Art of Motorcycle Maintenance* (New
York: Morrow, 1974); Anthony Scaduto, *Dylan* (New York: New
American Library, 1971); Hunter Davies, *The Beatles* (New York:
McGraw-Hill, 1968); Ron E. Roberts, *The New Communes* (Engle-
wood Cliffs, N.J.: Prentice-Hall, 1971); David Buchdahl, "Ameri-
can Realities," Ph.D. dissertation, University of Chicago, 1974.

The shift from a postmillennial optimism to a premillennial
pessimism, evident even among intellectual sophisticates in this
awakening, is evident in: Robert L. Heilbroner, *An Inquiry into the*

*Human Prospect* (New York: Norton, 1971); Hal Lindsey and C. C. Carlson, *The Late Great Planet Earth* (Grand Rapids, Mich.: Zondervan, 1973); and Alvin Toffler, *Future Shock* (New York: Bantam Books, 1971).

# Index